ENHANCING
CYBER CULTURE

Enhancing Cyber Culture

Stan Bradley

Published by Masterworks, 2024.

ENHANCING CYBER CULTURE

First edition. June 19, 2024.

Copyright © 2024 Stan Bradley.

ISBN: 979-8227287748

Written by Stan Bradley.

ENHANCING
CYBER CULTURE
BY STAN BRADLEY

SECTION ONE

SECTION TWO

SECTION THREE

SECTION FOUR

SECTION FIVE

SECTION SIX

ABOUT THIS BOOK

Enhancing Cyber Culture: Digital Literacy, Ethics, and Community in the 21st Century

Introduction

In the rapidly evolving landscape of the 21st century, cyber culture has emerged as a dominant force shaping our social, economic, and cultural environments. As digital technologies continue to advance, they increasingly permeate every aspect of our daily lives, from how we communicate and collaborate to how we learn and entertain ourselves. This monograph, "Enhancing Cyberculture: Digital Literacy, Ethics, and Community in the 21st Century," aims to explore the multifaceted dimensions of cyberculture and provide a comprehensive guide to understanding and improving our digital interactions.

The concept of cyberculture encompasses a wide range of phenomena, including the creation and dissemination of digital content, the formation of online communities, and the ethical considerations that arise in digital spaces. As we navigate this complex and interconnected world, it becomes crucial to foster a culture that promotes digital literacy, ethical behavior, and inclusive communities.

Digital Literacy

At the heart of enhancing cyberculture is the need for robust digital literacy. In an era where information is abundant and constantly evolving, the ability to critically evaluate and effectively use digital tools and resources is essential. Digital literacy goes beyond basic computer skills; it involves understanding the socio-technical systems that underpin digital environments and developing the capacity to engage with these systems thoughtfully and responsibly.

Ethical Considerations

As our interactions increasingly take place in virtual spaces, ethical considerations become paramount. Issues such as privacy, data security, and digital rights require careful deliberation to ensure that our digital practices align with broader societal values. This monograph will delve into the ethical challenges posed by digital technologies and propose frameworks for navigating these complexities with integrity and foresight.

Online Communities

The rise of the internet has given birth to diverse and vibrant online communities. These digital spaces offer opportunities for connection, collaboration, and cultural exchange that transcend geographical boundaries. However, they also present challenges related to inclusivity, moderation, and the potential for echo chambers. By examining the dynamics of online communities, we can develop strategies to foster more inclusive, respectful, and productive digital environments.

Conclusion

"Enhancing Cyberculture" seeks to equip readers with the knowledge and tools necessary to thrive in the digital age. By promoting digital literacy, ethical behavior, and strong online communities, we can harness the power of cyberculture to create a more connected, informed, and equitable world. Through this monograph, we invite you to join us on a journey to better understand and enhance the digital landscapes that shape our lives.

PREFACE: AN INTRODUCTION TO THE THEMES AND OBJECTIVES OF THE COLLECTION

In an ever-evolving world where technology permeates every aspect of life, the intersection of artificial intelligence and culture has become a fertile ground for exploration and innovation. This collection delves into the profound implications of AI in the realm of cultural theory and the burgeoning field of cyber arts. The objective is to navigate the complex landscape where machine intelligence and human creativity converge, offering insights into how these elements shape, enhance, and redefine our cultural experiences.

Cultural theory has long been concerned with understanding the systems of meaning that structure societies, encompassing various disciplines such as anthropology, sociology, and media studies. The introduction of AI into this domain brings a paradigm shift, compelling us to rethink foundational concepts and methodologies. AI's capability to process vast amounts of data, recognize patterns, and generate content presents both opportunities and challenges. It necessitates a re-examination of cultural narratives, authorship, and the nature of artistic expression.

One of the central themes of this collection is the augmentation of human creativity through AI. Historically, the creative process has been viewed as an inherently human endeavor, characterized by intuition, emotion, and subjectivity. However, AI challenges this notion by demonstrating its ability to produce art, music, literature, and other forms of creative output. This raises questions about the definition of creativity and the role of the artist. Is creativity exclusive to human cognition, or can machines genuinely contribute to the creative process? By exploring AI-generated art and its reception, we gain insights into how technology influences our understanding of creativity and originality.

The integration of AI in cultural production also prompts a critical examination of authorship and authenticity. In traditional art forms, the artist's identity and personal experience are integral to the value and meaning of the work. AI-generated content, however, complicates this relationship. When a machine produces a piece of art, who is the true author? Is it the programmer who designed the algorithm, the machine itself, or the collective data from which the AI learned? This collection investigates these questions, highlighting how AI reshapes our perceptions of authorship and authenticity in art.

Moreover, AI's role in cultural theory extends beyond creation to interpretation and analysis. Cultural artifacts—ranging from ancient texts to contemporary media—can be analyzed with unprecedented precision using AI tools. Natural language processing, image recognition, and sentiment analysis allow scholars to uncover patterns and insights that were previously inaccessible. This technological enhancement not only deepens our understanding of cultural phenomena but also democratizes access to knowledge. By making complex analyses more accessible, AI empowers a broader range of voices to participate in cultural discourse.

Another critical aspect explored in this collection is the ethical implications of AI in culture. As AI systems become more integrated into cultural production and analysis, issues of bias, representation, and equity come to the fore. AI algorithms are trained on existing data, which often reflect societal biases and inequalities. Consequently, AI-generated content can perpetuate and even exacerbate these biases. This collection addresses the ethical responsibilities of creators and scholars in ensuring that AI contributes to a more inclusive and equitable cultural landscape.

In the realm of cyber arts, AI is pushing the boundaries of what is possible, creating new genres and experiences. From virtual reality installations to interactive digital artworks, AI enables artists to explore uncharted territories. These innovations not only expand the vocabulary of contemporary art but also invite audiences to engage with art in novel ways. The immersive nature of cyber arts, facilitated by AI, transforms the spectator into an active participant, blurring the lines between creator and audience.

Furthermore, AI's capacity for personalization and customization is revolutionizing the cultural experience. Algorithms that tailor content to individual preferences can create highly personalized artistic encounters. This capability, while enhancing user engagement, also raises concerns about the homogenization of culture and the potential loss of serendipitous discovery. By examining the balance between personalization and diversity, this collection offers perspectives on how AI can enrich cultural experiences without compromising the breadth and richness of artistic expression.

The interplay between AI and culture also necessitates a reevaluation of education and training in the arts and humanities. As AI tools become integral to artistic and scholarly practices, there is a growing need for interdisciplinary education that bridges the gap between technology and the arts. This collection advocates for curricula that equip students with both technical skills and critical thinking abilities, preparing them to navigate and shape the future cultural landscape.

In exploring the relationship between AI and culture, this collection also pays homage to the historical precedents that have paved the way for current developments. The fascination with artificial beings and mechanical creativity dates back to ancient myths and early automatons. By tracing the lineage of these concepts, we gain a deeper appreciation of the contemporary discourse surrounding AI and creativity. This historical context underscores the enduring human curiosity about the nature of intelligence and the boundaries of the possible.

Ultimately, this collection aims to foster a nuanced understanding of how AI intersects with cultural theory and cyber arts. It invites readers to reflect on the transformative potential of AI while remaining cognizant of the ethical and societal implications. By embracing the opportunities and addressing the challenges, we can harness the power of AI to enhance cultural production, interpretation, and experience.

In conclusion, the integration of AI into cultural theory and cyber arts represents a significant paradigm shift with far-reaching implications. This collection offers a comprehensive exploration of this dynamic interplay, highlighting the ways in which AI is reshaping our understanding of creativity, authorship, authenticity, and cultural experience. Through critical analysis and diverse perspectives, it provides a roadmap for navigating the complexities of this new cultural frontier. By engaging with these themes, we can envision a future where AI and human creativity coalesce to enrich and expand the horizons of culture.

SECTION ONE

FOUNDATIONAL THEORISTS AND PHILOSOPHERS

Throughout history, foundational theorists and philosophers have significantly shaped our understanding of various domains of knowledge, laying the groundwork for modern advancements in artificial intelligence (AI), natural language processing, machine learning, and transformative technologies like the Generative Pre-trained Transformer (GPT). This exploration seeks to bridge the insights of these early thinkers with contemporary technological innovations, demonstrating how foundational ideas continue to influence and inform the rapidly evolving field of AI.

In the realm of philosophy, figures such as Aristotle, René Descartes, and Immanuel Kant have provided critical frameworks for understanding human cognition and language. Aristotle's works on logic and categorization laid the groundwork for structured thinking, which is essential in the development of AI algorithms. His emphasis on empirical observation and systematic classification can be seen as a precursor to the data-driven approaches that dominate AI research today. Descartes' proposition of mind-body dualism and his assertion "Cogito, ergo sum" ("I think, therefore I am") emphasized the centrality of rational thought and introspection in understanding intelligence, indirectly influencing the conceptualization of AI as a domain concerned with replicating rational decision-making processes in machines.

Immanuel Kant's contributions, particularly his exploration of the nature of human understanding and the limits of knowledge, resonate deeply with current AI challenges. Kant's theory of knowledge, which posits that our understanding of the world is shaped by inherent structures of the mind, parallels the idea that AI systems require predefined architectures to process and interpret data effectively. His insights into the nature of perception and cognition provide valuable perspectives on how AI might emulate or differ from human intelligence.

As we transition from classical philosophy to the modern era, the influence of early computer scientists and logicians becomes more pronounced. Alan Turing, often regarded as the father of computer science, introduced the concept of a universal machine capable of performing any computation given the appropriate algorithm. Turing's landmark paper "Computing Machinery and Intelligence" posed the question of whether machines can think and introduced the Turing Test as a criterion for determining machine intelligence. His work laid the theoretical foundation for AI, emphasizing the importance of algorithmic processes and formal systems in replicating cognitive functions.

The advent of AI as a distinct field of study in the mid-20th century was marked by seminal contributions from figures such as John McCarthy, Marvin Minsky, and Herbert Simon. John McCarthy, who coined the term "artificial intelligence," envisioned a future where machines could perform tasks that typically require human intelligence, such as reasoning, learning, and problem-solving. McCarthy's development of the LISP programming language facilitated advancements in AI research, particularly in symbolic reasoning and knowledge representation.

Marvin Minsky's work on artificial neural networks and cognitive architectures emphasized the importance of understanding the structure of intelligence. His exploration of how machines can simulate human problem-solving processes and adapt to new information contributed significantly to the development of machine learning. Herbert Simon's interdisciplinary approach, combining insights from psychology, economics, and computer science, highlighted the role of heuristics and bounded rationality in decision-making, influencing the development of AI systems that mimic human cognitive processes.

Machine learning, a subfield of AI, has its roots in the work of pioneers like Arthur Samuel and Frank Rosenblatt. Arthur Samuel's development of self-learning algorithms for playing checkers demonstrated the potential of machines to improve their performance through experience, laying the groundwork for modern reinforcement learning techniques. Frank Rosenblatt's invention of the perceptron, an early artificial neural network, provided a foundational model for understanding how machines could simulate the learning processes of the human brain.

The evolution of machine learning has been marked by significant theoretical advancements, particularly in the development of algorithms for supervised, unsupervised, and reinforcement learning. These approaches enable machines to learn from data, identify patterns, and make predictions, fundamentally transforming fields such as image recognition, natural language processing, and autonomous systems.

Natural language processing (NLP), a critical area of AI, seeks to enable machines to understand, interpret, and generate human language. The theoretical foundations of NLP are rooted in linguistic theories developed by figures such as Noam Chomsky, whose work on transformational grammar provided a framework for understanding the deep structure of language. Chomsky's theories emphasized the generative nature of language, suggesting that a finite set of rules can produce an infinite variety of sentences. This insight has informed the development of algorithms that enable machines to parse and generate natural language.

In recent years, the field of NLP has been revolutionized by the advent of deep learning techniques and the development of sophisticated models such as the Generative Pre-trained Transformer (GPT). GPT, developed by OpenAI, represents a significant leap forward in the ability of machines to generate human-like text. The model leverages a transformer architecture, which enables it to capture long-range dependencies in text and generate coherent, contextually relevant responses. GPT's ability to generate text based on pre-trained knowledge and fine-tune it for specific tasks exemplifies the transformative potential of AI in understanding and producing natural language.

The transformer architecture, introduced by Vaswani et al. in 2017, marked a paradigm shift in NLP by addressing limitations of previous models that struggled with long-range dependencies and parallelization. The attention mechanism, a core component of transformers, allows the model to weigh the importance of different words in a sentence, enabling it to capture nuanced contextual information. This innovation has led to significant improvements in various NLP tasks, including machine translation, text summarization, and question answering.

The success of models like GPT highlights the importance of pre-training and fine-tuning in achieving state-of-the-art performance in NLP. Pre-training involves training the model on a large corpus of text to learn general language patterns, while fine-tuning adapts the model to specific tasks using smaller, task-specific datasets. This two-step approach has proven highly effective in leveraging vast amounts of data to create models that perform well across a wide range of applications.

As we reflect on the contributions of foundational theorists and philosophers, it becomes evident that their insights continue to shape the development of AI and NLP. The quest to understand and replicate human intelligence has driven researchers to explore the theoretical underpinnings of cognition, language, and learning, resulting in transformative technologies that enhance our ability to process and interpret information.

The intersection of AI, machine learning, and natural language processing represents a dynamic and rapidly evolving field that promises to revolutionize our interaction with technology. By building on the foundational theories of past thinkers and integrating cutting-edge advancements, researchers are pushing the boundaries of what is possible, creating machines that not only perform complex tasks but also exhibit a degree of understanding and creativity that was once thought to be uniquely human.

In conclusion, the foundational theorists and philosophers have provided a rich tapestry of ideas that continue to influence the development of AI, natural language processing, and machine learning. From the early explorations of human cognition and language to the creation of sophisticated models like the Generative Pre-trained Transformer, the journey of AI reflects a deepening understanding of intelligence and the potential of machines to augment and enhance human capabilities. As we move forward, the ongoing dialogue between theoretical insights and technological innovations will undoubtedly yield new discoveries and applications, shaping the future of AI and its role in our society.

1 STRUCTURAL ANTHROPOLOGY, CULTURAL THEORY, AND THE LEGACY OF STRUCTURALISM

Claude Lévi-Strauss, a towering figure in the realm of anthropology, revolutionized the field with his development of structural anthropology, profoundly influencing cultural theory. His work laid the foundation for structuralism, a theoretical paradigm that has left an indelible mark on a myriad of academic disciplines, including literary criticism, sociology, and even the nascent field of artificial intelligence.

Lévi-Strauss was born in Brussels in 1908 to French parents of Jewish descent. His academic journey began with philosophy at the Sorbonne in Paris, where he developed a critical eye for the human condition and social structures. His early encounters with Marxist theory and psychoanalysis shaped his intellectual outlook, but it was his subsequent move to Brazil that steered him towards anthropology. Lévi-Strauss's experiences in Brazil, where he conducted fieldwork among indigenous tribes, provided him with firsthand insights into the richness and complexity of human cultures. These experiences were crucial in forming the basis of his later theories.

Structural anthropology, as pioneered by Lévi-Strauss, posits that underlying the diverse and multifaceted cultural expressions of humanity are universal structures of the human mind. He argued that these structures are the same for all human beings and that they manifest in the form of binary oppositions—such as life and death, nature and culture, and male and female. By examining these underlying structures, Lévi-Strauss believed we could gain a deeper understanding of the human condition. This approach was a significant departure from previous anthropological methods that focused primarily on cultural particularities and historical development.

Lévi-Strauss's structuralism was heavily influenced by the linguistic theories of Ferdinand de Saussure, who emphasized the importance of underlying structures in understanding language. Just as Saussure identified the rules and conventions governing the use of language, Lévi-Strauss sought to uncover the rules and conventions underlying cultural practices. He famously applied this method to the study of myths, arguing that myths from different cultures, despite their apparent differences, share a common structure. In his seminal work, "Mythologiques," Lévi-Strauss analyzed hundreds of myths from indigenous cultures across the Americas, revealing the universal patterns that underlie them. He demonstrated that myths operate like languages, with their own grammar and syntax, and that they function to resolve contradictions within human experience.

One of the central concepts in Lévi-Strauss's work is that of the "bricoleur" and the "engineer," which he introduced in his book "The Savage Mind." The bricoleur represents traditional, non-Western societies that use whatever materials and tools are at hand to address immediate problems. The engineer, on the other hand, symbolizes Western societies that rely on scientific principles and planned methodologies to solve problems. Lévi-Strauss argued that both modes of thinking are equally valid and effective, challenging the ethnocentric notion that Western scientific thought is superior to traditional knowledge systems.

Lévi-Strauss's structuralism had profound implications for cultural theory. By emphasizing the universality of human thought processes, he challenged the idea that cultures could be understood in isolation from one another. Instead, he proposed that all cultures are interconnected through shared cognitive structures. This perspective paved the way for a more holistic and integrative approach to the study of culture, one that recognizes the commonalities underlying cultural diversity.

The influence of Lévi-Strauss's ideas extended far beyond anthropology. In literary criticism, his structuralist approach inspired the development of narratology, the study of narrative structures. Scholars such as Roland Barthes and Gérard Genette applied structuralist principles to analyze the underlying structures of literary texts, uncovering the deep grammar that shapes storytelling across different cultures and genres. In sociology, structuralism provided new insights into the ways social institutions and practices are organized, highlighting the importance of underlying structures in shaping social life.

The impact of Lévi-Strauss's work is also evident in the field of artificial intelligence (AI). Structuralism's emphasis on underlying cognitive structures has parallels with the development of AI, particularly in the areas of machine learning and natural language processing. Just as Lévi-Strauss sought to uncover the universal structures of human thought, AI researchers aim to develop algorithms that can recognize and replicate these structures. For example, the use of deep learning techniques in AI involves training neural networks to identify patterns and structures in vast amounts of data, mirroring the structuralist approach of uncovering the underlying rules governing human cognition.

Moreover, the structuralist focus on binary oppositions can be seen in the development of AI systems that rely on binary classification algorithms. These algorithms operate by categorizing data into one of two possible classes, reflecting the structuralist idea that human thought is organized around binary oppositions. By drawing on structuralist principles, AI researchers are able to develop more sophisticated and accurate models of human cognition.

Lévi-Strauss's contributions to anthropology and cultural theory were not without controversy. Critics argued that his structuralist approach downplayed the importance of historical context and cultural specificity, reducing cultures to mere expressions of universal cognitive structures. They contended that Lévi-Strauss's focus on underlying structures overlooked the dynamic and fluid nature of cultural practices, which are constantly evolving in response to changing social and historical conditions. However, Lévi-Strauss's defenders argued that his work provided a valuable corrective to the parochialism and ethnocentrism that had previously dominated anthropology. By emphasizing the commonalities underlying cultural diversity, they contended, Lévi-Strauss's structuralism fostered a more inclusive and global perspective on human societies.

The legacy of Claude Lévi-Strauss is enduring and multifaceted. His pioneering work in structural anthropology has left an indelible mark on the study of human cultures, providing a framework for understanding the deep structures that shape our beliefs, practices, and social institutions. His ideas have transcended disciplinary boundaries, influencing fields as diverse as literary criticism, sociology, and artificial intelligence. In an era characterized by rapid technological advancements and increasing cultural interconnectedness, Lévi-Strauss's insights into the universal structures of human thought continue to resonate, offering valuable perspectives on the nature of human cognition and the complexities of cultural diversity.

As we look to the future, the relevance of Lévi-Strauss's work is likely to grow. The integration of structuralist principles into the development of AI promises to yield new insights into the ways we think and interact with the world around us. By harnessing the power of AI to uncover the underlying structures of human cognition, we can gain a deeper understanding of the universal patterns that connect us all. In this way, the legacy of Claude Lévi-Strauss lives on, shaping not only our understanding of the past but also our visions of the future.

The influence of structural anthropology extends beyond the academic sphere, informing contemporary debates on cultural identity and globalization. In a world increasingly characterized by cultural hybridity and transnational flows, Lévi-Strauss's emphasis on the interconnectedness of human societies provides a valuable framework for navigating the complexities of cultural exchange. His work reminds us that, despite our differences, we are all part of a shared human experience, bound together by the universal structures that underpin our thoughts and actions.

Claude Lévi-Strauss remains an iconic figure in the annals of anthropology, his contributions continuing to inspire and challenge scholars across disciplines. His structuralist approach, with its focus on uncovering the deep structures of human cognition, has opened up new avenues for understanding the richness and complexity of human cultures. In the ever-evolving landscape of cultural theory and AI, Lévi-Strauss's insights offer a timeless reminder of the enduring quest to comprehend the intricate web of meanings that define our shared humanity.

2 A DEEP DIVE INTO ANALYTICAL PSYCHOLOGY, ART, DREAMS AND HISTORICAL REFLECTIONS

Carl Gustav Jung, a Swiss psychiatrist and psychotherapist, made monumental contributions to the understanding of the human psyche. His work branched into various facets of psychology, art, dreams, and even touched upon the grim realities of his time, including the rise of Nazism. Jung's analytical psychology delves deep into the unconscious mind, offering profound insights into the human experience.

Jung's theories were a departure from the ideas of his mentor, Sigmund Freud. While Freud focused heavily on the sexual origins of neuroses, Jung broadened the scope, emphasizing the collective unconscious and archetypes. He believed that the unconscious was not just a repository of personal experiences but also contained universal symbols and themes shared by all humans. These archetypes, according to Jung, manifest in our dreams, art, and myths, influencing our behaviors and perceptions in profound ways.

Dreams were a significant area of exploration for Jung. He saw them as windows into the unconscious, revealing truths about the self that the conscious mind might be unaware of. Unlike Freud, who interpreted dreams primarily through the lens of repressed desires, Jung considered them a means of communication from the unconscious. He believed that dreams could provide insights, guidance, and even solutions to problems faced in waking life. By analyzing symbols and recurring themes in dreams, Jung helped individuals uncover hidden aspects of their personality and achieve greater self-awareness.

Art, for Jung, was another medium through which the unconscious could be expressed. He viewed artistic creativity as a manifestation of the inner workings of the psyche. Artists, in Jung's perspective, tap into the collective unconscious, bringing forth images and themes that resonate on a universal level. This process allows both the artist and the viewer to connect with deeper layers of meaning and experience. Jung himself engaged in artistic practices, creating mandalas and other works that he believed were expressions of his own unconscious mind.

The concept of the collective unconscious and archetypes is crucial in understanding Jung's perspective on art and dreams. Archetypes, such as the Hero, the Mother, and the Shadow, are fundamental motifs that recur across cultures and time periods. These archetypal images and narratives provide a framework through which individuals make sense of their experiences and the world around them. In dreams, these archetypes can appear in symbolic form, offering insights into personal and collective issues. In art, they manifest as recurring themes and symbols that evoke a sense of familiarity and profound significance.

Jung's analytical psychology also intersected with historical and cultural phenomena, including the rise of Nazism in Germany. Jung's reflections on this period reveal his concerns about the psychological underpinnings of mass movements and the shadow side of the collective psyche. He observed that the Nazi movement was not just a political phenomenon but also a manifestation of deep-seated archetypal forces within the collective unconscious. The figure of Adolf Hitler, for instance, could be seen as an embodiment of the dark, destructive aspects of the psyche that Jung termed the "Shadow."

Jung's engagement with the Nazis has been a subject of considerable debate and controversy. During the early 1930s, he held several positions within psychiatric organizations that were influenced by Nazi policies. Some critics have accused him of sympathizing with or failing to oppose the regime. However, a closer examination of his writings and actions suggests a more complex relationship. Jung was deeply critical of the totalitarian and anti-Semitic aspects of Nazism, and he used his platform to warn about the dangers of unchecked power and mass hysteria.

One of Jung's significant contributions during this time was his analysis of Hitler's psychology. Jung saw Hitler as a "medium" through which the collective unconscious of the German people was expressing itself. He described Hitler as a figure who embodied the dark, irrational forces that had been unleashed in Germany. Jung's insights into the psychological dynamics of Nazism highlighted the dangers of ignoring the unconscious and the potential for destructive energies to take hold of a society.

Jung's theories also have profound implications for understanding the nature of types and personality. His development of the theory of psychological types has had a lasting impact on psychology and popular culture. Jung proposed that individuals could be categorized based on their preferences in four dichotomies: Extraversion vs. Introversion, Sensing vs. Intuition, Thinking vs. Feeling, and Judging vs. Perceiving. These preferences form the basis of the Myers-Briggs Type Indicator (MBTI), a widely used personality assessment tool.

Jung's typology provides a framework for understanding individual differences and how people perceive and interact with the world. It emphasizes that there is no one "right" way to be; instead, different personality types offer unique strengths and perspectives. This understanding can enhance personal growth, improve relationships, and foster a greater appreciation of diversity.

Jung's influence extends beyond psychology into various fields, including art, literature, and spirituality. His ideas about the unconscious, archetypes, and individuation resonate with many creative and spiritual practices. Individuation, a core concept in Jung's theory, refers to the process of becoming one's true self. It involves integrating different aspects of the personality, including the conscious and unconscious, to achieve a state of wholeness. This journey of self-discovery and integration is reflected in many artistic and spiritual traditions, which seek to explore and express the depths of the human experience.

In literature, Jung's ideas have inspired numerous authors and poets. His exploration of the unconscious and archetypal themes has provided a rich source of material for storytelling. Writers have used Jungian concepts to create characters and narratives that delve into the complexities of the human psyche. The archetypal hero's journey, for example, mirrors the process of individuation, where the protagonist undergoes trials and transformations to achieve self-realization.

Jung's work has also had a significant impact on spiritual practices. His ideas about the collective unconscious and archetypes resonate with many religious and mystical traditions. Jung believed that spiritual experiences were expressions of the unconscious, providing a means of connecting with deeper truths and transcendent realities. He saw the process of individuation as a spiritual journey, where individuals seek to integrate the various aspects of their personality and connect with the divine within themselves.

Jung's engagement with alchemy is a testament to his interest in the intersection of psychology and spirituality. He viewed alchemy as a symbolic representation of the individuation process. The alchemical transformation of base metals into gold mirrored the psychological transformation of the self. Jung's analysis of alchemical texts and symbols provided insights into the deeper meanings and processes of psychological and spiritual growth.

Despite the profound impact of Jung's work, he was not without his critics. Some have argued that his theories are too abstract and lack empirical support. Others have questioned his engagement with controversial figures and movements, including his interactions with the Nazi regime. However, Jung's contributions to psychology and his exploration of the unconscious continue to inspire and challenge scholars, therapists, and individuals seeking to understand themselves and the world around them.

In conclusion, Carl Jung's work encompasses a vast and intricate exploration of the human psyche. His theories on analytical psychology, dreams, art, and personality types have provided valuable insights into the nature of the unconscious and the process of individuation. Jung's reflections on the rise of Nazism reveal his concerns about the psychological forces that drive mass movements and the dangers of ignoring the shadow side of the psyche. His ideas continue to influence various fields, offering a framework for understanding the complexities of human behavior and the journey toward self-realization. Through his exploration of the unconscious, Jung has left an enduring legacy that invites us to delve deeper into the mysteries of the mind and the profound connections between our inner and outer worlds.

3 SIMULACRA, SIMULATION, AND MODERN ETHICS IN THE AGE OF CYBER COMMUNICATION AND AI

Jean Baudrillard, a French sociologist, philosopher, and cultural theorist, is best known for his theories on simulacra and simulation, concepts that delve into the nature of reality and hyperreality in the modern world. Baudrillard's work explores the ways in which contemporary society has become dominated by symbols and signs, leading to a state where the distinction between reality and representation becomes blurred, ultimately culminating in the creation of hyperreality—a state in which reality itself is replicated to the point where it becomes indistinguishable from its representation.

Baudrillard's exploration of simulacra and simulation is articulated in his seminal work "Simulacra and Simulation." In this book, he discusses how contemporary culture is saturated with images and signs that no longer have any direct reference to the real world. Instead, these signs become self-referential, creating a simulated reality that precedes and determines what is perceived as real. Baudrillard identifies four stages of simulacra: the first stage is a faithful copy of the real; the second is a perversion of reality; the third pretends to be a faithful copy but is actually a copy with no original; and the fourth stage is pure simulation, where the simulacrum has no relation to any reality whatsoever. This progression leads to a hyperreality where the boundaries between the real and the imaginary are dissolved, and people live in a world of endless simulations.

The concept of hyperreality is evident in various aspects of modern life, from media and advertising to the digital realm. Baudrillard argues that in the contemporary era, media images and digital technologies create a simulated environment that shapes our perceptions and experiences. For instance, television and film present a version of reality that is often more compelling and believable than reality itself. This mediated experience influences individuals' understanding of the world, leading them to accept the simulated version of reality as the real one. In this sense, the representation becomes more significant than the actual event, and people become more attuned to the simulacra than to reality.

Baudrillard's notion of the "ecstasy of communication" further explores the implications of living in a hyperreal world. He describes this state as one where the proliferation of communication technologies and media channels has led to an overload of information, creating a superficial and instantaneous form of communication. This constant flow of information diminishes the depth and meaning of communication, as individuals are bombarded with images and messages that lack context and substance. The ecstasy of communication results in a society where the speed and volume of information take precedence over the content and quality of the message, leading to a fragmented and disoriented experience of reality.

The process of miniaturization is another key concept in Baudrillard's theory. He argues that technological advancements have led to the compression of time and space, creating a world where distances are eliminated, and events are experienced in real-time. This miniaturization of reality is exemplified by the rise of digital technologies and the internet, which allow for instantaneous communication and access to information from anywhere in the world. The result is a global village where traditional boundaries and distinctions are dissolved, and individuals are constantly connected to a network of information and communication.

Baudrillard's ideas on simulacra, simulation, and hyperreality have profound implications for understanding modern ethics in the context of cyber communication and artificial intelligence (AI). In a world dominated by simulations, ethical considerations become increasingly complex as the distinction between real and virtual experiences blurs. The rise of AI and digital technologies poses new challenges for ethical frameworks that were traditionally based on clear distinctions between human and machine, reality and representation.

One of the key ethical concerns in the age of AI and cyber communication is the question of authenticity. Baudrillard's concept of hyperreality suggests that in a world where simulations are more real than reality, the notion of authenticity becomes problematic. Digital technologies and AI have the ability to create hyperreal experiences that are indistinguishable from the real world, raising questions about the authenticity of these experiences. For example, virtual reality (VR) and augmented reality (AR) technologies can create immersive environments that mimic real-world experiences, leading individuals to question what is real and what is simulated. This blurring of boundaries challenges traditional notions of truth and authenticity, prompting a re-evaluation of ethical principles in the digital age.

Another ethical issue related to Baudrillard's theories is the impact of AI and cyber communication on human identity and agency. In a hyperreal world, individuals' identities are often shaped by the simulated environments and digital representations they encounter. Social media platforms, for instance, create curated versions of reality that influence how individuals perceive themselves and others. AI technologies, such as facial recognition and data analytics, further complicate issues of privacy and autonomy, as individuals' personal information is collected, analyzed, and used in ways that may not be fully understood or consented to. The ethical implications of these technologies include concerns about surveillance, data security, and the potential for manipulation and control.

Baudrillard's concept of the ecstasy of communication also raises ethical questions about the nature of human interaction in the digital age. The constant flow of information and the superficial nature of online communication can lead to a sense of disconnection and alienation. In a hyperconnected world, individuals may feel overwhelmed by the sheer volume of information and the pressure to constantly engage with digital content. This can result in a loss of meaningful and authentic human connections, as interactions become increasingly mediated by technology. Ethical considerations in this context include the need to balance the benefits of digital communication with the potential for negative social and psychological impacts.

The ethical challenges posed by AI and cyber communication also extend to the realm of decision-making and accountability. As AI systems become more advanced and integrated into various aspects of society, the question of who is responsible for the actions and decisions made by these systems becomes critical. Baudrillard's theories suggest that in a hyperreal world, the lines of accountability can become blurred, as individuals and institutions may rely on simulations and algorithms to make decisions. This raises ethical concerns about transparency, bias, and the potential for unintended consequences. Ensuring that AI systems are designed and implemented in ways that uphold ethical standards and human values is a key challenge for policymakers and technologists.

Baudrillard's work also has implications for the ethics of representation in the digital age. The proliferation of digital images and simulations raises questions about the power and influence of visual media in shaping perceptions and beliefs. In a hyperreal world, images and representations can take on a life of their own, detached from any original reference. This can lead to the manipulation of reality and the construction of alternative narratives that may serve particular interests or agendas. Ethical considerations in this context include the need for critical media literacy and the importance of maintaining a healthy skepticism towards digital representations.

In conclusion, Jean Baudrillard's theories on simulacra, simulation, the ecstasy of communication, and miniaturization provide a critical framework for understanding the complexities of modern ethics in the context of cyber communication and AI. His insights into the nature of hyperreality and the proliferation of simulations challenge traditional notions of authenticity, identity, and agency, prompting a re-evaluation of ethical principles in the digital age. As AI and digital technologies continue to evolve and reshape our world, Baudrillard's work offers valuable perspectives on the ethical implications of living in a hyperreal society, highlighting the need for critical reflection and ethical accountability in the development and use of these technologies.

4 SEMIOTICS, MYTHOLOGIES, AND THE DEATH OF THE AUTHOR

Roland Barthes, a seminal figure in literary theory and criticism, profoundly influenced the study of semiotics and the analysis of cultural phenomena through his exploration of mythologies and his provocative notion of the "death of the author." Barthes' work delves into the structures and functions of signs and symbols within society, and his theories have had a lasting impact on the fields of literary criticism, cultural studies, and semiotics.

Barthes was born in 1915 in Cherbourg, France. He pursued his education at the University of Paris, where he developed a keen interest in literature and linguistics. His early works were influenced by structuralism, a theoretical approach that seeks to understand the underlying structures that shape human culture and thought. Barthes' engagement with structuralism laid the groundwork for his later contributions to semiotics—the study of signs and symbols as elements of communicative behavior.

One of Barthes' most significant contributions to semiotics is his book "Mythologies," published in 1957. In this collection of essays, Barthes analyzes various cultural artifacts and practices, ranging from advertisements and fashion to food and popular culture, to reveal the ideological underpinnings that shape them. Barthes argues that these everyday objects and practices are imbued with meanings that go beyond their immediate, literal significance. He refers to these additional layers of meaning as "myths."

For Barthes, myths function as a type of speech, a system of communication that transforms history into nature. In other words, myths naturalize cultural and ideological constructs, making them appear as if they are inherent and self-evident truths. By doing so, myths obscure the historical and social processes that produce them, rendering them invisible and unquestionable. Barthes' analysis of myths is not limited to overtly ideological phenomena; he demonstrates that even the most mundane aspects of daily life can serve as vehicles for conveying and reinforcing dominant ideologies.

One of the most famous essays in "Mythologies" is Barthes' analysis of a photograph of a young black soldier saluting the French flag. Barthes deconstructs the image to reveal the multiple layers of meaning it conveys. On the surface, the image represents patriotism and national unity. However, Barthes argues that the image also serves to mask the realities of colonialism and racial inequality by presenting the black soldier as a symbol of inclusiveness and integration. Through this analysis, Barthes illustrates how myths operate to perpetuate dominant ideologies by transforming complex social realities into simplified, naturalized narratives.

Barthes' work in semiotics extends beyond "Mythologies." In his later writings, he delves deeper into the nature of signs and the ways they function within language and culture. One of his key contributions to semiotics is the distinction between denotation and connotation. Denotation refers to the literal, explicit meaning of a sign, while connotation encompasses the additional, culturally specific meanings that a sign carries. Barthes argues that connotation is crucial for understanding how signs operate within cultural contexts, as it is through connotation that signs acquire their ideological significance.

Barthes' exploration of semiotics culminates in his seminal essay "The Death of the Author," published in 1967. In this provocative text, Barthes challenges the traditional notion of the author as the central figure in the creation and interpretation of literary texts. He argues that the focus on the author as the source of meaning limits the possibilities for interpretation and reduces the text to a mere reflection of the author's intentions. Instead, Barthes proposes that the meaning of a text should be derived from the interplay of signs within the text itself, independent of the author's intentions.

By declaring the "death of the author," Barthes shifts the focus from the author to the reader. He contends that it is the reader who brings the text to life through the act of interpretation. In this view, the text is not a fixed, stable entity but a dynamic, open-ended field of meaning that is constantly being reinterpreted and redefined by its readers. This shift in focus has significant implications for literary criticism, as it challenges the authority of the author and empowers the reader as an active participant in the creation of meaning.

Barthes' notion of the "death of the author" also has broader implications for cultural theory and the study of media and communication. In a world saturated with texts and images, the idea that meaning is not fixed but constantly in flux resonates with contemporary understandings of media and culture. Barthes' work anticipates the rise of postmodernism, with its emphasis on the plurality of meanings and the decentering of traditional sources of authority.

The impact of Barthes' theories extends far beyond the realm of literary criticism. His ideas have influenced a wide range of disciplines, including cultural studies, media studies, and sociology. In cultural studies, Barthes' analysis of myths and his focus on the ideological functions of signs have provided a framework for understanding how culture operates to produce and reproduce social power relations. His work has also informed critical approaches to media, highlighting the ways in which media texts construct and convey meaning.

In media studies, Barthes' semiotic approach has been instrumental in analyzing how media representations shape our perceptions of reality. By examining the ways in which media texts use signs and symbols to construct meaning, scholars can uncover the ideological messages embedded within these texts. Barthes' insights into the functioning of myths are particularly relevant in the context of advertising and consumer culture, where images and symbols are used to create desires and shape consumer behavior.

Barthes' influence is also evident in the field of sociology, where his ideas have been used to explore the ways in which signs and symbols function within social systems. His work on semiotics provides a tool for analyzing how social practices and institutions are constructed and maintained through the use of signs. By examining the ways in which signs operate within social contexts, sociologists can gain a deeper understanding of the processes that shape social reality.

In addition to his contributions to semiotics and cultural theory, Barthes was also a prolific writer on the subject of literature and textuality. His works, such as "S/Z" and "The Pleasure of the Text," offer detailed analyses of literary texts and explore the ways in which texts produce meaning. In "S/Z," Barthes conducts a meticulous reading of Balzac's short story "Sarrasine," demonstrating how the text operates as a network of codes and signs that generate multiple layers of meaning. In "The Pleasure of the Text," Barthes examines the subjective experience of reading, exploring the ways in which readers derive pleasure from engaging with texts.

Barthes' exploration of textuality is marked by a playful and experimental approach to writing. His works often blur the boundaries between criticism and creativity, combining rigorous analysis with personal reflection and poetic expression. This approach reflects Barthes' belief that texts are not static objects but dynamic processes that invite multiple interpretations and engagements.

Roland Barthes' legacy is vast and multifaceted. His contributions to semiotics, cultural theory, and literary criticism have left an enduring impact on the study of language, culture, and communication. His insights into the functioning of signs and symbols continue to inform contemporary approaches to media and cultural analysis, while his provocative notion of the "death of the author" has reshaped our understanding of authorship and interpretation. Barthes' work challenges us to look beyond the surface of texts and cultural artifacts, to uncover the deeper structures and meanings that shape our perceptions of reality. In doing so, he has opened up new possibilities for critical inquiry and creative exploration, making him a central figure in the landscape of modern thought.

5 POWER, KNOWLEDGE, AND DISCOURSE

Michel Foucault, a French philosopher and social theorist, profoundly shaped contemporary thought through his explorations of power, knowledge, and discourse. His work delves into the ways in which power operates in society, not merely as a top-down force exerted by institutions but as a pervasive network of relations that shapes and is shaped by knowledge and language. Foucault's intellectual contributions span a wide array of fields, including history, sociology, criminology, and cultural studies, making him a pivotal figure in the landscape of modern intellectual thought.

Foucault's analysis of power moves beyond traditional conceptions that view power solely as a form of repression or domination. Instead, he posits that power is omnipresent and operates through the everyday practices and discourses that constitute social life. Power, for Foucault, is not just something that institutions like the state wield over individuals; it is embedded in the very fabric of social interactions and knowledge production. This idea is most comprehensively articulated in his concept of the "power/knowledge" nexus, which underscores the inseparable relationship between power and knowledge. According to Foucault, knowledge is never neutral or objective but is always intertwined with power relations. The production of knowledge is a means through which power is exercised, and conversely, power relations shape what is considered knowledge.

Foucault's notion of discourse is central to his analysis of power and knowledge. Discourse, in Foucault's framework, refers to the ways in which language and practice combine to produce and regulate what can be said, thought, and done within a particular context. Discourses are not merely ways of speaking or writing but are constitutive of social reality itself. They define the boundaries of knowledge and shape the identities and actions of individuals. By examining the historical development of various discourses, Foucault reveals how they serve to normalize certain ways of thinking and acting while marginalizing others. For instance, in his seminal work "The History of Sexuality," Foucault traces the development of sexual discourses and shows how they have been used to regulate bodies and desires, demonstrating how power operates through the discourse on sexuality.

Roland Barthes, another influential French intellectual, intersects with Foucault in his exploration of language, signs, and their impact on culture and society. Barthes is best known for his work on semiotics, the study of signs and symbols, and his theory of mythologies, which examines how cultural narratives and myths shape our understanding of the world. Like Foucault, Barthes challenges the idea that language and knowledge are neutral. Instead, he argues that they are imbued with ideological meanings that serve to reinforce existing power structures.

Barthes' concept of the "death of the author" complements Foucault's critique of traditional authority and the production of knowledge. In his essay "The Death of the Author," Barthes argues that the meaning of a text should not be determined by the intentions of its author but by the interpretations of its readers. This shift from authorial intent to reader interpretation decentralizes the authority of the author and opens up the text to multiple meanings and interpretations. This idea parallels Foucault's emphasis on the contingent and constructed nature of knowledge and challenges the notion of fixed or singular truths.

Intellectual rigor and critical analysis are hallmarks of both Foucault and Barthes. Their works invite readers to question the taken-for-granted assumptions about power, knowledge, and language that shape our everyday lives. Foucault's historical investigations into the origins and transformations of various social institutions, such as prisons, hospitals, and schools, reveal how these institutions are not merely neutral sites of administration but are deeply implicated in the exercise of power. His concept of biopower, which he develops in works like "Discipline and Punish" and "The Birth of the Clinic," examines how modern states regulate populations through an array of techniques and practices aimed at managing life, health, and bodies. Biopower operates through a combination of disciplinary practices that target individual bodies and regulatory mechanisms that target populations, thereby linking the micro-level of individual subjectivity with the macro-level of state governance.

Barthes, with his acute sense of cultural critique, exposes how everyday objects and practices are laden with ideological significance. In "Mythologies," he deconstructs a wide range of cultural artifacts, from advertisements to wrestling matches, to show how they function as myths that naturalize and perpetuate dominant ideologies. Barthes' semiotic analysis reveals the hidden meanings and power relations embedded in cultural texts, encouraging readers to look beyond the surface and question the deeper structures of meaning that shape their perceptions and beliefs.

Both Foucault and Barthes engage with the concept of subjectivity, exploring how individuals are constituted as subjects through various discourses and practices. Foucault's later work, particularly his lectures at the Collège de France, focuses on the technologies of the self—practices and techniques through which individuals shape their own identities and conduct. He examines how subjectivity is not a given but is produced through the interplay of power and knowledge. Barthes, in his autobiographical work "Roland Barthes by Roland Barthes," similarly reflects on the fragmented and constructed nature of the self, challenging the notion of a unified, coherent identity.

The intellectual contributions of Foucault and Barthes have significant implications for contemporary social and cultural theory. Their insights into the workings of power, knowledge, and discourse provide powerful tools for analyzing a wide range of social phenomena, from the dynamics of social institutions to the production of cultural meaning. In the realm of social media and digital communication, their theories offer valuable perspectives for understanding how new forms of power and knowledge are being produced and circulated.

Social media platforms, with their algorithms and data-driven practices, exemplify the complex interplay of power and knowledge that Foucault describes. These platforms generate vast amounts of data about users, which are then used to shape and influence behavior, preferences, and interactions. The algorithms that govern social media feeds operate as modern-day techniques of biopower, regulating and managing digital populations. Barthes' semiotic analysis can be applied to the content shared on social media, revealing how images, hashtags, and memes function as contemporary myths that convey and reinforce ideological messages.

In the context of artificial intelligence and machine learning, Foucault's and Barthes' theories invite critical reflection on the ways in which these technologies are embedded in power relations and discursive practices. AI systems, which are often perceived as neutral and objective, are in fact shaped by the data and algorithms that reflect existing social biases and inequalities. The production of knowledge by AI systems is a deeply political process, raising important ethical questions about accountability, transparency, and justice.

Foucault's and Barthes' intellectual legacies continue to resonate in contemporary debates about the nature of knowledge, power, and subjectivity. Their works challenge us to think critically about the ways in which our realities are constructed and to recognize the pervasive influence of power in shaping our perceptions and experiences. By examining the historical and cultural contexts in which knowledge is produced and circulated, they provide a framework for understanding the complexities of modern society and the potential for resistance and transformation.

In summary, Michel Foucault and Roland Barthes have profoundly influenced our understanding of power, knowledge, and discourse. Their works offer critical insights into the ways in which language, signs, and practices shape social reality and perpetuate power relations. By deconstructing the taken-for-granted assumptions that underpin our understanding of the world, Foucault and Barthes challenge us to think critically about the nature of knowledge and the ways in which it is produced and circulated. Their intellectual contributions continue to inspire and inform contemporary social and cultural theory, providing valuable tools for analyzing the complexities of modern life.

6 THE COMMODIFICATION OF ART IN POSTMODERNISM

Benjamin H. D. Buchloh is a prominent art historian and critic whose work has significantly shaped the discourse around postmodern art. Born in 1941, Buchloh has spent much of his career analyzing and critiquing the developments in contemporary art, particularly focusing on the shifts that occurred in the latter half of the 20th century. His insights into postmodern art have been influential in understanding the complexities and contradictions of this era.

Postmodernism in art is characterized by its reaction against the principles and practices of modernism. Where modernism was often concerned with the pursuit of new forms, originality, and the avant-garde, postmodernism is marked by a skeptical approach to grand narratives, an embrace of pastiche, and a focus on the multiplicity of meanings and interpretations. Buchloh's contributions to the study of postmodern art are invaluable in dissecting these characteristics and exploring how they manifest in various artistic practices.

One of Buchloh's central concerns is the critique of what he perceives as the commodification of art in the postmodern era. He argues that the commercial aspects of the art world have increasingly influenced the production and reception of art, often at the expense of critical and avant-garde practices. This critique is part of a broader analysis of how art functions within the capitalist system, reflecting Buchloh's deep engagement with Marxist theory. By examining how art is commodified, Buchloh highlights the tensions between artistic autonomy and market forces, a theme that recurs throughout his work.

Buchloh is also known for his rigorous examination of specific artists and movements that have defined postmodern art. His essays and critiques often focus on the works of artists such as Andy Warhol, Gerhard Richter, and Hans Haacke, among others. Through these studies, Buchloh explores how these artists navigate the complex terrain of postmodernity, engaging with issues such as the role of mass media, the appropriation of historical styles, and the critique of institutional power.

In his analysis of Andy Warhol, for example, Buchloh delves into the ways in which Warhol's work embodies the postmodern condition. Warhol's use of mass-produced images and his embrace of celebrity culture challenge traditional notions of artistic originality and authorship. Buchloh argues that Warhol's art reflects a broader cultural shift towards a society dominated by media images and consumer culture. This perspective aligns with the postmodern critique of the supposed autonomy of art, suggesting that art is inextricably linked to the broader social and economic contexts in which it is produced.

Gerhard Richter is another artist whose work Buchloh has extensively analyzed. Richter's diverse body of work, which includes both abstract and photorealistic paintings, exemplifies the postmodern rejection of a singular artistic style or narrative. Buchloh interprets Richter's art as a response to the historical traumas of the 20th century, particularly the legacy of World War II and the Holocaust. By oscillating between abstraction and figuration, Richter's work resists easy categorization and reflects the fragmented nature of postmodern identity and memory.

Hans Haacke's work, on the other hand, is examined by Buchloh through the lens of institutional critique. Haacke's art often explicitly addresses the power structures within the art world, including the relationships between art institutions, corporate sponsorship, and political interests. Buchloh sees Haacke's work as a powerful example of how postmodern art can serve as a form of social and political critique, challenging the complicity of art institutions in the broader dynamics of power and capitalism.

Buchloh's engagement with postmodern art is not limited to individual artists but also encompasses broader movements and trends. One such trend is the resurgence of conceptual art in the postmodern era. Conceptual art, with its emphasis on ideas and processes over aesthetic objects, aligns with the postmodern suspicion of traditional artistic values. Buchloh's analysis of conceptual art highlights how this movement challenges the commodification of art by prioritizing intellectual engagement over visual pleasure.

In addition to his critiques of individual artists and movements, Buchloh has also contributed to the theoretical understanding of postmodernism itself. He has written extensively on the historical conditions that gave rise to postmodern art, situating it within the broader context of late capitalism. Buchloh's theoretical work often intersects with the writings of other influential theorists, such as Theodor Adorno and Walter Benjamin, whose critiques of culture and society provide a foundation for Buchloh's own analyses.

One of the key themes in Buchloh's theoretical work is the idea of historical memory and its representation in postmodern art. He argues that postmodern art often engages with history in complex and ambivalent ways, oscillating between nostalgia and critique. This engagement with history is evident in the widespread use of appropriation in postmodern art, where artists borrow and recontextualize images and styles from different historical periods. Buchloh interprets this practice as both a critique of the modernist obsession with originality and an exploration of the fragmented nature of historical consciousness in the postmodern era.

Buchloh's writings also address the implications of technological advancements for postmodern art. The rise of digital media and the proliferation of images have fundamentally transformed the ways in which art is produced and consumed. Buchloh is critical of how these technological changes have further entrenched the commodification of art, as digital reproduction facilitates the mass distribution and commercialization of artistic images. At the same time, he acknowledges the potential for digital media to democratize art and challenge traditional hierarchies within the art world.

Throughout his career, Buchloh has been a vocal advocate for the critical and oppositional potential of art. He argues that, despite the pervasive influence of commodification and market forces, art retains the capacity to resist and critique dominant power structures. This belief in the transformative power of art underpins much of Buchloh's writing and reflects his commitment to a vision of art that is deeply engaged with social and political issues.

In summary, Benjamin H. D. Buchloh's contributions to the study of postmodern art are characterized by a deep engagement with the complexities and contradictions of this era. Through his critiques of individual artists, movements, and broader theoretical issues, Buchloh provides a nuanced understanding of how postmodern art navigates the tensions between commodification, historical memory, and social critique. His work highlights the ways in which postmodern art challenges traditional notions of artistic autonomy and originality, reflecting the broader cultural and economic shifts of the late 20th century. As an influential voice in contemporary art criticism, Buchloh continues to shape the discourse around postmodern art, offering critical insights that remain relevant in our ongoing exploration of art and its place in society.

7 DECONSTRUCTION AND DIFFÉRANCE

Jacques Derrida, a French philosopher, is best known for his development of deconstruction and the concept of différance, both of which have significantly influenced post-structuralism. Derrida's work emerged in the context of post-war philosophy, a period marked by the reevaluation of many established philosophical ideas and traditions. His thought was also profoundly shaped by existentialism, the dominant intellectual movement in France during the mid-20th century. Derrida's contributions to philosophy and critical theory have fundamentally altered our understanding of language, meaning, and interpretation, enhancing and challenging many aspects of contemporary thought.

Deconstruction, as formulated by Derrida, is a method of critical analysis that seeks to uncover the complexities, contradictions, and instabilities within texts. It is not merely a technique for dismantling arguments but a way of understanding the inherent instability of language and meaning. Deconstruction reveals that texts do not have fixed, singular meanings but are instead open to multiple interpretations, shaped by the play of language and the context in which they are read. Derrida's approach challenges the traditional idea that meaning is directly tied to the author's intention, suggesting instead that meaning is always deferred and never fully present.

The concept of différance is central to Derrida's philosophy. It is a neologism that combines the meanings of two French verbs: "différer," meaning both "to differ" and "to defer." Différance highlights the dual process by which meaning is produced in language. On one hand, it refers to the way words differ from one another, creating meaning through their differences. On the other hand, it indicates the deferral of meaning, as each word points to other words in an endless chain of signification. This dual process undermines the idea of fixed, stable meanings, emphasizing instead the fluid and dynamic nature of language.

Derrida's ideas emerged as part of the broader intellectual movement known as post-structuralism, which sought to move beyond the structuralist emphasis on underlying structures and systems. While structuralism, influenced by linguists like Ferdinand de Saussure, focused on the stable structures of language and culture, post-structuralism highlighted the instability and fluidity of these structures. Derrida's deconstruction is a key aspect of this shift, as it challenges the notion of stable structures and exposes the inherent contradictions within any system of meaning.

Post-structuralism, and Derrida's work in particular, developed in the context of post-war philosophy, a period characterized by intense philosophical reflection and critique. After the devastation of World War II, many European intellectuals sought to understand the conditions that had led to such widespread destruction and to rethink the foundations of Western thought. Existentialism, led by figures such as Jean-Paul Sartre and Simone de Beauvoir, was one of the dominant philosophical movements of this time. Existentialism emphasized individual freedom, responsibility, and the search for meaning in an absurd and often chaotic world.

Derrida's thought was deeply influenced by existentialism, though he moved beyond many of its central tenets. While existentialists focused on the individual's confrontation with a meaningless world, Derrida turned his attention to the structures of language and meaning that shape our understanding of the world. He was particularly interested in how these structures are inherently unstable and open to multiple interpretations. This shift from individual existential concerns to the broader structures of language and meaning is a key aspect of Derrida's philosophical project.

Derrida's work also engages with the broader themes of post-war philosophy, particularly the critique of Enlightenment rationality and the questioning of grand narratives. Post-war philosophers, influenced by the horrors of the Holocaust and the atomic bomb, became skeptical of the idea that human reason and progress could lead to a better world. Derrida's deconstruction is part of this broader critique, as it challenges the idea that language and meaning can be fully controlled or mastered. Instead, he emphasizes the ways in which meaning is always deferred, always in flux.

One of the key implications of Derrida's thought is the idea that interpretation is an endless process. There is no final, definitive meaning to be found in a text, as meaning is always shifting and evolving. This has significant implications for a wide range of fields, from literary criticism to philosophy to political theory. Derrida's work suggests that our understanding of texts, concepts, and even ourselves is always provisional and open to revision. This emphasis on the fluidity of meaning challenges many traditional ideas about knowledge and interpretation, opening up new possibilities for critical inquiry and thought.

Derrida's influence extends beyond philosophy and literary theory to a wide range of disciplines. His ideas have been taken up by scholars in fields as diverse as law, anthropology, psychoanalysis, and architecture. In each of these fields, deconstruction has been used to challenge established ideas and to reveal the complexities and contradictions within various systems of thought and practice. Derrida's work has thus had a profound impact on contemporary thought, reshaping our understanding of language, meaning, and interpretation.

Despite his significant influence, Derrida's work has also been the subject of much debate and controversy. Critics have accused him of promoting a form of relativism that undermines the possibility of meaningful communication and understanding. They argue that if meaning is always deferred and unstable, then it becomes difficult, if not impossible, to make definitive claims or to engage in meaningful dialogue. Derrida, however, resisted this characterization of his work. He argued that deconstruction is not about abandoning meaning or communication but about recognizing the complexities and instabilities that are always present in our attempts to understand the world.

Derrida's thought also engages with the political implications of language and meaning. He was deeply concerned with the ways in which power operates through language and how deconstruction can be used as a tool to challenge and resist various forms of domination. For Derrida, deconstruction is a form of critical practice that seeks to reveal the hidden assumptions and power dynamics that shape our understanding of the world. This has led to the development of what is sometimes called "deconstructive politics," which seeks to use the insights of deconstruction to critique and transform social and political structures.

In the realm of ethics, Derrida's work has also had a significant impact. He challenges traditional notions of ethical certainty and emphasizes the importance of responsibility and decision-making in the face of uncertainty. For Derrida, ethics is not about following predetermined rules or principles but about engaging with the complexities and ambiguities of each situation. This emphasis on ethical responsibility in the face of uncertainty is a key aspect of Derrida's thought and has influenced a wide range of contemporary ethical debates.

Derrida's engagement with existentialism is evident in his focus on themes of death, finitude, and the limits of human understanding. He often returns to the question of mortality and the ways in which our awareness of death shapes our understanding of meaning and existence. This existential dimension of Derrida's thought adds a depth and richness to his philosophical project, as he grapples with the fundamental questions of human existence and the limits of our ability to understand and control our world.

In his later work, Derrida explored themes of hospitality, justice, and forgiveness, further expanding the ethical and political dimensions of his thought. He argued that true hospitality requires an openness to the other that goes beyond mere tolerance or acceptance. This radical hospitality challenges us to rethink our ethical and political commitments and to recognize the ways in which our understanding of justice and forgiveness is always provisional and open to revision.

In summary, Jacques Derrida's contributions to philosophy and critical theory have had a profound and lasting impact on contemporary thought. His development of deconstruction and the concept of différance has reshaped our understanding of language, meaning, and interpretation, challenging traditional ideas and opening up new possibilities for critical inquiry. Derrida's engagement with post-structuralism, post-war philosophy, and existentialism reflects his deep commitment to understanding the complexities and instabilities of human existence.

His work continues to inspire and challenge scholars across a wide range of disciplines, offering new insights into the nature of language, meaning, and power. Through his innovative and often provocative ideas, Derrida has enhanced our understanding of the world and the ways in which we make sense of it, leaving a lasting legacy in the field of philosophy and beyond.

8 THE WORK OF ART IN THE AGE OF MECHANICAL REPRODUCTION: INSIGHTS IN THE DIGITAL AND AI ERA

Walter Benjamin's seminal essay "The Work of Art in the Age of Mechanical Reproduction," published in 1936, has profoundly influenced how we understand art, culture, and technology. Benjamin's analysis centers on the transformation of art in the context of modernity, focusing on how technological advancements, specifically mechanical reproduction, alter the perception and value of art. His insights remain strikingly relevant in the current digital age, where computers, cyber technologies, and artificial intelligence, such as GPT (Generative Pre-trained Transformer), further complicate and extend the questions he raised.

In his essay, Benjamin begins by examining how the reproducibility of art changes its nature and function. Before the advent of mechanical reproduction, art was primarily unique and tied to a specific time and place, embodying what Benjamin calls its "aura." This aura encompasses the authenticity, originality, and presence of a work of art, aspects that are inherently linked to its existence as a singular object. The aura represents the unique experience one has in the presence of the original artwork, an experience rooted in its historical and cultural context.

However, with the rise of technologies such as photography and film, the ability to reproduce art mechanically leads to a fundamental shift. Reproduction detaches the art object from its original context, allowing it to be disseminated and accessed widely. This process diminishes the aura, as the reproduced artwork loses its unique presence and becomes more of a commodity. Benjamin argues that this shift democratizes art, making it accessible to a broader audience, but it also transforms the nature of art itself, as its value is no longer tied to its uniqueness but to its reproducibility and mass distribution.

Benjamin's concerns about the impact of mechanical reproduction on art extend to the way it changes the role of the artist and the audience. The artist's role becomes less about creating a unique, original piece and more about engaging with the processes of reproduction and mass communication. Similarly, the audience's experience of art shifts from a contemplative engagement with a singular object to a more distracted consumption of widely available reproductions. This new mode of interaction with art reflects broader changes in society, where mass media and technology increasingly mediate and shape our experiences.

The themes Benjamin explores in his essay are amplified and extended in the digital age, where computers and cyber technologies have revolutionized the production, reproduction, and consumption of art. Digital technologies enable even greater ease and fidelity in reproducing and disseminating art. The internet allows for the instantaneous distribution of digital reproductions to a global audience, further eroding the aura of the original work. Art in the digital age can be manipulated, altered, and shared in ways that were unimaginable in Benjamin's time.

One of the most significant developments in the digital realm is the advent of artificial intelligence, particularly in the form of generative models like GPT. GPT, developed by OpenAI, is a powerful tool that uses machine learning to generate text based on a vast corpus of human language data. It exemplifies the potential of AI to create new forms of art and communication, raising new questions about creativity, authorship, and authenticity.

GPT and similar AI technologies can generate text, music, visual art, and more, blurring the lines between human and machine creativity. These technologies challenge traditional notions of authorship, as the outputs they produce result from complex algorithms rather than individual human creativity. In a sense, GPT can be seen as an extension of the mechanical reproduction processes Benjamin discussed, but with the added dimension of generating new, original content rather than merely reproducing existing works.

The implications of AI-generated art are profound. On one hand, these technologies democratize creative production, enabling individuals without traditional artistic skills to create compelling works. On the other hand, they raise questions about the value and authenticity of art produced by machines. If art can be generated algorithmically, what does this mean for the role of the artist and the uniqueness of their vision? How do we evaluate and appreciate art that lacks a human author?

Benjamin's concept of the aura becomes even more complex in the context of AI-generated art. While mechanical reproduction diminished the aura by detaching the artwork from its original context, AI-generated art complicates the notion of originality itself. If an AI can produce infinite variations of an artwork, each potentially unique but lacking a human origin, how do we conceptualize authenticity and originality?

Furthermore, AI technologies like GPT can analyze and mimic existing artistic styles, creating works that are indistinguishable from those produced by human artists. This ability to replicate styles challenges our understanding of creativity and innovation. If an AI can generate a painting in the style of Van Gogh or compose a symphony in the manner of Beethoven, does this devalue the original works or expand our appreciation of these styles?

The rise of digital and AI technologies also transforms the way we interact with and consume art. Virtual galleries, online exhibitions, and digital art platforms enable new forms of engagement and interaction. These platforms allow for a more participatory and interactive experience, where audiences can not only view but also remix and reinterpret artworks. This shift reflects Benjamin's observation that mechanical reproduction changes the audience's relationship with art, making it more interactive and less contemplative.

However, the digital age also introduces new challenges related to intellectual property and ownership. The ease of copying and distributing digital art raises questions about the rights of artists and creators. In a world where digital reproductions can be easily shared and modified, how do we protect the interests of artists and ensure they are compensated for their work? These issues are further complicated by AI-generated art, where questions of ownership and authorship become even more ambiguous.

Benjamin's insights into the political implications of art and technology remain relevant today. He argued that mechanical reproduction could be used both to democratize art and to serve political agendas. In the digital age, the internet and social media platforms can amplify artistic voices and foster global cultural exchange. However, these same technologies can also be used for propaganda and manipulation, reflecting the dual potential of technology that Benjamin identified.

The digital age has also seen the rise of new forms of art that engage with and critique the very technologies that enable their creation. Digital artists often explore themes related to technology, surveillance, and the digital economy, reflecting contemporary concerns about the impact of technology on society. These works can be seen as part of a broader tradition of art that seeks to critically engage with the conditions of its production, a theme that resonates with Benjamin's analysis.

In conclusion, Walter Benjamin's "The Work of Art in the Age of Mechanical Reproduction" provides a critical framework for understanding the impact of technological advancements on art and culture. His insights into the transformation of art in the context of mechanical reproduction remain highly relevant in the digital age, where computers, cyber technologies, and AI further complicate and extend the questions he raised. The rise of AI-generated art challenges traditional notions of creativity, authorship, and authenticity, while digital technologies transform the ways we produce, consume, and interact with art. As we navigate these changes, Benjamin's work offers valuable perspectives on the evolving relationship between art, technology, and society.

9 AI, EXISTENTIALISM AND THE UNIVERSES

Jean-Paul Sartre, a towering figure in 20th-century philosophy, is best known for his contributions to existentialism and phenomenology. His work profoundly influenced not only philosophical discourse but also literature, psychology, political theory, and more. Sartre's existentialism emphasizes individual freedom, responsibility, and the subjective experience of existence, while his engagement with phenomenology provides a rigorous method for exploring consciousness and the structures of experience. In the contemporary context, the rise of artificial intelligence (AI) presents new opportunities and challenges for existential and phenomenological inquiries, raising questions about consciousness, agency, and the nature of existence in a universe increasingly shaped by technology.

Sartre's existentialism is rooted in the idea that existence precedes essence. This means that individuals are not born with a predetermined nature or purpose; rather, they must create their own essence through their actions and choices. This radical freedom comes with the weight of responsibility, as individuals are wholly accountable for their actions and the person they become. Sartre famously declared, "Man is condemned to be free," highlighting the paradoxical nature of freedom as both an empowering and burdensome condition. Existentialism thus confronts individuals with the necessity of making meaningful choices in an indifferent and often absurd universe.

Phenomenology, the philosophical method developed by Edmund Husserl and later adopted and adapted by Sartre, focuses on the structures of experience from the first-person perspective. Phenomenology seeks to describe phenomena as they are experienced, without recourse to preexisting theories or assumptions. Sartre's phenomenological approach in works like "Being and Nothingness" aims to uncover the fundamental structures of human existence, such as consciousness, perception, and intentionality. He posits that consciousness is always directed toward something, a concept known as intentionality, and that this directedness is foundational to the human experience of the world.

In "Being and Nothingness," Sartre explores the concept of nothingness, which he argues is a central aspect of human consciousness. Nothingness refers to the capacity of consciousness to negate, question, and transcend given realities. It is through this capacity that individuals can envision possibilities beyond their immediate circumstances and exercise their freedom. Sartre's analysis of nothingness also leads to his famous concept of bad faith, a form of self-deception in which individuals deny their freedom and responsibility by conforming to societal roles and expectations.

The advent of AI introduces new dimensions to existential and phenomenological questions. AI systems, particularly those employing machine learning and neural networks, are capable of processing vast amounts of data and performing complex tasks that were once thought to require human intelligence. These advancements prompt us to reconsider what it means to be conscious, to make decisions, and to exercise agency. While AI lacks the subjective experience and intentionality that characterize human consciousness, its capabilities challenge our understanding of these concepts and their significance.

One of the central questions raised by AI in the context of existentialism is whether AI systems can possess a form of agency or autonomy. Traditional existentialism asserts that human beings are unique in their capacity for self-directed action and self-definition. However, as AI systems become more sophisticated and capable of autonomous behavior, the boundaries between human and machine agency become increasingly blurred. Can AI systems be said to "choose" or "act" in any meaningful sense, or are their actions merely the result of programmed algorithms and data inputs? This question touches on the nature of freedom and responsibility, core tenets of existential philosophy.

Moreover, the development of AI invites a reexamination of the concept of consciousness. Phenomenology emphasizes the importance of subjective experience, yet AI operates without subjective awareness. This raises questions about the possibility and nature of machine consciousness. Some theorists argue that consciousness might emerge from sufficiently complex computational processes, while others maintain that subjective experience is inherently tied to biological organisms. Sartre's phenomenological approach, with its focus on the structures of experience, provides a valuable framework for exploring these questions, even as it underscores the profound differences between human and artificial intelligences.

The existential challenge of finding meaning in an increasingly automated and technologically mediated world is another significant issue. As AI systems take on more roles traditionally performed by humans, individuals may struggle with feelings of redundancy and purposelessness. Sartre's existentialism emphasizes the importance of creating one's own meaning through authentic choices and actions. In a world where AI can perform many tasks more efficiently than humans, the search for meaning becomes more pressing. Individuals must navigate the existential tension between technological advancement and the quest for authentic existence.

Sartre's existentialism also speaks to the ethical implications of AI. The freedom and responsibility central to existentialist thought demand that we consider the ethical consequences of creating and deploying AI systems. As creators and users of AI, humans must grapple with the moral dimensions of their choices, ensuring that AI technologies are developed and used in ways that respect human dignity and promote the common good. Sartre's emphasis on responsibility and the ethical implications of freedom provides a critical lens through which to evaluate the societal impact of AI.

The concept of universes, both literal and metaphorical, also intersects with existential and phenomenological questions in intriguing ways. Sartre's existentialism is concerned with the human condition within the universe, emphasizing the individual's role in creating meaning within an indifferent cosmos. The exploration of literal universes, as in astrophysics and cosmology, expands our understanding of the physical universe and our place within it. These discoveries can deepen the existential questions about the nature of existence, the limits of human knowledge, and the search for meaning.

The metaphorical universe of AI and digital technologies represents a new frontier for existential inquiry. Virtual realities, simulated environments, and digital worlds created by AI offer new contexts for human experience and interaction. These digital universes challenge traditional notions of reality and identity, raising questions about what it means to exist and interact in virtual spaces. Sartre's phenomenological method can help us explore these new forms of existence, analyzing the structures of experience within digital environments and their implications for our understanding of self and other.

The interaction between AI and human beings in these digital universes also raises existential questions about authenticity and alienation. Sartre's concept of bad faith, the denial of one's freedom and responsibility, can be applied to the ways individuals may lose themselves in virtual realities, escaping from the demands of authentic existence. Conversely, digital technologies can also offer new opportunities for self-expression and connection, challenging us to find authentic ways of being in these new contexts.

In summary, Jean-Paul Sartre's existentialism and phenomenology provide profound insights into the nature of human existence, freedom, and responsibility. His work challenges us to confront the fundamental questions of what it means to be, to choose, and to create meaning in an indifferent universe. The rise of AI and digital technologies introduces new dimensions to these questions, prompting us to reconsider our understanding of consciousness, agency, and the search for authenticity. Sartre's philosophical framework offers valuable tools for navigating these challenges, emphasizing the importance of freedom, responsibility, and the pursuit of meaning in an ever-evolving universe. As we continue to explore the frontiers of technology and existence, Sartre's existentialism remains a vital and relevant guide for understanding the complexities of the human condition.

10 MEDIA THEORY AND THE GLOBAL VILLAGE

Marshall McLuhan, a Canadian philosopher and media theorist, revolutionized our understanding of the relationship between media and society. His groundbreaking ideas about media theory and the concept of the global village have profoundly influenced how we think about communication, technology, and culture. McLuhan's insights are particularly relevant in the digital age, where the proliferation of digital media has transformed our world in ways that he anticipated with remarkable prescience.

McLuhan's most famous dictum, "the medium is the message," encapsulates his belief that the nature of a medium influences society more profoundly than the content it conveys. This idea suggests that each medium, whether print, radio, television, or digital, has its own unique effects and consequences on human perception, cognition, and social organization. By focusing on the characteristics of the medium itself rather than the content it delivers, McLuhan shifted the focus of media studies to the structural and functional aspects of communication technologies.

In his seminal work, "Understanding Media: The Extensions of Man," McLuhan explores how different media extend human senses and alter our perceptions of the world. He categorizes media into "hot" and "cool" based on their levels of engagement and the degree of participation they require from the audience. Hot media, like print and radio, provide high-definition information and require less audience involvement. Cool media, like television and telephone, offer lower resolution and invite greater audience participation. This distinction helps explain how different media shape our sensory experiences and interactions with the world.

McLuhan's concept of the global village is another cornerstone of his media theory. He argued that electronic media, particularly television and later the internet, would transform the world into a single interconnected community. In the global village, distance and time are compressed, allowing people to experience events and communicate with others instantaneously, regardless of geographic location. This idea foreshadows the digital age, where the internet and social media have indeed created a highly interconnected and interdependent world.

The digital age has amplified McLuhan's theories in profound ways. The advent of the internet, smartphones, and social media platforms has created a hyper-connected global village where information flows rapidly and ubiquitously. Digital media have not only transformed how we communicate but also how we think, learn, and interact with the world. The characteristics of digital media, such as interactivity, immediacy, and networked connectivity, align with McLuhan's insights about the transformative power of media.

Digital media, much like McLuhan's concept of cool media, require active participation from users. Social media platforms like Facebook, Twitter, and Instagram engage users in constant interaction, shaping their perceptions and social dynamics. These platforms enable real-time communication and instant sharing of information, creating a sense of global presence and community. The global village McLuhan envisioned is now a digital reality where people can connect, share, and collaborate across vast distances in real time.

One of the key implications of McLuhan's media theory in the digital age is the transformation of social structures and cultural practices. Digital media have redefined notions of identity, community, and privacy. Online identities can be constructed, curated, and modified, allowing for greater flexibility and experimentation. However, this also raises questions about authenticity and the fragmentation of the self in the digital world. The blurring of public and private boundaries on social media platforms further complicates issues of privacy and surveillance.

The global village, while fostering greater connectivity and access to information, also presents challenges related to information overload and the spread of misinformation. The sheer volume of information available online can overwhelm users, making it difficult to discern credible sources from unreliable ones. This has significant implications for public discourse and democratic processes, as the rapid spread of misinformation can shape public opinion and influence political outcomes.

McLuhan's idea that media are extensions of human senses is vividly illustrated by the impact of digital technologies on our sensory experiences. The use of smartphones and other digital devices has become an integral part of daily life, extending our sensory capabilities and altering our interactions with the world. Augmented reality (AR) and virtual reality (VR) technologies further expand these sensory extensions, creating immersive experiences that blur the line between the physical and digital worlds.

In the digital age, McLuhan's notion of the medium shaping our sensory experiences is evident in how we consume news, entertainment, and information. Digital platforms curate content algorithms that tailor information to individual preferences, creating echo chambers and filter bubbles. These personalized media environments can reinforce existing beliefs and limit exposure to diverse perspectives, impacting social cohesion and understanding.

McLuhan's insights also have implications for education and learning in the digital age. The traditional classroom model, based on print culture and linear learning, is being transformed by digital technologies that support interactive and multimodal learning experiences. Online education platforms, digital textbooks, and educational apps offer new ways of accessing and engaging with information, emphasizing collaboration and experiential learning. McLuhan's ideas about media as extensions of human faculties suggest that digital technologies can enhance cognitive processes and learning outcomes, but they also require a rethinking of pedagogical approaches.

The rise of artificial intelligence (AI) and machine learning further extends McLuhan's theories into new territories. AI technologies, such as natural language processing and machine vision, augment human capabilities and automate complex tasks, reshaping various industries and aspects of daily life. The integration of AI into digital media platforms enhances personalization and user engagement but also raises ethical concerns about data privacy, algorithmic bias, and the implications of machine autonomy.

McLuhan's work encourages us to critically examine the broader societal and cultural impacts of these technological advancements. As AI systems become more integrated into communication and media, they influence not only how information is processed and disseminated but also how knowledge is produced and validated. The intersection of AI and digital media creates new forms of interaction and representation, challenging traditional notions of authorship, creativity, and intellectual property.

The global village concept also resonates with contemporary discussions about globalization and cultural exchange. Digital media facilitate the global flow of cultural products, ideas, and practices, fostering cross-cultural understanding and collaboration. However, this interconnectedness also brings to light issues of cultural homogenization, digital colonialism, and the unequal distribution of technological resources. McLuhan's theories provide a framework for understanding these dynamics and the tensions between global connectivity and cultural diversity.

In conclusion, Marshall McLuhan's media theory and the concept of the global village offer valuable insights into the transformative power of media and communication technologies. His ideas about the medium as the message, the sensory extensions of media, and the global village anticipated many of the developments in the digital age. As digital technologies continue to reshape our world, McLuhan's work remains a critical tool for analyzing the societal, cultural, and ethical implications of these changes. The digital age amplifies and extends McLuhan's theories, highlighting the need for ongoing critical reflection on the role of media in shaping human experience and social structures.

11 THE SOCIETY OF THE SPECTACLE

Guy Debord, a French Marxist theorist, writer, and filmmaker, is most famous for his influential work "The Society of the Spectacle," published in 1967. Debord's critique of contemporary capitalist society revolves around the concept of the spectacle, a term he uses to describe the pervasive and all-encompassing nature of modern media and consumer culture. According to Debord, the spectacle is a social relation mediated by images, where reality is replaced by representations and appearances. This idea presciently anticipates many aspects of today's media-saturated world, including the phenomena of simulacra and virtual realities.

Debord's analysis begins with the assertion that in societies where modern conditions of production prevail, all of life presents itself as an immense accumulation of spectacles. Everything that was directly lived has moved away into representation. In this context, the spectacle is not just a collection of images, but a social relationship between people that is mediated by images. It is a worldview that has been actualized, and it manifests itself in every aspect of life. The spectacle serves to unify and explain the reality in which people live, but it does so by replacing genuine social interaction with mediated, image-based relationships.

The spectacle, according to Debord, serves the interests of the ruling class by perpetuating a false reality that keeps individuals passive and distracted. It promotes a way of life centered on consumption, where commodities are imbued with symbolic meanings that people aspire to acquire. The spectacle is both a symptom and an instrument of the capitalist system, reinforcing the power structures that sustain it. It distracts individuals from the real conditions of their existence and from the potential for genuine social change.

Debord's concept of the spectacle has profound implications for understanding contemporary media culture. The proliferation of screens and digital media has created a world where images and representations are more pervasive than ever. Social media, advertising, television, and other forms of mass communication constantly bombard individuals with images that shape their perceptions of reality. These images often present a distorted view of the world, emphasizing superficial appearances and consumerist ideals.

The notion of simulacra, developed by Jean Baudrillard, complements Debord's theory of the spectacle by exploring how representations and signs have come to replace reality itself. Simulacra are copies or images that no longer have any original referent, existing only as representations of other representations. In a world dominated by simulacra, the distinction between reality and representation becomes blurred, leading to a hyperreal condition where the simulation is more real than reality itself.

Baudrillard's concept of simulacra extends Debord's critique by suggesting that the spectacle has evolved to a point where it no longer merely mediates reality but actually constitutes it. In this hyperreal world, individuals interact with representations and signs that have no grounding in any original reality. For example, digital images and virtual experiences can create environments that feel more real and immediate than the physical world, further entrenching individuals in the logic of the spectacle.

Virtual reality (VR) and augmented reality (AR) technologies exemplify the contemporary manifestation of the spectacle and simulacra. These technologies create immersive experiences that can replicate or enhance reality, allowing users to engage with environments and scenarios that are entirely constructed. VR and AR blur the lines between the real and the virtual, offering experiences that are simultaneously real in their impact on the user and artificial in their construction.

In the context of Debord's and Baudrillard's theories, virtual realities can be seen as the ultimate expression of the spectacle. They create spaces where individuals can escape from the mundane aspects of their lives and immerse themselves in carefully crafted, commodified experiences. These virtual environments often emphasize visual spectacle and interactivity, appealing to the desire for novelty and entertainment. However, they also perpetuate the alienation and passivity that Debord critiques, as individuals become more engaged with artificial representations than with their real social and political conditions.

The rise of social media platforms further illustrates the pervasive influence of the spectacle in contemporary society. Platforms like Facebook, Instagram, and Twitter create virtual spaces where individuals present curated versions of their lives through images and posts. These representations often emphasize idealized or aspirational aspects of life, contributing to a culture of comparison and competition. The spectacle of social media encourages individuals to see themselves and others through the lens of commodified images, reinforcing consumerist values and distracting from genuine social engagement.

Moreover, the algorithms that drive social media platforms amplify the logic of the spectacle by prioritizing content that generates engagement, often favoring sensational or emotionally charged images and stories. This creates echo chambers and filter bubbles where individuals are exposed to a narrow range of perspectives, reinforcing existing beliefs and biases. The spectacle of social media thus not only shapes individual perceptions but also influences broader social and political dynamics.

Debord's critique of the spectacle also has implications for the nature of political engagement in the digital age. The spectacle's emphasis on images and representations extends to the realm of politics, where media coverage and political campaigns often focus on appearances and soundbites rather than substantive issues. Politicians and public figures become spectacles themselves, their images carefully managed to appeal to public sentiments. This reduces complex political realities to simplified, commodified representations, obscuring the underlying power dynamics and systemic issues.

The commodification of culture and information in the digital age reinforces the spectacle's power. Online platforms and media companies profit from the production and dissemination of images, turning every aspect of life into a potential commodity. Personal data, user-generated content, and online interactions are all monetized, further entrenching the spectacle's logic of consumption and passive engagement. The digital economy thrives on the continuous production and circulation of images, perpetuating the alienation and fragmentation that Debord critiques.

Despite the pervasive influence of the spectacle, Debord's work also points to the possibility of resistance and transformation. He emphasizes the need for critical awareness and the reclamation of genuine social interactions. By recognizing the mechanisms of the spectacle and challenging its representations, individuals can begin to dismantle the false realities it creates and reconnect with the real conditions of their existence. This requires a shift from passive consumption to active engagement, from mediated representations to direct social relations.

The potential for resistance is evident in various forms of digital activism and counter-spectacle practices. Grassroots movements and alternative media use digital platforms to challenge dominant narratives and create spaces for marginalized voices. These efforts seek to disrupt the spectacle's hegemony by providing alternative perspectives and fostering genuine social connections. However, the challenge remains to sustain these efforts and resist the spectacle's tendency to co-opt and commodify dissent.

In conclusion, Guy Debord's "The Society of the Spectacle" provides a critical framework for understanding the pervasive influence of media and consumer culture in contemporary society. His insights into the nature of the spectacle, the commodification of images, and the alienation of social relations remain profoundly relevant in the digital age. The concepts of simulacra and virtual realities further extend Debord's critique, highlighting the ways in which representations have come to constitute reality itself. As digital technologies continue to shape our world, Debord's work challenges us to critically examine the impact of the spectacle on our perceptions, relationships, and political engagement, and to seek ways to reclaim genuine social interaction and transformative action.

12 POSTMODERNISM AND CULTURAL THEORY

Fredric Jameson is a renowned American literary critic and Marxist political theorist whose work on postmodernism and cultural theory has profoundly influenced contemporary thought. His exploration of postmodernism, particularly its relationship with late capitalism, provides a critical framework for understanding the complexities and contradictions of our current era. Central to Jameson's analysis are the concepts of schizophrenia, as borrowed from Lacanian psychoanalysis, and the pervasive influence of multinational corporations in shaping culture and society in the digital age.

Jameson's seminal work, "Postmodernism, or, The Cultural Logic of Late Capitalism," published in 1991, offers a comprehensive critique of postmodern culture and its entanglement with the economic conditions of late capitalism. He argues that postmodernism represents a fundamental shift in the cultural logic of society, characterized by the dissolution of traditional boundaries and the proliferation of fragmented and commodified cultural forms. Unlike the modernist period, which was marked by a sense of historical continuity and depth, postmodern culture is dominated by superficiality, pastiche, and a waning of affect.

One of Jameson's key insights is the relationship between postmodern culture and the economic conditions of late capitalism. He contends that the cultural forms of postmodernism are deeply intertwined with the dynamics of a globalized capitalist economy. In this context, culture becomes a commodity, produced and consumed in a manner similar to other goods and services. The result is a culture of constant novelty and spectacle, where the distinction between high and low culture is eroded, and everything is subsumed under the logic of the market.

Jameson's use of the term "schizophrenia" to describe the postmodern condition is drawn from the psychoanalytic theories of Jacques Lacan. Lacan's concept of schizophrenia refers to a breakdown in the relationship between signifiers, resulting in a fragmented and incoherent sense of self. In a postmodern context, Jameson uses schizophrenia metaphorically to capture the disorienting and fragmented nature of contemporary experience. The rapid proliferation of images, texts, and commodities in postmodern culture creates a sense of disconnection and disorientation, where individuals struggle to construct coherent narratives or identities.

This fragmented experience is exacerbated by the influence of digital technologies, which accelerate the pace of cultural production and consumption. The digital age, with its emphasis on instantaneity and interconnectivity, amplifies the characteristics of postmodern culture described by Jameson. Social media platforms, streaming services, and online marketplaces facilitate the constant flow of information and commodities, further entrenching the logic of late capitalism. In this digital landscape, individuals are bombarded with a relentless stream of images and information, contributing to a sense of temporal and spatial dislocation.

The role of multinational corporations in shaping postmodern culture is another critical aspect of Jameson's analysis. He argues that these corporations are not merely economic entities but also cultural producers, deeply involved in the creation and dissemination of cultural forms. The influence of corporations extends to every aspect of cultural production, from film and television to fashion and music. This corporate dominance results in a homogenization of culture, where diverse cultural expressions are subsumed under the logic of profitability and marketability.

In the digital age, the power of corporations is further amplified by their control over digital platforms and technologies. Companies like Google, Facebook, Amazon, and Apple exert enormous influence over the production, distribution, and consumption of cultural content. These corporations not only shape the cultural landscape but also collect vast amounts of data on users, further entrenching their power and control. The digital economy, driven by data and algorithms, exemplifies the logic of late capitalism, where everything, including cultural expressions and personal information, is commodified.

Jameson's critique extends to the impact of postmodern culture on politics and ideology. He argues that the proliferation of images and representations in postmodern culture contributes to a sense of cynicism and apathy, undermining the potential for collective political action. The spectacle of media and entertainment distracts individuals from the underlying economic and political structures that shape their lives. This depoliticization is reinforced by the fragmentation of experience, where individuals are isolated and disconnected from larger social and political movements.

The influence of Lacanian psychoanalysis in Jameson's work provides a theoretical framework for understanding the psychological dimensions of postmodern culture. Lacan's emphasis on the symbolic order and the role of language in shaping the unconscious resonates with Jameson's analysis of the cultural logic of late capitalism. The breakdown of coherent narratives and the proliferation of fragmented signifiers in postmodern culture can be understood through Lacan's concept of the symbolic order, where the stability of meaning is constantly undermined.

In the context of digital technologies, the Lacanian concept of the "mirror stage" offers a useful analogy for understanding the construction of identity in the digital age. The mirror stage refers to the process by which an infant recognizes their reflection in a mirror, leading to the formation of the "I" or self. In the digital age, social media platforms function as virtual mirrors, where individuals construct and present their identities through curated images and narratives. This digital self-construction is often fragmented and performative, reflecting the broader characteristics of postmodern culture.

The commodification of culture and identity in the digital age raises significant ethical and political questions. The logic of late capitalism, as described by Jameson, prioritizes profit over human well-being, leading to the exploitation of labor, the erosion of privacy, and the homogenization of cultural expressions. Digital technologies, while offering new opportunities for connection and creativity, also contribute to these dynamics by facilitating the commodification of personal data and the proliferation of superficial cultural forms.

Jameson's analysis of postmodernism and late capitalism provides a critical framework for understanding these contemporary challenges. His insights into the relationship between culture and economy highlight the need for a more nuanced and critical approach to digital technologies and their impact on society. By recognizing the ways in which digital platforms and multinational corporations shape cultural production and consumption, we can begin to address the ethical and political implications of the digital age.

In conclusion, Fredric Jameson's work on postmodernism and cultural theory offers a comprehensive critique of the cultural logic of late capitalism. His analysis of the fragmentation and commodification of culture, informed by Lacanian psychoanalysis, provides valuable insights into the psychological and social dimensions of the postmodern condition. In the digital age, these insights are particularly relevant as digital technologies and multinational corporations further entrench the logic of late capitalism. By critically engaging with Jameson's work, we can better understand the complexities and contradictions of our contemporary cultural landscape and explore new possibilities for resistance and transformation.

13 PRAGMATISM, EDUCATION, AND THE IMPACT OF AI AND COMPUTING IN THE DIGITAL AGE

John Dewey, one of the foremost American philosophers and educators, profoundly influenced the fields of philosophy, education, and social reform through his development of pragmatism and his innovative ideas on education. Dewey's philosophy emphasizes the importance of experience, experimentation, and democratic engagement in the learning process. His ideas continue to be relevant today, particularly in the context of technological advancements such as artificial intelligence (AI) and computing. Dewey's pragmatic approach provides a valuable framework for understanding the implications of these technologies for education and society.

Pragmatism, as developed by Dewey, is a philosophical tradition that prioritizes the practical consequences of ideas and actions. It posits that the truth of a concept is determined by its practical effects and usefulness in real-world situations. Dewey applied this principle to education, arguing that learning should be an active, experiential process that engages students in meaningful activities. He believed that education should not be about the passive absorption of information but about fostering critical thinking, problem-solving, and the ability to apply knowledge in practical contexts.

Dewey's vision of education was deeply democratic. He believed that schools should be communities where students learn to engage with others, participate in democratic processes, and develop the skills necessary for active citizenship. This approach contrasts sharply with traditional models of education that emphasize rote memorization and authoritarian structures. Dewey's emphasis on experience and interaction aligns well with the possibilities offered by modern technology, which can facilitate collaborative learning and interactive, hands-on experiences.

One of Dewey's lesser-known but intriguing pieces is his essay on "machines evolving into God." In this essay, Dewey explores the potential for machines and technology to evolve to a point where they possess capabilities far beyond current human understanding. This idea, although speculative, touches on themes that are highly relevant in the context of AI and computing. The rapid advancements in these fields have led to debates about the potential for machines to achieve superintelligence and the ethical implications of such developments.

The idea of machines evolving into entities with god-like capabilities raises profound philosophical and ethical questions. Dewey's pragmatic philosophy provides a framework for addressing these questions by focusing on the practical consequences of technological advancements. Instead of getting lost in abstract speculation, Dewey's approach encourages us to consider how these technologies can be used to enhance human life and promote democratic values. This perspective is crucial in discussions about AI and computing, where the focus often shifts to dystopian scenarios and existential risks.

In the context of education, AI and computing technologies offer significant opportunities and challenges. On one hand, these technologies can enhance personalized learning, provide access to vast resources of information, and facilitate new forms of interactive and experiential learning. AI-driven educational tools can adapt to individual students' needs, offering customized feedback and support that can help students learn more effectively. Computing technologies can also support collaborative projects, enabling students to work together across distances and engage with real-world problems.

However, the integration of AI and computing in education also raises important ethical and practical issues. One concern is the potential for these technologies to exacerbate existing inequalities. Access to advanced educational technologies is often limited by socioeconomic factors, which can widen the gap between privileged and underprivileged students. Dewey's commitment to democratic education emphasizes the need to ensure that technological advancements are accessible to all students, regardless of their background.

Another concern is the potential for AI and computing to undermine the human aspects of education. Dewey believed that education should be a deeply social and interactive process, where students engage with teachers and peers in meaningful ways. There is a risk that over-reliance on technology could lead to more isolated and less socially engaged forms of learning. Dewey's philosophy encourages us to use technology in ways that enhance, rather than replace, human interaction and democratic participation.

Dewey's ideas also provide a framework for thinking about the ethical implications of AI and computing beyond education. The potential for machines to evolve into entities with advanced capabilities raises questions about the nature of intelligence, consciousness, and ethical agency. Dewey's pragmatic approach suggests that we should evaluate these technologies based on their practical effects and their ability to promote human flourishing. This means considering not just the technical capabilities of AI, but also their impact on human values, social structures, and democratic processes.

The idea of machines evolving into god-like entities intersects with debates about the role of the supernatural and the limits of human understanding. Dewey was skeptical of traditional religious and supernatural explanations, arguing that they often hindered critical thinking and scientific inquiry. Instead, he advocated for a naturalistic and empirical approach to understanding the world. In the context of AI and computing, this perspective encourages us to focus on the empirical and practical aspects of technological advancements, rather than getting caught up in speculative or mystical thinking.

Dewey's emphasis on empirical inquiry and practical consequences is particularly relevant in the field of computing, where the rapid pace of innovation often outstrips our ability to fully understand and control these technologies. By applying a pragmatic approach, we can develop more grounded and responsible strategies for managing the development and deployment of AI and computing technologies. This means prioritizing transparency, accountability, and ethical considerations in the design and use of these technologies.

The integration of AI and computing into various aspects of society also raises questions about the nature of work and human agency. Dewey's philosophy highlights the importance of meaningful work and active engagement in shaping our identities and communities. As machines take over more tasks traditionally performed by humans, we need to consider how to ensure that people still have opportunities for meaningful work and participation. This might involve rethinking economic and social structures to better distribute the benefits of technological advancements and ensure that all individuals can contribute to and benefit from these changes.

Dewey's ideas on education, democracy, and technological advancement offer valuable insights for navigating the complexities of the digital age. His pragmatic philosophy encourages us to focus on the practical effects of technology and to use these advancements to enhance human well-being and democratic participation. By applying Dewey's principles, we can develop more equitable, inclusive, and responsible approaches to integrating AI and computing into education and society.

In conclusion, John Dewey's contributions to pragmatism and education provide a robust framework for understanding and addressing the challenges and opportunities posed by technological advancements in AI and computing. His emphasis on experience, democratic engagement, and practical consequences aligns well with the potential of these technologies to transform education and society. Dewey's ideas encourage us to use technology in ways that enhance human interaction, promote democratic values, and ensure equitable access to the benefits of technological progress. As we navigate the complexities of the digital age, Dewey's philosophy remains a vital guide for creating a more just and humane society.

SECTION TWO

CONTEMPORARY THINKERS AND CULTURAL CRITICS

Contemporary thinkers and cultural critics have increasingly turned their attention to the burgeoning fields of AI and cybertechnology, recognizing their profound impact on society and culture. These technologies are not only reshaping industries and economies but also transforming the ways in which we understand and interact with the world. By enhancing cultural theory with insights from these fields, contemporary thinkers are developing new frameworks for interpreting the complex interplay between technology and culture.

AI, or artificial intelligence, represents one of the most significant technological advancements of our time. Its ability to process vast amounts of data and learn from it has opened up new possibilities for automation, prediction, and decision-making. However, AI also raises important questions about agency, ethics, and control. Contemporary thinkers such as Shoshana Zuboff and Nick Bostrom have explored the implications of AI on privacy, surveillance, and the future of humanity. Zuboff, in her seminal work "The Age of Surveillance Capitalism," argues that AI-driven data collection and analysis have created a new form of capitalism where personal data is commodified and used to predict and manipulate behavior. This, she suggests, has significant implications for individual autonomy and democratic governance.

Nick Bostrom, on the other hand, delves into the existential risks posed by AI. In "Superintelligence: Paths, Dangers, Strategies," Bostrom outlines the potential for AI to surpass human intelligence and the possible scenarios that could arise from such an event. His work raises critical questions about the alignment of AI goals with human values and the safeguards necessary to prevent catastrophic outcomes. These thinkers contribute to a growing body of literature that examines the ethical and societal implications of AI, urging policymakers and technologists to consider the broader impacts of their work.

Cybertechnology, encompassing the internet, digital communication, and cybersecurity, is another area of focus for contemporary cultural critics. The internet has revolutionized the way we access information, communicate, and organize, but it has also given rise to new forms of social interaction and cultural expression. Scholars such as Manuel Castells and Zeynep Tufekci have analyzed the ways in which digital networks influence social movements and political participation. Castells, in "The Rise of the Network Society," argues that the internet has enabled new forms of social organization that transcend traditional geographic and institutional boundaries. This networked society, he suggests, has profound implications for power dynamics and social change.

Zeynep Tufekci, in "Twitter and Tear Gas: The Power and Fragility of Networked Protest," examines the role of digital platforms in contemporary social movements. She argues that while these platforms can amplify voices and mobilize large groups quickly, they also introduce new vulnerabilities and challenges. The ease of online organization can lead to shallow forms of engagement and make movements susceptible to surveillance and repression. Tufekci's work highlights the dual-edged nature of cybertechnology, demonstrating how it can both empower and undermine social movements.

Enhancing cultural theory with insights from AI and cybertechnology involves integrating these technologies into broader discussions about culture, society, and power. Cultural theorists such as Donna Haraway and Bruno Latour have pioneered this approach, blending concepts from technology studies with cultural analysis. Haraway's "Cyborg Manifesto" is a foundational text in this regard, proposing the cyborg as a metaphor for the hybridization of human and machine. Haraway argues that this hybridity challenges traditional binaries such as nature/culture and human/machine, offering new ways of thinking about identity and agency in a technologically mediated world.

Bruno Latour's actor-network theory (ANT) provides another framework for integrating technology into cultural theory. ANT posits that both human and non-human actors (such as technologies) are part of networks that shape social and cultural outcomes. Latour's work encourages us to consider how technologies are not merely tools but active participants in the construction of social reality. This perspective is particularly useful for analyzing the complex interactions between AI, cybertechnology, and society, as it acknowledges the agency of these technologies in shaping cultural practices and norms.

The integration of AI and cybertechnology into cultural theory also involves examining the ways in which these technologies influence cultural production and consumption. The rise of digital media and algorithmic content curation has transformed the landscape of cultural production, creating new opportunities and challenges for artists, creators, and audiences. Scholars such as Lev Manovich and Tarleton Gillespie have explored the implications of these changes for cultural practices and industries. Manovich's work on software studies examines how software shapes cultural production, arguing that digital tools and platforms influence the aesthetics and distribution of cultural artifacts. Gillespie, in "Custodians of the Internet," analyzes the role of algorithms and content moderation in shaping online discourse, highlighting the power of tech companies in curating and controlling information.

The impact of AI on cultural production is particularly evident in the realm of creative AI, where machine learning algorithms are used to generate art, music, and literature. This raises questions about authorship, creativity, and the nature of artistic expression. Can an algorithm be considered a creator? What does it mean for art to be generated by a machine rather than a human? These questions challenge traditional notions of creativity and require a reevaluation of cultural theory to account for the contributions of AI.

Moreover, AI and cybertechnology are also transforming the ways in which we consume culture. Algorithmic recommendation systems, such as those used by streaming services and social media platforms, personalize content delivery based on user preferences and behavior. This has significant implications for cultural diversity and the democratization of cultural access. While these systems can help users discover new content, they can also reinforce existing biases and create filter bubbles that limit exposure to diverse perspectives. Cultural critics such as Safiya Umoja Noble and Cathy O'Neil have highlighted the potential for algorithmic bias and discrimination, urging greater transparency and accountability in the design and implementation of these technologies.

Safiya Umoja Noble's "Algorithms of Oppression" examines how search engines perpetuate racial and gender biases, shaping the ways in which information is accessed and understood. Noble's work underscores the importance of critically examining the design and impact of AI systems on marginalized communities. Similarly, Cathy O'Neil's "Weapons of Math Destruction" explores the societal harms caused by biased algorithms, advocating for ethical standards and regulatory frameworks to mitigate these risks.

In addition to these critiques, contemporary thinkers are also exploring the potential for AI and cybertechnology to enhance cultural theory by providing new tools and methodologies for research and analysis. Digital humanities, for example, leverages computational techniques to analyze large datasets and uncover patterns in cultural artifacts. This interdisciplinary field combines traditional humanities scholarship with data science, enabling new forms of cultural analysis that were previously unimaginable.

AI-driven text analysis, network analysis, and visualization tools can reveal insights into cultural trends, discourse, and social dynamics. By integrating these tools into cultural theory, researchers can gain a deeper understanding of the complexities of culture and its interactions with technology. This approach also encourages collaboration between humanities scholars, data scientists, and technologists, fostering interdisciplinary dialogue and innovation.

Furthermore, the integration of AI and cybertechnology into cultural theory also prompts a reexamination of the ethical and philosophical dimensions of technology. Contemporary thinkers such as Luciano Floridi and Frank Pasquale have emphasized the need for a robust ethical framework to guide the development and deployment of AI. Floridi's work on the philosophy of information explores the ethical implications of digital technologies, advocating for a human-centric approach that prioritizes the well-being and dignity of individuals.

Frank Pasquale, in "The Black Box Society," argues for greater transparency and accountability in the use of AI and algorithmic systems. He highlights the dangers of opaque algorithms that make decisions affecting individuals' lives, calling for regulatory measures to ensure fairness and justice. These ethical considerations are essential for developing a culturally informed understanding of AI and cybertechnology, as they address the broader societal impacts and responsibilities associated with these technologies.

In conclusion, contemporary thinkers and cultural critics are increasingly recognizing the need to incorporate insights from AI and cybertechnology into cultural theory. By examining the ethical, societal, and cultural implications of these technologies, they are developing new frameworks for understanding the complex interplay between technology and culture. This interdisciplinary approach not only enhances our understanding of contemporary cultural dynamics but also provides valuable insights for navigating the challenges and opportunities of a technologically mediated world. Through critical analysis and ethical reflection, contemporary thinkers are contributing to a more nuanced and holistic understanding of the transformative impact of AI and cybertechnology on culture and society.

14 POSTMODERNISM AND THE CRITIQUE OF REPRESENTATION

Craig Owens was a profound and influential thinker in the realm of postmodernism and the critique of representation. His work has left an indelible mark on various fields, including art, pedagogy, and e-learning, while his exploration of icons and their implications continues to resonate in contemporary discourse.

Owens's engagement with postmodernism revolved around the critique of representation, which is central to understanding the complexities of contemporary art and cultural theory. Postmodernism, characterized by its skepticism toward grand narratives and emphasis on fragmentation, pastiche, and irony, provided a fertile ground for Owens's critical inquiries. He was particularly interested in how representations in art and media could both reflect and shape cultural and social realities.

Owens argued that traditional forms of representation often reinforced dominant ideologies and power structures. By critically examining these representations, he sought to uncover the underlying assumptions and biases that they perpetuated. This critique was not merely an academic exercise but a call to rethink how images and symbols function in society. Owens believed that by deconstructing these representations, it was possible to challenge and subvert the norms and values they upheld.

One of Owens's significant contributions was his analysis of the role of the icon in postmodern culture. Icons, whether in the form of religious imagery, celebrity figures, or cultural symbols, hold a particular power in shaping public consciousness. Owens explored how icons function as both representations and objects of worship, blurring the lines between reality and simulation. In a postmodern context, icons are not just reflections of cultural values but active participants in the construction of meaning.

Owens's critique of representation extended to his views on pedagogy and e-learning. He recognized that the ways in which knowledge is transmitted and received are deeply intertwined with questions of representation. Traditional educational models, which often rely on hierarchical structures and didactic methods, can reinforce existing power dynamics and limit critical engagement. Owens advocated for more participatory and dialogical approaches to pedagogy, where learners are encouraged to question and challenge the material presented to them.

In the realm of e-learning, Owens saw both potential and peril. On one hand, digital technologies offer new opportunities for interactive and personalized learning experiences. They can democratize access to knowledge and foster collaborative learning environments. On the other hand, the proliferation of digital media also raises concerns about the commodification of education and the superficiality of information consumption. Owens was critical of the ways in which e-learning platforms could replicate the same issues of representation and power that he identified in traditional media.

To navigate these challenges, Owens called for a critical pedagogy that is aware of the dynamics of representation in both physical and virtual classrooms. This involves not only integrating technology in meaningful ways but also fostering critical digital literacy. Learners need to be equipped with the skills to critically assess the information they encounter online, understanding the sources, contexts, and potential biases of digital content.

Owens's work on postmodernism and representation also intersected with broader cultural and political issues. He was particularly interested in how marginalized groups are represented in art and media. The politics of representation, as he saw it, involves recognizing who gets to be represented, how they are depicted, and what voices are included or excluded in cultural narratives. Owens's analysis highlighted the ways in which minority groups, such as women, people of color, and LGBTQ+ individuals, are often marginalized or stereotyped in mainstream media.

By bringing these issues to the forefront, Owens contributed to a broader movement within cultural studies and critical theory that seeks to challenge and transform dominant narratives. His work has inspired countless artists, scholars, and activists to use representation as a tool for social change. By creating alternative images and stories, they can offer new perspectives and challenge the status quo.

In the context of art, Owens's critique of representation often focused on the strategies used by postmodern artists to disrupt traditional forms of depiction. Artists such as Cindy Sherman, Barbara Kruger, and Sherrie Levine employed techniques like appropriation, pastiche, and parody to question the authenticity and originality of images. By recontextualizing familiar images and symbols, these artists exposed the constructed nature of representation and invited viewers to reconsider their assumptions about reality and art.

Owens was particularly drawn to the work of these artists because they exemplified the postmodern rejection of the notion that art could be a transparent window to the world. Instead, their work highlighted the ways in which all representation is mediated by cultural codes and power relations. By disrupting conventional modes of representation, they forced viewers to confront the ideological underpinnings of visual culture.

For example, Cindy Sherman's photographic series, where she staged herself in various guises, challenged the traditional roles and stereotypes assigned to women. Her work demonstrated how identity is constructed through images and how these constructions can be both limiting and liberating. Similarly, Barbara Kruger's text-based works, with their provocative slogans overlaid on black-and-white photographs, critiqued consumer culture and the ways in which it manipulates desires and identities. Sherrie Levine's rephotographs of famous works of art questioned notions of originality and authorship, emphasizing the endless circulation and replication of images in contemporary culture.

Owens's analysis extended beyond visual art to encompass broader cultural phenomena. He was keenly aware of the ways in which representation operates in mass media and popular culture. The rise of television, advertising, and later digital media, created new forms of representation that were both pervasive and powerful. Owens's critique of these media forms was grounded in the belief that they played a crucial role in shaping social consciousness and cultural norms.

One of the central concerns in Owens's critique was the idea of the simulacrum, a concept he borrowed from Jean Baudrillard. Simulacra are copies that depict things that either had no original, to begin with, or that no longer have an original. In a world saturated with images and representations, the distinction between reality and simulation becomes increasingly blurred. Owens argued that this collapse of the real into the hyperreal had profound implications for how we understand and interact with the world.

In the realm of pedagogy, Owens's insights into the nature of representation and the simulacrum highlighted the importance of developing critical media literacy. He believed that educators should not only teach students how to interpret texts and images but also how to critically engage with the media environments they inhabit. This involves understanding the mechanisms of representation, the interests they serve, and the effects they produce.

E-learning, with its reliance on digital platforms and multimedia content, presents unique challenges and opportunities in this regard. Owens saw the potential for e-learning to offer more dynamic and interactive educational experiences. However, he was also wary of the ways in which digital technologies could reinforce superficial engagement and passive consumption of information. He advocated for e-learning approaches that prioritize critical thinking, active participation, and reflective inquiry.

The shift to digital learning environments, accelerated by the advent of the internet and later by global events such as the COVID-19 pandemic, has brought these issues into sharper focus. Owens's ideas remain relevant as educators grapple with how to create meaningful and equitable learning experiences in a digital age. The proliferation of online courses, virtual classrooms, and educational apps has transformed the landscape of education, but it has also raised questions about access, quality, and the commodification of knowledge.

In his critique of traditional educational models, Owens emphasized the need for a pedagogy that is inclusive and responsive to diverse learners. This means recognizing the different ways in which students engage with and make sense of information, as well as the various cultural and social contexts they bring to their learning. By fostering an environment that values critical engagement and diverse perspectives, educators can help students develop the skills and dispositions necessary to navigate a complex and mediated world.

Owens's work also has significant implications for how we think about icons in contemporary culture. Icons, whether they are religious figures, celebrities, or cultural symbols, hold a particular power in shaping our perceptions and values. Owens's analysis of icons was not just about their visual representation but also about their cultural and social significance. Icons function as focal points for collective identities and aspirations, but they can also be sites of contestation and struggle.

In a postmodern context, icons are often subject to reappropriation and reinterpretation. This can be seen in the ways in which contemporary artists and activists use iconic images to challenge dominant narratives and propose alternative visions. By disrupting and recontextualizing these images, they expose the power dynamics at play and invite new ways of seeing and understanding.

Owens's engagement with the politics of representation was deeply intertwined with his commitment to social justice. He believed that by critically examining and challenging dominant representations, it was possible to create a more inclusive and equitable society. This involves not only changing the images and narratives that circulate in culture but also addressing the structural inequalities that underpin them.

In conclusion, Craig Owens's work on postmodernism, representation, and icons offers profound insights into the ways in which images and symbols shape our cultural and social realities. His critique of traditional forms of representation and his advocacy for more inclusive and participatory approaches to pedagogy and e-learning remain highly relevant in today's media-saturated world. By challenging the assumptions and biases embedded in representations, Owens's work continues to inspire efforts to create a more critical, reflective, and equitable society.

15 THE ANTI-AESTHETIC AND POSTMODERN CULTURE

Hal Foster, an influential figure in contemporary art criticism and theory, has significantly shaped the discourse on postmodern culture through his seminal work "The Anti-Aesthetic." This collection of essays, which he edited, offers a critical examination of the paradigms that define postmodernism, particularly in relation to art, photography, and the intersections with crime. Foster's insights challenge traditional notions of aesthetics and representation, pushing the boundaries of how we understand and engage with cultural production.

"The Anti-Aesthetic" emerged during a time when the art world was undergoing profound transformations. Postmodernism, as Foster articulated, rejects the grand narratives and universal truths that characterized modernism. Instead, it embraces fragmentation, plurality, and a skepticism towards metanarratives. This shift has profound implications for how art is produced, interpreted, and valued. Foster argues that postmodern culture is marked by a critical stance against the notion of a singular, authoritative aesthetic. This anti-aesthetic approach seeks to democratize art by questioning the hierarchies and power structures that have traditionally governed it.

Photography, as a medium, occupies a central place in Foster's critique of postmodern culture. In the context of postmodernism, photography is not merely a tool for documentation or representation but a site of contestation and critical inquiry. Foster explores how photography challenges the boundaries between reality and representation, often blurring the lines and calling into question the very nature of truth and objectivity. The reproducibility of photographs and their widespread dissemination in mass media further complicate these boundaries, making photography a potent medium for postmodern critique.

In his examination of photography, Foster draws attention to the work of artists who use the medium to subvert conventional aesthetics and narratives. For instance, the photographs of Cindy Sherman, which depict the artist in various guises and personas, challenge the notion of identity as fixed and stable. Sherman's work exemplifies the postmodern preoccupation with performance and the construction of self, revealing how identity is often mediated through images and cultural representations. By adopting different roles and appearances, Sherman disrupts the viewer's expectations and invites a critical engagement with the images.

Foster also highlights the work of photographers like Richard Prince, whose rephotographs of advertising images critique the commodification of culture. Prince's work appropriates and recontextualizes commercial photographs, exposing the underlying ideologies and power dynamics at play. This practice of appropriation is a key strategy in postmodern art, as it reveals the constructed nature of images and their role in shaping social and cultural norms. Through these examples, Foster illustrates how photography can serve as a powerful tool for questioning and deconstructing dominant narratives.

Art, in the broader sense, is another focal point of Foster's critique. Postmodern art is characterized by its rejection of the idea that art should be autonomous and separated from everyday life. Instead, it embraces the notion that art is inherently political and social, intertwined with the broader cultural and economic contexts in which it is produced. Foster argues that postmodern artists seek to challenge and destabilize the traditional boundaries of art, often by incorporating elements of popular culture, mass media, and everyday objects into their work.

One of the key figures in Foster's discussion of postmodern art is the artist Barbara Kruger. Kruger's work, which combines photographic images with provocative text, critiques consumer culture and the ways in which it shapes identities and desires. Her use of bold, declarative statements overlaid on black-and-white images creates a powerful visual impact, forcing the viewer to confront the messages embedded in the images. Kruger's work exemplifies the postmodern strategy of using art to challenge and critique societal norms, revealing the power dynamics that underpin them.

Foster also examines the work of artists like Jeff Koons and Damien Hirst, whose practices blur the lines between high art and popular culture. Koons's sculptures and installations, which often feature kitsch objects and banal subjects, challenge the traditional distinctions between art and commodity. By elevating everyday objects to the status of art, Koons questions the value systems and hierarchies that determine what is considered art. Similarly, Hirst's works, which often involve provocative and controversial subjects, such as dead animals and medical imagery, challenge the viewer's sensibilities and provoke critical reflection on the nature of art and its relationship to life and death.

The intersection of art and crime is another intriguing aspect of Foster's critique. In postmodern culture, the boundaries between art and crime are often blurred, as artists explore themes of transgression, subversion, and illegality. Foster argues that this blurring of boundaries reflects a broader cultural fascination with crime and deviance, as well as a critique of the institutions and systems that define and regulate these concepts.

One notable example of this intersection is the work of the street artist Banksy. Banksy's graffiti and public art installations often involve acts of illegal defacement of property, challenging the legal and moral boundaries of art. His works, which often carry political and social messages, critique various aspects of contemporary society, from consumerism and capitalism to war and government surveillance. By operating outside the conventional frameworks of the art world, Banksy embodies the postmodern rejection of traditional notions of art and authority, using crime as a medium for artistic expression and critique.

Foster also explores the work of artists who engage with themes of criminality and transgression in more metaphorical ways. For instance, the photographs of Nan Goldin, which document the lives of marginalized and subcultural communities, often depict scenes of drug use, violence, and sexual transgression. Goldin's work challenges the viewer to confront the realities of these communities, revealing the ways in which societal norms and legal systems marginalize and criminalize certain behaviors and identities. By documenting these aspects of life, Goldin's work serves as a powerful critique of the social and legal structures that define and regulate criminality.

In his critique of postmodern culture, Foster also addresses the role of institutions, such as museums and galleries, in shaping and defining art. He argues that these institutions often reinforce traditional hierarchies and power structures, determining what is considered valuable and worthy of preservation. Postmodern artists, therefore, seek to challenge and subvert these institutional frameworks, often by creating works that exist outside the conventional spaces of the art world or by engaging in practices that critique the role of institutions in the production and dissemination of art.

The concept of the anti-aesthetic, as Foster articulates it, is central to understanding the postmodern critique of representation and value in art. The anti-aesthetic rejects the idea that art should adhere to a specific set of aesthetic criteria or standards. Instead, it embraces a plurality of forms, styles, and practices, reflecting the diverse and fragmented nature of contemporary culture. This rejection of traditional aesthetics is not merely a negation but a call to rethink the ways in which art can engage with and critique the world.

In conclusion, Hal Foster's work on the anti-aesthetic and postmodern culture offers a profound and critical examination of the ways in which art, photography, and the intersections with crime challenge traditional notions of representation and value. By highlighting the strategies of appropriation, subversion, and critique employed by postmodern artists, Foster reveals how these practices disrupt conventional aesthetics and power structures. His insights into the role of institutions, the politics of representation, and the intersections of art and crime continue to resonate in contemporary cultural discourse, offering valuable perspectives on the complexities and contradictions of postmodern culture. Through his critique, Foster invites us to reconsider the ways in which we engage with and understand art, challenging us to embrace a more critical and inclusive approach to cultural production and interpretation.

16 ESSAYS ON LITERATURE AND ART

Guy Davenport was an American writer, scholar, and critic whose essays on literature and art delve deeply into the intersections of culture, history, and human creativity. His works are marked by an erudite and eclectic approach, weaving together a wide array of references and insights to offer fresh perspectives on both classical and contemporary themes. Davenport's essays not only illuminate the works and lives of artists and writers but also engage with broader questions about authenticity, imitation, and the nature of human consciousness.

One of the central themes in Davenport's essays is the concept of the counterfeiter, an idea that resonates across various domains of art and literature. Counterfeiters, in Davenport's view, are not merely those who create forgeries or fakes but also those who engage in imitation and pastiche as a form of homage or critique. This concept is particularly relevant in the context of postmodernism, where the boundaries between original and copy are often blurred, and the act of imitation itself can be a creative and subversive gesture.

Davenport explores the figure of the counterfeiter through a variety of lenses, from the classical tradition of literary imitation to the modernist experiments with pastiche and parody. He examines how writers and artists throughout history have engaged with the works of their predecessors, sometimes with reverence and sometimes with irreverence, but always with an acute awareness of the tension between originality and imitation. For Davenport, this interplay is not merely a technical or stylistic issue but a profound commentary on the nature of artistic creation and the continuity of cultural memory.

In his essays, Davenport often returns to the idea that all art is, in some sense, a form of imitation. He cites examples from classical literature, where the notion of mimesis, or the imitation of life, is a foundational concept. This classical perspective is then juxtaposed with the modern and postmodern contexts, where imitation becomes more self-conscious and ironic. The counterfeiter, in Davenport's analysis, is both a trickster and a sage, someone who reveals the constructed nature of all representations while simultaneously participating in the ongoing creation of cultural meaning.

Davenport's exploration of the counterfeiter extends to his discussion of the Turing Test, a concept from the field of artificial intelligence that raises important questions about the nature of human and machine intelligence. Named after the British mathematician and logician Alan Turing, the Turing Test is designed to assess a machine's ability to exhibit intelligent behavior indistinguishable from that of a human. In this context, the counterfeiter becomes a metaphor for the machine, which attempts to mimic human thought and communication so convincingly that it can deceive human interlocutors.

Davenport's interest in the Turing Test is not merely technical but deeply philosophical. He is concerned with what it means to be human and how we understand and measure intelligence and creativity. The Turing Test, for Davenport, is not just a challenge for machines but also a mirror that reflects our own assumptions and biases about consciousness and identity. In his essays, he explores the implications of the Turing Test for our understanding of art and literature, suggesting that the boundaries between human and machine, like those between original and counterfeit, are more fluid and permeable than we might think.

One of the fascinating aspects of Davenport's writing is his ability to draw connections between seemingly disparate topics. For example, he links the idea of the counterfeiter in literature and art to broader themes of authenticity and identity in the modern world. In a culture increasingly dominated by digital media and virtual realities, the question of what is real and what is imitation becomes ever more pressing. Davenport's essays suggest that the act of counterfeiting, whether in the form of artistic imitation or artificial intelligence, forces us to confront these questions in new and challenging ways.

Davenport's engagement with these themes is enriched by his deep knowledge of history and his ability to bring historical figures and events to life in his writing. His essays often feature vivid portraits of artists and writers, situating their work within the broader cultural and historical contexts that shaped their creative endeavors. This historical perspective is crucial to Davenport's analysis, as it allows him to trace the evolving meanings of imitation and authenticity across different periods and traditions.

For instance, in his discussions of Renaissance art, Davenport highlights how the masters of this period engaged in deliberate imitation of classical models, not as mere copying but as a way of achieving a deeper understanding and reinterpretation of their cultural heritage. Similarly, he examines the role of imitation in modernist literature, where writers like James Joyce and T.S. Eliot used pastiche and allusion to create complex, multilayered texts that both reference and transform their sources. In these discussions, Davenport demonstrates how the act of imitation can be a powerful tool for innovation and critique.

Davenport's essays also explore the ethical dimensions of counterfeiting and imitation. He is keenly aware of the potential for deception and exploitation inherent in these practices, but he also recognizes their creative potential. The counterfeiter, in Davenport's view, occupies a liminal space between authenticity and artifice, challenging us to reconsider our assumptions about what is genuine and what is fake. This ethical ambiguity is central to many of Davenport's analyses, as he grapples with the complexities and contradictions of cultural production.

In his exploration of the Turing Test, Davenport similarly addresses the ethical and philosophical questions raised by artificial intelligence. He is particularly interested in the implications of machines that can mimic human thought and creativity, and what this means for our understanding of consciousness and identity. Davenport suggests that the Turing Test, like the act of counterfeiting, forces us to confront the limitations and possibilities of human intelligence. By blurring the boundaries between human and machine, the Turing Test challenges us to rethink our definitions of what it means to be truly intelligent or creative.

Davenport's essays are characterized by their rich, allusive style and their ability to synthesize diverse strands of thought into coherent and compelling arguments. His writing is dense with references to literature, art, philosophy, and history, reflecting his wide-ranging intellectual curiosity and his commitment to interdisciplinary inquiry. This eclecticism is one of the hallmarks of Davenport's work, as he weaves together insights from different fields to illuminate the complexities of his subjects.

In his discussions of literature and art, Davenport often employs a close reading approach, analyzing specific texts and artworks in detail to draw out their deeper meanings. This method allows him to uncover the layers of significance embedded in these works, revealing how they engage with and transform their cultural contexts. Davenport's close readings are informed by his extensive knowledge of literary and artistic traditions, as well as his keen sensitivity to the nuances of language and form.

Davenport's essays also frequently incorporate elements of narrative and biography, bringing the lives and experiences of artists and writers into his analyses. This biographical dimension adds a humanistic depth to his work, as he explores the personal and historical contexts that shaped the creative processes of his subjects. By situating these figures within their broader cultural and historical milieus, Davenport provides a rich, multifaceted understanding of their contributions to literature and art.

In conclusion, Guy Davenport's essays on literature and art offer a profound and multifaceted exploration of themes related to imitation, authenticity, and the nature of human creativity. Through his discussions of counterfeiting and the Turing Test, Davenport engages with some of the most pressing questions of our time, challenging us to rethink our assumptions about what it means to create and understand art. His erudite and eclectic approach, combined with his deep historical knowledge and keen analytical insights, makes his work an invaluable resource for anyone interested in the intersections of culture, history, and human consciousness.

17 CONTEMPORARY ART CRITICISM

Bruce Hainley is a prominent figure in contemporary art criticism, known for his incisive and often provocative analyses of modern and contemporary art. His work delves deeply into the practices and philosophies of various artists, offering insights that challenge conventional perspectives and encourage new ways of thinking about art. One of his significant contributions is his exploration of the artist Elaine Sturtevant, particularly through his writings in "Under the Sign of [sic] (Sturtevant's Volte-Face)." This text examines Sturtevant's unique approach to art-making, which involves the replication of works by other artists, a practice that raises essential questions about originality, authorship, and the nature of art itself.

Sturtevant, who is often simply referred to by her last name, built her career on meticulously recreating works by contemporary artists such as Andy Warhol, Jasper Johns, and Roy Lichtenstein. Her practice was not mere imitation or forgery; rather, it was a conceptual strategy that interrogated the very foundations of artistic creation and perception. By replicating these iconic works, Sturtevant prompted viewers to reconsider the value and meaning attributed to originality and authorship in art. Hainley's analysis of Sturtevant's work is both an homage to her revolutionary practice and a critical examination of its implications for contemporary art.

Hainley's writing style is both erudite and accessible, blending rigorous academic analysis with a conversational tone that engages a broad audience. In "Under the Sign of [sic]," he delves into the complexities of Sturtevant's volte-face, a term that denotes a complete reversal of opinion or attitude. This concept is central to understanding Sturtevant's work, as her practice involves a deliberate and strategic inversion of traditional artistic values. By replicating the works of her contemporaries, Sturtevant subverted the art market's emphasis on originality and individual genius, instead highlighting the reproducibility and fluidity of artistic ideas.

Hainley explores how Sturtevant's work complicates the notion of the artist as a unique creator. Her practice suggests that art is not solely the product of individual inspiration but is instead part of a larger cultural and historical dialogue. This perspective aligns with postmodern theories that challenge the romanticized notion of the solitary genius and instead view art as a collaborative and intertextual practice. Hainley's analysis underscores how Sturtevant's work disrupts the conventional art historical narrative, inviting viewers to engage with art in a more critical and reflective manner.

In addition to his exploration of Sturtevant's work, Hainley is known for his broader contributions to contemporary art criticism. He has written extensively on a wide range of artists and art movements, offering insights that illuminate the complexities and nuances of contemporary art. His critiques often focus on the intersections of art, culture, and politics, examining how artworks reflect and shape societal values and ideologies. Hainley's ability to contextualize art within broader cultural and historical frameworks is a hallmark of his critical approach, allowing him to draw connections between disparate ideas and highlight the multifaceted nature of contemporary art.

Hainley's engagement with contemporary art extends to his analysis of various art forms and media, including the influence of technology and digital culture on artistic practices. One notable aspect of his work is his exploration of the role of electronic and digital media in contemporary art, which he refers to as "electro." This term encompasses a wide range of practices and technologies, from digital photography and video art to internet-based works and interactive installations. Hainley's analysis of electro art examines how these technologies transform the ways in which art is created, distributed, and experienced.

The advent of digital technology has had a profound impact on the art world, challenging traditional notions of medium and materiality. Hainley's critique of electro art considers how digital technologies blur the boundaries between different art forms, creating new possibilities for artistic expression. He explores how artists use digital tools to create immersive and interactive experiences that engage viewers in novel ways. This shift towards interactivity and immersion reflects broader cultural trends towards greater connectivity and participation, highlighting the evolving relationship between art and technology.

Hainley's analysis also addresses the democratizing potential of digital technologies. The internet and social media platforms have enabled artists to reach global audiences without the need for traditional gatekeepers such as galleries and museums. This has led to a more inclusive and diverse art world, where artists from different backgrounds and regions can share their work and gain recognition. However, Hainley also critically examines the challenges and limitations of this digital shift, including issues of accessibility, commercialization, and the commodification of digital art.

One of the central themes in Hainley's exploration of electro art is the concept of reproducibility. Digital technologies enable the easy replication and distribution of artworks, challenging the traditional emphasis on the uniqueness and authenticity of the original. This shift has significant implications for the art market and the value systems that underpin it. Hainley's critique considers how reproducibility transforms the relationship between the artist, the artwork, and the audience, suggesting that digital art requires new modes of engagement and appreciation.

Hainley's writings on electro art often intersect with his broader concerns about the commodification of art and the influence of market forces on artistic practices. He explores how digital technologies both challenge and reinforce existing power dynamics within the art world. On one hand, digital platforms can democratize access to art and create new opportunities for marginalized voices. On the other hand, they can also perpetuate existing inequalities, as commercial interests increasingly shape the production and distribution of digital art. Hainley's critique encourages a critical examination of these dynamics, urging readers to consider the ethical and political implications of digital art.

In addition to his critical writings, Hainley has contributed to the art world through his curatorial work and collaborations with artists. His deep understanding of contemporary art and his ability to articulate its complexities have made him a valuable interlocutor for artists seeking to engage with critical theory and cultural analysis. Hainley's collaborative approach reflects his belief in the importance of dialogue and exchange in the creation and interpretation of art. Through his curatorial projects and writings, he has fostered a more inclusive and dynamic art world, where diverse perspectives and practices can thrive.

Hainley's contributions to contemporary art criticism are characterized by their intellectual rigor, critical insight, and commitment to challenging conventional perspectives. His exploration of Sturtevant's work in "Under the Sign of [sic]" exemplifies his ability to engage deeply with complex and provocative artistic practices, offering new ways of understanding and appreciating contemporary art. By examining the intersections of art, culture, and technology, Hainley's writings provide a comprehensive and nuanced critique of the contemporary art landscape.

In conclusion, Bruce Hainley's work as a contemporary art critic and scholar offers valuable insights into the evolving nature of art in the modern world. His analysis of Sturtevant's practice and the concept of the volte-face challenges traditional notions of originality and authorship, prompting a reevaluation of the foundations of artistic creation. Hainley's exploration of electro art highlights the transformative impact of digital technologies on artistic practices and the art market, encouraging a critical engagement with the possibilities and challenges of the digital age. Through his incisive and thought-provoking critiques, Hainley has made significant contributions to the field of contemporary art criticism, fostering a deeper understanding of the complexities and nuances of modern and contemporary art.

18 FILM AND POSTMODERN AESTHETICS

Hal Hartley is a filmmaker whose work epitomizes the postmodern aesthetics that emerged prominently in late 20th-century cinema. Known for his distinctive style, characterized by deadpan humor, philosophical dialogue, and a unique visual sensibility, Hartley's films explore the complexities of contemporary life and human relationships through a lens that is at once ironic and deeply reflective. One of his most celebrated works, "Henry Fool," serves as a prime example of his approach to filmmaking and his engagement with postmodern themes.

"Henry Fool," released in 1997, tells the story of an unlikely friendship between Henry, an enigmatic and rebellious writer, and Simon Grim, a socially awkward garbage man who discovers his own literary genius under Henry's unconventional tutelage. The film is a meditation on art, identity, and the transformative power of literature, set against the backdrop of a mundane suburban existence. Hartley's signature style is evident in the film's witty dialogue, offbeat characters, and a narrative that oscillates between the absurd and the profound.

Hartley's approach to film is deeply rooted in postmodern aesthetics, which often involve a rejection of grand narratives and a focus on fragmentation, irony, and self-referentiality. In "Henry Fool," these elements are woven into the fabric of the story and the characters. The film's title character, Henry, embodies the postmodern anti-hero: flawed, morally ambiguous, and perpetually in conflict with societal norms. His presence disrupts the status quo, challenging the other characters to reconsider their own lives and aspirations.

The film's narrative structure reflects the postmodern penchant for subverting traditional storytelling conventions. Rather than following a linear, cause-and-effect progression, "Henry Fool" unfolds in a more episodic and fragmented manner. This allows Hartley to explore different facets of the characters and their relationships without being confined to a strict plot trajectory. The dialogue, often stylized and theatrical, further enhances this sense of fragmentation, as characters engage in philosophical debates and introspective monologues that blur the line between reality and artifice.

One of the key themes in "Henry Fool" is the nature of artistic creation and the role of the artist in society. Henry presents himself as a misunderstood genius, railing against the mediocrity and conformity of the world around him. His influence on Simon, who transforms from a timid and overlooked figure into a celebrated poet, raises questions about the sources of artistic inspiration and the often arbitrary nature of artistic success. Hartley uses their dynamic to explore the tension between authenticity and pretension, and the ways in which art can both illuminate and obfuscate the truth.

The character of Simon Grim serves as a counterpoint to Henry's flamboyant persona. Initially depicted as a passive and unremarkable individual, Simon's latent talent is revealed through his interactions with Henry. This transformation is depicted with Hartley's characteristic blend of humor and pathos, as Simon navigates the newfound complexities of his identity as a writer. The film's portrayal of Simon's rise to literary fame satirizes the literary establishment and the fickle nature of critical acclaim, underscoring the postmodern skepticism towards authority and canonical values.

Hartley's visual style in "Henry Fool" also reflects his postmodern sensibilities. The film employs a minimalist aesthetic, with careful attention to composition and framing. Hartley often uses static shots and long takes, allowing the actors' performances and the dialogue to take center stage. This visual restraint contrasts with the more frenetic editing styles common in contemporary cinema, creating a sense of deliberate pacing that invites the viewer to engage more deeply with the characters and their interactions.

The use of music in "Henry Fool" is another notable aspect of Hartley's postmodern approach. The film's score, composed by Hartley's frequent collaborator Jeffrey Taylor, combines classical motifs with contemporary sounds, creating a musical landscape that echoes the film's thematic concerns. The juxtaposition of different musical styles mirrors the film's blending of high and low culture, a hallmark of postmodern art. This synthesis of disparate elements reflects the eclectic and inclusive nature of postmodern aesthetics, where boundaries between genres and forms are fluid and constantly shifting.

"Henry Fool" also engages with the theme of identity and the performative aspects of selfhood. The characters in the film are constantly negotiating their identities, both in relation to themselves and to others. Henry, with his larger-than-life persona and grandiose declarations, can be seen as a performance artist of sorts, crafting his identity through his interactions and his writings. Simon's journey from obscurity to recognition involves a similar process of self-construction, as he learns to navigate the public and private dimensions of his new identity as a poet.

Hartley's filmography, including "Henry Fool," often explores the idea that identity is not fixed but is instead a fluid and dynamic process. This aligns with postmodern theories of subjectivity, which reject the notion of a stable, unified self in favor of a more fragmented and contingent understanding of identity. In "Henry Fool," the characters' evolving identities are depicted with a mix of humor and poignancy, highlighting the complexities and contradictions inherent in the search for self-definition.

The film's exploration of morality and ethics further underscores its postmodern sensibilities. Henry's character embodies a kind of anarchic individualism, challenging conventional moral codes and societal norms. His influence on Simon introduces a moral ambiguity that complicates the straightforward dichotomy of right and wrong. Hartley uses this moral complexity to critique the simplistic moralism often found in mainstream narratives, instead presenting a more nuanced and ambivalent view of human behavior.

"Henry Fool" also addresses the relationship between the individual and society, a recurring theme in Hartley's work. The film portrays a suburban milieu that is both familiar and alienating, a setting that reflects the characters' struggles with conformity and isolation. Henry's rebellion against societal expectations and Simon's eventual integration into the literary world highlight the tensions between personal freedom and social conformity. Hartley's depiction of this suburban landscape serves as a microcosm for broader societal dynamics, illustrating the ways in which individuals navigate the pressures and constraints of contemporary life.

Hartley's use of intertextuality and references to other works of literature and film further exemplifies his postmodern approach. "Henry Fool" is replete with allusions to literary traditions and philosophical ideas, creating a rich tapestry of references that adds depth and complexity to the narrative. These intertextual elements invite viewers to engage with the film on multiple levels, encouraging a more active and interpretive mode of spectatorship.

In addition to its literary and philosophical dimensions, "Henry Fool" also engages with broader cultural and political themes. The film's critique of the literary establishment and its satirical portrayal of the publishing industry reflect Hartley's skepticism towards institutional authority and the commodification of art. This critique is emblematic of postmodernism's broader challenge to dominant cultural narratives and its emphasis on marginalized voices and alternative perspectives.

Hartley's films, including "Henry Fool," are characterized by their ability to blend humor with serious philosophical inquiry. This distinctive tonal balance allows Hartley to address weighty themes without resorting to didacticism or sentimentality. Instead, his films invite viewers to reflect on the absurdities and complexities of life, using humor as a means of engaging with profound existential questions. This approach aligns with the postmodern aesthetic, which often employs irony and parody to subvert conventional expectations and provoke critical reflection.

"Henry Fool" is a testament to Hal Hartley's unique vision as a filmmaker and his contribution to postmodern cinema. The film's exploration of art, identity, and morality, combined with its distinctive visual and narrative style, exemplifies Hartley's ability to engage with contemporary themes in a way that is both intellectually rigorous and emotionally resonant. Through his work, Hartley challenges viewers to reconsider their assumptions about art and life, offering a perspective that is both deeply human and refreshingly unconventional.

In conclusion, Hal Hartley's "Henry Fool" is a quintessential example of postmodern aesthetics in contemporary cinema. The film's exploration of originality, identity, and morality, along with its distinctive visual and narrative style, reflects Hartley's engagement with the complexities and contradictions of modern life. By blending humor with philosophical inquiry, Hartley creates a film that is both thought-provoking and entertaining, inviting viewers to engage with the rich tapestry of ideas and themes that define his work. Through his innovative approach to filmmaking, Hartley continues to be a significant voice in the landscape of contemporary cinema, offering insights that challenge and inspire.

19 CONTEMPORARY CULTURAL ANALYSIS

Matthew Barnett is a significant figure in contemporary cultural analysis, contributing deeply to the understanding of how culture operates in the modern world. His work encompasses a broad spectrum of themes, from media and technology to identity and politics, providing a comprehensive look at the forces that shape contemporary society. Barnett's approach is characterized by an interdisciplinary methodology, combining insights from sociology, anthropology, and media studies to offer nuanced perspectives on cultural phenomena.

Barnett's analysis begins with the recognition that culture is not a static entity but a dynamic process that evolves in response to various social, economic, and political factors. He emphasizes that contemporary culture is particularly marked by its global interconnectedness, where the flow of information, people, and goods transcends traditional boundaries. This globalization of culture has profound implications for how identities are formed and how cultural practices are maintained and transformed.

One of the central themes in Barnett's work is the role of media and technology in shaping contemporary culture. He argues that digital technologies have fundamentally altered the way we communicate, consume information, and perceive the world. The rise of social media platforms, for instance, has created new forms of social interaction and community, but it has also raised concerns about privacy, surveillance, and the spread of misinformation. Barnett's analysis of digital culture examines both the opportunities and challenges presented by these technologies, highlighting their impact on social norms, political engagement, and individual identities.

In his exploration of media, Barnett also addresses the concept of the "mediatized society," where media not only reflect but also construct social reality. He suggests that the pervasive influence of media in contemporary life means that our understanding of events and issues is increasingly mediated through various forms of representation. This has implications for how we perceive truth and authenticity, as well as for the ways in which power and authority are exercised. Barnett's work often focuses on the interplay between media narratives and public discourse, analyzing how media shape our perceptions of reality and influence public opinion.

Identity is another key focus of Barnett's cultural analysis. He explores how contemporary identities are constructed and negotiated in a globalized and mediated world. Barnett argues that identity is increasingly understood as fluid and multifaceted, rather than fixed and stable. This reflects broader societal shifts towards recognizing and valuing diversity and pluralism. However, it also brings new challenges in terms of social cohesion and belonging. Barnett's work examines the tensions between individual identity and collective belonging, exploring how people navigate these dynamics in their everyday lives.

Barnett is particularly interested in how cultural identities are formed and expressed through consumption practices. He suggests that in contemporary society, consumption is not merely about acquiring goods but also about constructing and communicating identity. This perspective draws on theories of symbolic consumption, which posit that the things we buy and use carry meanings that help us define who we are and how we relate to others. Barnett's analysis of consumer culture explores how brands and commodities function as symbols of identity and how marketing practices tap into our desires and aspirations.

In addition to his focus on media and identity, Barnett addresses the political dimensions of contemporary culture. He examines how cultural practices and representations are intertwined with issues of power, inequality, and resistance. Barnett argues that culture is both a site of domination and a space for contestation, where different groups struggle over meanings and values. This perspective is informed by critical cultural studies, which emphasize the role of culture in sustaining and challenging social hierarchies.

One area where Barnett's political analysis is particularly evident is in his work on cultural politics and social movements. He explores how cultural expressions, from art and music to digital activism, can serve as forms of political resistance and social change. Barnett analyzes how marginalized groups use cultural practices to assert their identities and challenge dominant narratives. He also examines the role of culture in shaping political ideologies and mobilizing collective action.

Barnett's work is characterized by a commitment to understanding the lived experiences of individuals and communities. He employs ethnographic methods to capture the nuances of cultural practices and to highlight the perspectives of those who are often excluded from mainstream narratives. This bottom-up approach allows Barnett to provide rich, detailed accounts of how culture operates at the grassroots level, revealing the complexities and contradictions that characterize contemporary life.

In his analysis of contemporary culture, Barnett also engages with the concept of cultural hybridity. He explores how cultural practices are increasingly characterized by the blending and mixing of different traditions and influences. This hybridity reflects the global flows of people, ideas, and commodities, creating new forms of cultural expression and identity. Barnett's work examines the creative potential of cultural hybridity, as well as the tensions and conflicts that can arise from it.

Barnett's approach to cultural analysis is inherently interdisciplinary, drawing on a range of theoretical frameworks and methodologies. He integrates insights from sociology, anthropology, media studies, and cultural studies to provide a holistic understanding of cultural phenomena. This interdisciplinary approach allows Barnett to address the complexities of contemporary culture and to highlight the interconnections between different aspects of social life.

One of the strengths of Barnett's work is his ability to connect macro-level analyses of cultural trends with micro-level insights into individual experiences. He examines how broad social and economic changes, such as globalization and technological innovation, shape everyday practices and identities. At the same time, he pays close attention to the ways in which individuals and communities interpret and respond to these changes. This dual focus allows Barnett to capture the dynamic interplay between structure and agency in contemporary culture.

Barnett's contributions to cultural analysis extend beyond academia to engage with broader public debates. He is an active participant in discussions about the role of culture in addressing social and political challenges, such as inequality, racism, and climate change. Barnett's work often emphasizes the importance of cultural understanding and empathy in fostering social justice and cohesion. He advocates for cultural policies that support diversity, inclusion, and creativity, and he highlights the role of cultural institutions in promoting critical engagement and dialogue.

In conclusion, Matthew Barnett's work in contemporary cultural analysis offers valuable insights into the complex and dynamic nature of culture in the modern world. His interdisciplinary approach, which combines theoretical rigor with empirical depth, provides a comprehensive understanding of how media, technology, identity, and politics intersect to shape our cultural landscape. Barnett's analysis highlights the transformative potential of culture, as well as the challenges and contradictions it presents. Through his work, Barnett contributes to a deeper understanding of the forces that shape contemporary society and offers a critical lens through which to engage with the cultural phenomena that define our times.

20 CYBERFEMINISM AND CYBORG MANIFESTO

Donna Haraway is a prominent scholar whose work has significantly influenced the fields of feminist theory, science and technology studies, and cultural studies. Her most well-known contribution is "A Cyborg Manifesto: Science, Technology, and Socialist-Feminism in the Late Twentieth Century," an essay that has become a foundational text in the study of cyberfeminism. Haraway's manifesto offers a radical rethinking of the relationships between humans, machines, and animals, challenging traditional boundaries and proposing new ways of understanding identity, embodiment, and politics in the context of advanced technological societies.

"A Cyborg Manifesto," first published in 1985, is a provocative and ambitious work that uses the figure of the cyborg as a metaphor for exploring complex intersections of gender, technology, and power. Haraway defines a cyborg as a hybrid entity, part human and part machine, that transcends conventional dichotomies such as nature/culture, human/animal, and male/female. By embracing the cyborg as a symbol of boundary transgression, Haraway seeks to destabilize fixed categories and highlight the fluid and constructed nature of identities.

One of the central themes in Haraway's manifesto is the critique of traditional feminism, which she argues has often relied on essentialist notions of womanhood and binary oppositions. Haraway calls for a more inclusive and flexible approach to feminist politics, one that recognizes the diversity of women's experiences and the multiple, intersecting axes of oppression they face. She proposes the cyborg as a figure that embodies this new kind of feminism, which she terms "socialist-feminism," capable of addressing the complexities of life in a technologically mediated world.

Haraway's cyborg is a creature of social reality as well as a creature of fiction. It represents a new form of subjectivity that is not bound by the limitations of traditional humanism. This posthuman subject challenges the idea of a stable, unified self and instead embraces fragmentation, multiplicity, and contradiction. By doing so, Haraway aligns herself with postmodern and poststructuralist critiques of the subject, but she also extends these critiques to engage with issues of technology and materiality.

The manifesto explores how advanced technologies, particularly in the realms of biology and information science, have blurred the lines between organisms and machines. Haraway discusses the implications of biotechnologies such as genetic engineering and reproductive technologies, which challenge conventional notions of natural and artificial life. She also examines the rise of information technologies and their impact on communication, labor, and social organization. In doing so, Haraway highlights the ways in which these technologies can both reinforce and disrupt existing power structures.

Haraway's vision of the cyborg is deeply political. She argues that the cyborg's hybridity and boundary-crossing nature make it a potent symbol for resisting oppressive systems and imagining new forms of social and political organization. The cyborg, as a metaphor, allows Haraway to articulate a vision of coalition politics that transcends identity categories and emphasizes solidarity based on shared interests and goals. This approach challenges the essentialist tendencies within feminist and other identity-based movements and calls for more dynamic and fluid forms of political engagement.

In addition to its theoretical insights, "A Cyborg Manifesto" is notable for its playful and provocative style. Haraway employs a range of rhetorical strategies, including irony, parody, and humor, to engage readers and invite them to think critically about the issues she raises. This style reflects Haraway's commitment to making theory accessible and relevant to a broad audience, and it has contributed to the essay's enduring impact and popularity.

The manifesto has inspired a wide range of responses and interpretations, both within and outside academic circles. It has been influential in the development of cyberfeminism, a movement that explores the intersections of gender and technology and advocates for the empowerment of women in digital and technological spaces. Cyberfeminists have built on Haraway's ideas to address issues such as online harassment, digital labor, and the representation of women in technology industries. They have also used the figure of the cyborg to explore new forms of identity and embodiment in virtual and augmented realities.

Haraway's work has also resonated with scholars and activists in other fields, including environmental studies, disability studies, and queer theory. Her emphasis on the interconnectedness of humans, animals, and machines has inspired new ways of thinking about ecological relationships and the ethics of human-animal interactions. Her critique of essentialism and her embrace of hybridity and fluidity have provided valuable frameworks for understanding the experiences and identities of disabled and queer individuals.

In her later work, Haraway has continued to explore the themes introduced in "A Cyborg Manifesto," while also addressing new issues and expanding her theoretical framework. For example, in her book "Staying with the Trouble: Making Kin in the Chthulucene," Haraway introduces the concept of "making kin" as a way of fostering more sustainable and just relationships among humans and other species. She argues that in the face of environmental crises and technological transformations, it is crucial to cultivate practices of care, solidarity, and mutual responsibility.

"Staying with the Trouble" extends Haraway's earlier critiques of human exceptionalism and anthropocentrism. She challenges the notion that humans are separate from or superior to other forms of life, advocating instead for an ethic of multispecies coexistence. This perspective builds on the insights of "A Cyborg Manifesto" but places greater emphasis on the material and ecological dimensions of our entanglements with technology and other species.

Haraway's concept of the Chthulucene, introduced in "Staying with the Trouble," represents a new epoch that follows the Anthropocene. While the Anthropocene is defined by human dominance and the profound impact of human activities on the planet, the Chthulucene emphasizes interconnectedness, resilience, and the ongoing co-evolution of all life forms. Haraway calls for a shift from the destructive practices of the Anthropocene to more collaborative and life-affirming ways of living in the Chthulucene.

In exploring these themes, Haraway continues to draw on the figure of the cyborg, but she also introduces new metaphors and concepts to capture the complexities of contemporary life. For example, she uses the term "companion species" to describe the relationships between humans and other animals, emphasizing the mutual dependencies and co-constitutive nature of these interactions. This concept reflects Haraway's broader commitment to challenging hierarchical and dualistic thinking, whether in the context of gender, species, or technology.

Haraway's work has had a profound impact on a wide range of academic disciplines and has also influenced popular culture and activism. Her ideas have inspired artists, writers, and activists to explore new forms of expression and to engage with pressing social and political issues in innovative ways. The figure of the cyborg, in particular, has become a powerful symbol of resistance and transformation, resonating with diverse audiences and contexts.

One of the strengths of Haraway's work is her ability to weave together complex theoretical insights with concrete examples and personal reflections. This approach makes her writing both intellectually rigorous and deeply engaging, allowing readers to connect with her ideas on multiple levels. Haraway's interdisciplinary and multimodal methodology exemplifies the kind of integrative and transformative thinking she advocates for in her work.

In conclusion, Donna Haraway's "A Cyborg Manifesto" is a landmark text in feminist theory, science and technology studies, and cultural studies. It offers a radical rethinking of identity, embodiment, and politics in the context of advanced technological societies, using the figure of the cyborg as a metaphor for boundary transgression and hybrid subjectivity. Haraway's work challenges traditional categories and calls for more inclusive and flexible forms of feminist politics. Her later work continues to explore these themes while also addressing new issues related to ecology, multispecies coexistence, and the ethics of human-animal relationships. Haraway's contributions have had a lasting impact on academic scholarship, popular culture, and activism, inspiring new ways of thinking about the relationships between humans, machines, and other forms of life. Through her innovative and interdisciplinary approach, Haraway has provided valuable frameworks for understanding the complexities of contemporary life and for imagining more just and sustainable futures.

SECTION THREE

ART MOVEMENTS AND ARTISTS

The Techno Revolution in art emerged as a response to the rapid advancements in technology and digital media. This movement, which began to gain momentum in the late 20th century, saw artists integrating new technologies into their creative processes, fundamentally altering the ways art is produced, distributed, and consumed. The Techno Revolution was characterized by the use of computers, digital imaging, and the internet, allowing artists to explore new forms of expression and to reach global audiences instantaneously. One of the most significant aspects of this movement was the creation of digital art, which encompassed everything from digital painting and 3D modeling to interactive installations and virtual reality experiences. Artists like Nam June Paik, often referred to as the father of video art, pioneered the use of technology in art, creating works that incorporated video, television, and computer graphics. His work laid the foundation for future generations of artists to explore the limitless possibilities of digital media.

Modernism, which emerged in the late 19th and early 20th centuries, was a broad cultural, artistic, and literary movement that sought to break away from traditional forms and conventions. This movement was driven by a desire to reflect the rapidly changing world, characterized by industrialization, urbanization, and the aftermath of World War I. Modernist artists sought to capture the essence of modern life through experimentation with new techniques and materials. They rejected the realism and naturalism that had dominated art for centuries, instead embracing abstraction, fragmentation, and a focus on the inner psyche. Key figures in the Modernist movement included Pablo Picasso, whose work in Cubism deconstructed objects into geometric shapes, and Wassily Kandinsky, who is often credited with creating the first purely abstract paintings. Other notable Modernist artists include Marcel Duchamp, whose readymades challenged traditional notions of art, and Jackson Pollock, whose drip paintings epitomized the spontaneity and energy of Abstract Expressionism.

Postmodernism, which emerged in the mid-20th century as a reaction against Modernism, questioned the ideas of progress, originality, and the universality of experience that had defined the previous era. Postmodernist artists embraced pluralism, irony, and pastiche, often blurring the boundaries between high and low culture, and between different artistic disciplines. This movement was characterized by a skepticism towards grand narratives and an emphasis on the subjective nature of reality. Postmodernist artists such as Andy Warhol and Roy Lichtenstein drew heavily on popular culture and mass media, using techniques like silkscreen printing and comic strip imagery to create works that were both accessible and provocative. Their work challenged the notion of artistic originality and the idea of the artist as a solitary genius. Cindy Sherman, another prominent Postmodernist, used photography to explore issues of identity, gender, and representation, creating a series of self-portraits in which she adopted various roles and personas. Her work highlighted the constructed nature of identity and the ways in which it is mediated by images and cultural narratives.

Contemporary art, which encompasses a wide range of practices and styles from the late 20th century to the present day, reflects the diversity and complexity of the modern world. This period has seen the rise of globalization, the digital age, and increasing social and political awareness, all of which have influenced the art being produced. Contemporary artists often engage with pressing issues such as environmentalism, social justice, and identity politics, using a variety of media and approaches to explore these themes. The rise of installation art, performance art, and multimedia works has expanded the possibilities of artistic expression, allowing artists to create immersive and interactive experiences for viewers. Ai Weiwei, a Chinese contemporary artist and activist, uses his work to critique political and social issues, often incorporating traditional Chinese craftsmanship with modern technology and materials. His installations, such as "Sunflower Seeds" at Tate Modern, engage with themes of mass production, individuality, and cultural heritage.

Cyber art, also known as digital or new media art, represents the forefront of artistic innovation in the 21st century. This movement builds on the advancements of the Techno Revolution, exploring the possibilities of cyberspace and digital technologies. Cyber art includes a wide range of practices, from internet art and virtual reality to artificial intelligence and interactive installations. Artists working in this field often engage with the implications of living in a digitally connected world, exploring themes of identity, surveillance, and the nature of reality. One of the pioneering figures in cyber art is Rafael Lozano-Hemmer, whose interactive installations use technology to create participatory experiences that engage with urban space and the body. His work often involves the use of biometric data, such as heartbeats and breath, to create dynamic and responsive environments. Another notable cyber artist is Hito Steyerl, whose video installations and essays critically examine the impact of digital technologies on society, exploring issues of surveillance, data privacy, and the militarization of technology. Her work challenges viewers to consider the ethical and political dimensions of our increasingly mediated world.

The evolution from the Techno Revolution to Contemporary Art and Cyber Art highlights the dynamic and ever-changing nature of artistic practice. Each of these movements reflects the technological, social, and cultural transformations of their respective eras, demonstrating the ways in which art both responds to and shapes the world around us. As we move further into the digital age, the boundaries between art and technology continue to blur, opening up new possibilities for creative expression and challenging our perceptions of what art can be. The artists working within these movements have pushed the limits of traditional media and embraced new technologies, creating works that engage with the complexities of contemporary life and invite viewers to question and reflect on their own experiences. From the abstract explorations of Modernism to the critical interrogations of Postmodernism and the innovative practices of Contemporary and Cyber Art, the history of art is a testament to the enduring human drive to understand and represent the world in new and meaningful ways. As we look to the future, it is clear that the dialogue between art and technology will continue to evolve, offering endless opportunities for creativity and exploration.

21 THE READYMADE AND CONCEPTUAL ART IN POSTMODERNISM

Marcel Duchamp was an artist whose innovations reshaped the boundaries of what art could be, profoundly influencing the development of postmodern art. His introduction of the "readymade" fundamentally questioned the nature of artistic creativity and the role of the artist, opening up new avenues for conceptual art.

Duchamp's career spanned a range of artistic movements, including Impressionism, Fauvism, and Cubism, but his most revolutionary contribution came with his readymades. These were everyday objects that Duchamp selected and designated as art, challenging traditional notions of craftsmanship and aesthetics. The readymade was born out of Duchamp's desire to move away from what he saw as the tyranny of retinal art, art that appealed only to the eye. He wanted to shift the focus to the intellectual engagement with the artwork.

The first readymade, "Bicycle Wheel" (1913), consisted of a bicycle wheel mounted on a wooden stool. By selecting an object and repositioning it in a new context, Duchamp forced viewers to reconsider the object's intrinsic value and the criteria by which art is judged. His most famous readymade, "Fountain" (1917), a porcelain urinal signed "R. Mutt," further disrupted conventional art forms. "Fountain" was submitted to the Society of Independent Artists in New York and rejected, despite the society's policy of accepting all entries from members. This act of submission and subsequent rejection sparked intense debate about the definition of art and the role of the artist in determining what constitutes an artwork.

Duchamp's readymades were not created to be beautiful or expressive in the traditional sense. Instead, they served as a critique of the art market and the commodification of art. By using mass-produced objects, Duchamp questioned the uniqueness of the artwork and the artist's touch, which were highly valued in traditional art. This approach prefigured later developments in conceptual art, where the idea behind the work is often more important than the work itself.

In addition to his readymades, Duchamp's "The Bride Stripped Bare by Her Bachelors, Even" (The Large Glass) (1915-1923) is a complex work that further illustrates his conceptual approach. The Large Glass is a two-panel piece made of glass, dust, and various materials, depicting a mechanistic and enigmatic narrative. Duchamp provided cryptic notes and diagrams to accompany the piece, suggesting a deep engagement with ideas of chance, sexuality, and the interplay between male and female energies. The work defied easy interpretation and invited viewers to engage with it intellectually, foreshadowing the interactive nature of much postmodern art.

Duchamp's influence on postmodern art cannot be overstated. His readymades paved the way for artists like Andy Warhol, who used mass-produced images in his work, and Joseph Kosuth, whose conceptual pieces directly addressed the nature of art. Warhol's Brillo Boxes and Campbell's Soup Cans echoed Duchamp's challenge to the uniqueness of art objects, while Kosuth's works, such as "One and Three Chairs" (1965), explored the relationship between the object, its representation, and its linguistic description, a clear nod to Duchamp's legacy.

Duchamp's emphasis on the conceptual aspect of art also resonated with the postmodern critique of the art establishment. Postmodernism questioned the grand narratives and universal truths upheld by modernism, instead embracing multiplicity, fragmentation, and the role of context in shaping meaning. Duchamp's readymades, by their very nature, highlighted the contingency of meaning and the importance of context. A urinal is not just a urinal when placed in an art gallery; it becomes a statement, a question, a provocation.

Moreover, Duchamp's use of humor and irony prefigured the playful and often subversive nature of postmodern art. Works like "L.H.O.O.Q." (1919), a cheap postcard reproduction of the Mona Lisa onto which Duchamp drew a mustache and goatee, lampooned the reverence for iconic artworks and the seriousness of art criticism. This irreverence for established norms and the blending of high and low culture became hallmarks of postmodern art.

Duchamp's impact extends beyond visual arts into other areas of cultural production. His ideas influenced the Fluxus movement of the 1960s, which blurred the boundaries between art and life, performance and object. Artists like Yoko Ono and Nam June Paik drew on Duchamp's legacy to create works that were participatory and ephemeral, challenging the notion of the art object as a permanent, marketable commodity.

In the realm of literature and theory, Duchamp's concepts found resonance with post-structuralist thinkers like Roland Barthes and Jacques Derrida, who explored the instability of meaning and the role of the reader/viewer in constructing it. Barthes' idea of the "death of the author," which argues that the interpretation of a text is not fixed by the author's intentions but is instead created by the reader, parallels Duchamp's assertion that the viewer plays a crucial role in determining the meaning of an artwork. Derrida's deconstruction similarly echoes Duchamp's dismantling of the hierarchical distinctions between art and non-art, original and copy.

Duchamp's legacy is also evident in the digital age, where the proliferation of images and the ease of reproduction have further blurred the boundaries of art. The internet has democratized the creation and dissemination of art, aligning with Duchamp's idea that art is not confined to traditional mediums or institutions. Online platforms allow for new forms of readymades and conceptual pieces, where the context and interaction are as significant as the content itself.

In the educational sphere, Duchamp's work encourages a pedagogical approach that values critical thinking and creativity over technical skill alone. Art education programs that emphasize conceptual development and the exploration of ideas over the mere replication of techniques can trace their philosophical underpinnings back to Duchamp's revolutionary approach.

Duchamp's influence is pervasive, extending to various disciplines and continually inspiring new generations of artists and thinkers. His challenge to traditional aesthetics and his elevation of the conceptual over the visual remain foundational to contemporary art practices. As artists continue to explore the boundaries of what art can be, Duchamp's legacy as a pioneer of conceptual art and a catalyst for postmodernist thought endures, reminding us that art is as much about ideas as it is about objects.

22 MINIMALIST ART AND EXISTENTIAL ENGAGEMENT

Donald Judd, an influential figure in the minimalist movement, sought to redefine the boundaries of art by emphasizing simplicity, precision, and the use of industrial materials. His work is characterized by a reduction to fundamental forms and an exploration of spatial relationships, which together foster a deeper, almost existential contemplation of the viewer's interaction with art and space.

Judd began his career in the late 1950s as a painter, but he soon found that the two-dimensional medium was insufficient for his artistic goals. He moved towards three-dimensional works, creating objects that rejected traditional notions of sculpture. Instead of modeling or carving, Judd constructed his pieces using materials like stainless steel, aluminum, Plexiglas, and plywood. This shift marked a significant departure from the traditional sculptural techniques and aligned him with the burgeoning minimalist movement.

Minimalism, as championed by Judd, was not merely about simplicity for its own sake. It was a reaction against the emotional excesses of Abstract Expressionism and the overt symbolism of earlier modern art. Judd's work sought to strip away the extraneous and focus on the essential, creating pieces that were self-sufficient and devoid of metaphorical or narrative content. His art was about the object itself and its relationship to the space around it, an approach that demanded a new kind of viewer engagement.

Judd's pieces are often described as "specific objects," a term he coined to denote works that exist between painting and sculpture. These objects are typically modular, repeating geometric forms that emphasize order and clarity. An iconic example is his series of "stacks," where identically sized rectangular boxes are affixed to the wall in a vertical column, with equal spacing between each unit. The effect is a rhythmic play of light and shadow, encouraging viewers to consider the interplay of the objects with their environment.

The existential aspect of Judd's work lies in its insistence on direct, unmediated experience. By removing any representational content, Judd's objects invite viewers to confront the materials and forms directly. This confrontation with the "thingness" of the object encourages a deeper awareness of one's presence in space, mirroring existentialist themes of existence and being. The viewer's perception and interpretation become central to the experience, highlighting the subjective nature of meaning and the importance of individual engagement.

Judd's work is also notable for its use of industrial fabrication techniques. He often collaborated with manufacturers to produce his pieces, emphasizing precision and uniformity. This method further distanced his work from traditional craftsmanship and aligned it with contemporary industrial aesthetics. The use of such techniques underscores the neutrality and impersonality of his objects, reinforcing the minimalist ethos of removing the artist's hand and emotional input from the work.

The influence of architecture is evident in Judd's work, both in scale and conceptual approach. His larger installations, particularly those at his Marfa, Texas compound, blur the lines between art and architecture. At Marfa, Judd transformed a series of decommissioned army buildings into spaces for art, creating a permanent installation of his work in dialogue with the surrounding landscape. This setting allows for an immersive experience where the viewer can engage with the objects over time, fostering a contemplative interaction that extends beyond a typical gallery visit.

Judd's writings further illuminate his philosophical approach to art. In his influential essay "Specific Objects," Judd argued for the autonomy of the art object, advocating for works that exist on their own terms rather than representing or symbolizing something else. This emphasis on autonomy reflects existentialist concerns with authenticity and the importance of confronting reality directly. Judd believed that art should not serve as an illusion or a conduit for narrative, but rather as a concrete reality that engages the viewer's perception and cognition.

The legacy of Judd's minimalist approach can be seen in the work of numerous contemporary artists and designers. His emphasis on simplicity, functionality, and the intrinsic qualities of materials has resonated across disciplines, influencing architecture, design, and even philosophy. The minimalist movement, with its roots in Judd's principles, continues to inform contemporary practices that value clarity, efficiency, and direct engagement with space and material.

Judd's exploration of color, while often understated, plays a crucial role in his work. He frequently used colors in their purest forms, applied to the industrial materials of his sculptures. This use of color enhances the perception of form and space, creating a visual harmony that aligns with his minimalist principles. The colors are not symbolic but are chosen for their ability to interact with the material and the surrounding environment, further emphasizing the existential engagement of the viewer with the object.

In addition to his work in visual art, Judd also made significant contributions to design and furniture. His furniture designs, like his art, are characterized by simplicity, functionality, and the use of industrial materials. These pieces are not merely utilitarian objects but are considered extensions of his artistic practice, embodying the same principles of order, clarity, and material honesty. Judd's furniture underscores the holistic nature of his vision, where art, design, and architecture converge in a unified aesthetic experience.

Judd's impact extends beyond the realm of art into broader cultural and philosophical discussions. His work challenges viewers to reconsider their relationship with objects and spaces, encouraging a heightened awareness of the present moment and their physical surroundings. This existential dimension of his work resonates with broader philosophical inquiries into the nature of existence, perception, and reality.

Moreover, Judd's emphasis on the viewer's experience aligns with phenomenological approaches to art, which focus on the subjective perception of the viewer. Phenomenology, as developed by philosophers like Maurice Merleau-Ponty, emphasizes the importance of direct experience and the embodied nature of perception. Judd's work, with its insistence on unmediated engagement and spatial awareness, can be seen as a practical application of these philosophical ideas.

The enduring relevance of Judd's work lies in its ability to provoke thought and encourage a deeper engagement with the material world. His minimalist approach, with its focus on essential forms and direct experience, offers a counterpoint to the complexity and abstraction of much contemporary art. By stripping away the extraneous, Judd's work reveals the fundamental structures of perception and existence, inviting viewers to reflect on their own presence and engagement with the world around them.

In the contemporary art world, Judd's influence is evident in the ongoing exploration of minimalism and its principles. Artists continue to draw inspiration from his emphasis on form, material, and spatial relationships, creating works that challenge viewers to engage directly with the object and their environment. This legacy is a testament to the power of Judd's vision and his ability to distill complex philosophical ideas into tangible, concrete forms.

Judd's work also raises important questions about the role of the artist and the nature of artistic creation. By emphasizing industrial fabrication and the use of impersonal materials, Judd challenged traditional notions of artistic authorship and the value of the artist's hand. This approach aligns with existentialist themes of authenticity and the rejection of illusion, advocating for a direct and honest engagement with the material world.

In conclusion, Donald Judd's contribution to the minimalist movement and his exploration of existential themes have left a profound impact on the art world. His emphasis on simplicity, precision, and the use of industrial materials challenged traditional notions of art and opened new avenues for artistic expression. Through his work, Judd encouraged a deeper, more contemplative engagement with art and space, inviting viewers to confront the materiality of objects and their own presence in the world. His legacy continues to influence contemporary art and design, highlighting the enduring relevance of his vision and the power of minimalism to provoke thought and foster a deeper understanding of existence.

23 ENIGMATIC VISIONS

Mark Rothko was an influential American painter known for his contributions to Abstract Expressionism (AbEx). His work is characterized by large canvases with fields of color that aim to evoke emotional responses. Rothko's paintings often feature rectangular blocks of color with soft edges, creating a sense of depth and contemplation.

Key Elements of Rothko's Work:

- Large Canvases: Rothko's works are typically large, enveloping the viewer and creating an immersive experience.

- Fields of Color: He used large, flat areas of color, often with soft, blurred edges, to create a sense of calm and meditation.

- Emotional Impact: Rothko aimed to evoke deep emotional responses from viewers, often focusing on themes of human emotion and the sublime.

- Abstract Form: His paintings lack clear, recognizable forms, instead emphasizing color and composition to convey meaning.

Abstract Expressionism (AbEx):

- Movement: Abstract Expressionism emerged in the 1940s and 1950s in America, focusing on spontaneous, automatic, or subconscious creation.

- Key Artists: Besides Rothko, key figures include Jackson Pollock, Willem de Kooning, and Barnett Newman.

- Techniques: AbEx artists used techniques like action painting, color field painting, and gestural abstraction.

Painting Medium:

- Oil on Canvas: Rothko primarily used oil paints, layering colors to achieve a luminous, glowing effect.

- Layering and Blending: He meticulously layered colors, blending them to create subtle transitions and depth.

Rothko's paintings, with their meditative quality and focus on color and emotion, remain powerful examples of Abstract Expressionism's impact on modern art.

24 A MINIMALIST EXPERIMENT: REDEFINING THE BOUNDARIES OF PAINTING

Frank Stella, an iconic figure in contemporary art, emerged as a pioneering force within the minimalist movement during the late 1950s and early 1960s. His work, characterized by its boldness, precision, and abstract forms, challenged conventional notions of painting and redefined the boundaries of artistic expression. Stella's journey into minimalism was not merely a stylistic choice but a profound experiment in understanding and manipulating the essence of painting itself.

Stella's early works, such as the Black Paintings, epitomize his minimalist approach. These paintings, created between 1958 and 1960, are marked by their stark simplicity and monochromatic palette. The Black Paintings are a series of rectangular canvases with meticulously applied black stripes separated by thin lines of unpainted canvas. The uniformity and repetition in these works draw attention to the physical properties of the paint and the canvas, emphasizing the flatness of the surface and rejecting the illusion of depth. Stella's statement, "What you see is what you see," encapsulates his philosophy during this period. He sought to strip away any representational or symbolic content, focusing solely on the material and formal aspects of the painting.

This reductive approach was a radical departure from the expressive, gestural techniques of Abstract Expressionism, which dominated the art scene at the time. Stella's minimalism was a deliberate counterpoint to the emotional intensity and spontaneous brushwork of artists like Jackson Pollock and Willem de Kooning. Instead, Stella embraced precision, control, and the inherent qualities of the medium. His paintings became objects in their own right, rather than windows into an imagined world.

Stella's experimentation did not end with the Black Paintings. He continued to explore the possibilities of minimalist painting through various series and evolving techniques. In the early 1960s, he began creating the Aluminum Paintings and Copper Paintings, which featured metallic paints applied in geometric patterns. These works introduced a new dimension of reflectivity and surface texture, further emphasizing the materiality of the painting. The metallic sheen of the paint interacted with light in unique ways, creating a dynamic visual experience that changed depending on the viewer's perspective and the lighting conditions.

Throughout the 1960s and 1970s, Stella's work evolved to incorporate more complex and dynamic compositions. The Protractor Series, for example, introduced vibrant colors and intricate patterns based on protractor shapes. These paintings retained the minimalist emphasis on geometric forms and precise execution but expanded the visual vocabulary to include curves, arcs, and intersecting lines. The Protractor Series demonstrated Stella's ability to push the boundaries of minimalism while maintaining a rigorous formal discipline.

Stella's minimalist experiment extended beyond painting to include reliefs and three-dimensional works. In the late 1970s and 1980s, he began creating large-scale, wall-mounted reliefs that combined painting and sculpture. These works, often constructed from materials like aluminum and fiberglass, featured complex, layered structures that protruded from the wall. Stella's reliefs challenged traditional distinctions between painting and sculpture, blurring the lines between the two and exploring new possibilities for spatial interaction.

One of the defining characteristics of Stella's minimalist approach is his use of repetition and seriality. By repeating simple geometric forms and motifs across multiple works, Stella created a sense of continuity and coherence within his oeuvre. This serial approach allowed him to investigate the variations and permutations of a given form, revealing the subtle nuances and complexities that could emerge from seemingly simple elements. The use of repetition also reinforced the viewer's awareness of the painting as an object, emphasizing its physical presence and the process of its creation.

Stella's minimalist experiment was also deeply informed by his engagement with the history of art and his dialogue with other artists. He drew inspiration from a wide range of sources, including Islamic art, Russian Constructivism, and the works of early modernist painters like Kazimir Malevich and Piet Mondrian. Stella's minimalist aesthetic can be seen as part of a broader tradition of abstract art that seeks to distill visual experience to its essential components. However, Stella's approach was uniquely his own, characterized by a relentless focus on materiality, form, and the experiential qualities of the artwork.

In addition to his visual innovations, Stella's minimalist experiment had a profound impact on the theoretical discourse of contemporary art. His work challenged critics and art historians to reconsider the nature of painting and the role of the artist. Stella's insistence on the autonomy of the artwork, its self-referential quality, and its resistance to external interpretation resonated with the ideas of contemporary critics like Michael Fried and Clement Greenberg. These critics championed Stella's work as a paradigmatic example of modernist painting, emphasizing its purity, rigor, and formal coherence.

Despite his association with minimalism, Stella's work defies easy categorization. His career has been marked by a continual process of experimentation and evolution, encompassing a wide range of styles and techniques. From the stark austerity of the Black Paintings to the exuberant complexity of his later reliefs, Stella has consistently pushed the boundaries of what painting can be. His work embodies a spirit of exploration and innovation, challenging viewers to see and experience art in new and unexpected ways.

Stella's influence on subsequent generations of artists cannot be overstated. His minimalist experiment paved the way for a diverse array of practices that engage with the material and formal properties of art. Artists like Donald Judd, Sol LeWitt, and Dan Flavin, among others, have drawn inspiration from Stella's work, extending and expanding the principles of minimalism in their own unique ways. Stella's legacy is evident not only in the work of these artists but also in the broader trajectory of contemporary art, which continues to grapple with questions of form, materiality, and the nature of artistic experience.

In reflecting on Stella's minimalist experiment, it is clear that his contributions to art are both profound and enduring. His work challenges us to reconsider our assumptions about painting, to appreciate the beauty and complexity of simple forms, and to recognize the power of art to transform our perception of the world. Through his rigorous exploration of materiality, form, and process, Stella has left an indelible mark on the history of art, demonstrating the enduring relevance and vitality of minimalism as a mode of artistic inquiry.

25 GRIDS, SERIES, AND THE PLANNING OF CONCEPTUAL ART IN CONTEMPORARY AND POSTMODERN MOVEMENTS

Sol LeWitt was a pivotal figure in the transition from modern to postmodern art, renowned for his work that emphasized the concepts of grids, permutations, planning, and series. His approach to art was grounded in the belief that the idea or concept behind the work was paramount, often overshadowing the physical execution. This philosophy placed him firmly within the realms of both contemporary and postmodern art, where the process and system behind creating art became as important, if not more so, than the finished product itself.

LeWitt's early work in the 1960s and 1970s laid the foundation for his influential role in the conceptual art movement. He is best known for his wall drawings and structures (a term he preferred over sculptures), which explored geometric forms and mathematical permutations. His art often began with a grid, a simple yet profound tool that provided a framework for endless variations and complexity. This grid-based approach allowed LeWitt to explore a systematic method of art-making, where the final appearance of the work was determined by a set of rules or instructions.

The grid in LeWitt's art served as a fundamental structure that facilitated exploration within a defined space. It was a means to achieve precision and consistency while allowing for infinite variations. For instance, his "Wall Drawing #273" consists of a grid of squares that are systematically filled with lines in different directions, creating a dynamic and visually engaging pattern. This piece exemplifies how a simple grid can generate a complex visual experience through the application of a systematic method.

LeWitt's use of permutations further exemplifies his conceptual approach. Permutations in his work often involved variations in color, line, and form within the constraints of a grid. By changing one element while keeping others constant, LeWitt could explore the vast possibilities inherent in a single conceptual framework. His series "Incomplete Open Cubes" is a prime example, where he presented variations of cubes with missing edges. Each permutation offered a new perspective on the form, highlighting the relationships between completeness and absence, structure and space.

LeWitt's commitment to planning and systems was revolutionary. He often created detailed instructions or diagrams for his wall drawings, which could be executed by others. This approach challenged traditional notions of authorship and craftsmanship in art. By delegating the execution of his work to assistants or even museum staff, LeWitt underscored the importance of the idea over the hand of the artist. This method democratized the art-making process, allowing for the creation of art that was both reproducible and unique, depending on the interpreters' adherence to or deviation from the original instructions.

The concept of series in LeWitt's work is crucial to understanding his artistic philosophy. By working in series, LeWitt could systematically explore all possible variations of a particular idea. This approach is evident in works like his "Serial Project #1" (1966), which involved a systematic exploration of all the possible variations of a simple geometric form. Each piece in the series represents a different permutation, together forming a comprehensive examination of the conceptual possibilities.

LeWitt's emphasis on planning and conceptual systems resonated deeply within the contemporary art world. It paved the way for artists who sought to foreground the intellectual processes behind their work rather than the aesthetic qualities alone. His influence can be seen in the works of artists like Donald Judd, whose minimalist sculptures explore similar themes of geometry and repetition, and Solange Pessoa, whose installations often engage with systematic structures and organic permutations.

In the context of modern and postmodern art, LeWitt's contributions were crucial in bridging the two movements. Modern art, with its emphasis on formalism and the avant-garde, laid the groundwork for LeWitt's systematic explorations. However, his rejection of traditional aesthetics and his embrace of conceptual frameworks aligned him more closely with postmodernism, which questioned the very foundations of art and sought to deconstruct established norms.

Postmodern art often engages with themes of plurality, fragmentation, and the questioning of grand narratives. LeWitt's work embodies these themes through its exploration of infinite possibilities within a constrained system. By using grids, permutations, and series, he created art that was at once systematic and open-ended, inviting viewers to engage with the process and the idea behind the work. This approach mirrored the postmodernist rejection of singular interpretations and embraced the multiplicity of meanings.

LeWitt's work also intersects with contemporary art's preoccupation with the role of the artist and the nature of creativity. In an era where digital technology and automation have transformed artistic production, LeWitt's systems-based approach seems prescient. His art anticipated the rise of algorithmic and generative art, where artists create systems or programs that generate visual outcomes. The conceptual framework LeWitt established continues to influence contemporary artists who explore the intersections of technology, mathematics, and art.

One of the most compelling aspects of LeWitt's legacy is his ability to make complex ideas accessible through visual simplicity. His use of basic geometric forms and clear systems allows viewers to grasp the underlying concepts without needing extensive art historical knowledge. This accessibility is a hallmark of both contemporary and postmodern art, which often seeks to engage broader audiences and challenge elitist notions of art appreciation.

LeWitt's art also invites viewers to reflect on the nature of perception and the act of seeing. By presenting variations within a grid and series, he encourages an active engagement with the work, prompting viewers to notice subtle differences and patterns. This interactive element aligns with postmodern art's emphasis on viewer participation and the co-creation of meaning. In works like "Wall Drawing #51," where lines are drawn from the center of a wall to random points on a grid, the viewer's perception plays a crucial role in interpreting the work's dynamic visual structure.

The influence of LeWitt's approach extends beyond visual art into architecture and design. His principles of modularity, repetition, and variation have been applied in architectural practices that seek to balance uniformity and diversity. For instance, the use of modular systems in building design, where individual units can be configured in multiple ways to create varied spatial experiences, echoes LeWitt's grid-based permutations. This cross-disciplinary impact underscores the far-reaching implications of LeWitt's conceptual innovations.

LeWitt's writings, particularly his "Sentences on Conceptual Art" and "Paragraphs on Conceptual Art," provide valuable insights into his artistic philosophy. He articulated a vision of art that prioritized ideas over execution and embraced the possibility of multiple interpretations. These writings have become foundational texts in the study of conceptual art, offering a framework for understanding the movement's principles and objectives.

In conclusion, Sol LeWitt's work represents a critical juncture in the evolution of contemporary and postmodern art. His use of grids, permutations, planning, and series challenged traditional notions of art-making and opened new avenues for conceptual exploration. By emphasizing the idea over the execution, LeWitt redefined the role of the artist and the nature of creativity, influencing generations of artists across disciplines. His legacy is evident in the continued relevance of his principles in today's art world, where the boundaries between art, technology, and conceptual thought continue to blur. LeWitt's contributions underscore the enduring power of conceptual art to provoke thought, challenge conventions, and expand our understanding of what art can be.

26 POP ART AND CONSUMER CULTURE

Andy Warhol stands as an iconic figure in the realm of contemporary art, his name synonymous with the Pop Art movement that emerged in the mid-20th century. Warhol's innovative approach to art profoundly altered the landscape of modern aesthetics, and his works continue to influence both the art world and popular culture.

Warhol's journey into the world of art began in Pittsburgh, Pennsylvania, where he was born in 1928. From a young age, Warhol demonstrated a keen interest in visual arts. After graduating from the Carnegie Institute of Technology, he moved to New York City, where he initially found success as a commercial illustrator. However, it was his transition to fine art in the late 1950s and early 1960s that truly defined his career and left an indelible mark on the art world.

The essence of Warhol's contribution to art is encapsulated in the Pop Art movement, a genre that emerged as a reaction against the abstract expressionism dominating the post-World War II art scene. Pop Art sought to blur the boundaries between "high" art and "low" culture by incorporating imagery from advertising, comic books, and everyday consumer products. Warhol's fascination with consumer culture and mass production became the hallmark of his work, manifesting in his famous depictions of Campbell's soup cans, Coca-Cola bottles, and Marilyn Monroe.

Warhol's art was characterized by its emphasis on repetition and seriality, mimicking the processes of mass production. His use of the silkscreen printing technique allowed him to create multiple copies of a single image, challenging traditional notions of originality and authorship in art. This method not only aligned with the mass-produced nature of the subjects he portrayed but also democratized art by making it more accessible to a broader audience.

One of Warhol's most iconic series, his Campbell's Soup Cans, exemplifies his approach to art and his commentary on consumer culture. By transforming a mundane grocery item into a work of art, Warhol elevated the ordinary to the extraordinary, prompting viewers to reconsider their perceptions of everyday objects. The repetition of the soup cans, each one identical yet subtly unique, mirrored the uniformity of products in a supermarket aisle, highlighting the pervasive influence of consumerism in American society.

Similarly, Warhol's portraits of celebrities such as Marilyn Monroe, Elvis Presley, and Elizabeth Taylor reflect his fascination with fame and the cult of celebrity. By reproducing their images in vibrant, eye-catching colors, Warhol both celebrated and critiqued the superficiality and ephemeral nature of stardom. His Marilyn Diptych, created shortly after Monroe's death, juxtaposes vibrant, repetitive images of the actress with a fading, black-and-white version, symbolizing the fleeting nature of fame and the darker undercurrents of celebrity culture.

Warhol's impact extended beyond the art world into the realms of music, film, and fashion. He produced experimental films that challenged conventional narratives and aesthetics, such as "Chelsea Girls" and "Empire." His collaboration with the Velvet Underground, a seminal rock band, further demonstrated his interdisciplinary approach to art. The iconic banana cover of their debut album, designed by Warhol, remains one of the most recognizable images in music history.

Beyond his art, Warhol himself became a cultural icon, embodying the ethos of Pop Art. His enigmatic persona, characterized by his distinctive silver wigs and aloof demeanor, added to his mystique and amplified his influence. Warhol's studio, The Factory, became a hub for artists, musicians, and socialites, fostering a creative environment that blurred the lines between art and life. The Factory was as much a part of Warhol's artistic output as his paintings, serving as a microcosm of the vibrant, chaotic, and often hedonistic culture of 1960s New York. The Factory's influence extended into the digital age, with Warhol's experiments with computers in the 1980s foreshadowing the blending of art and technology that has become prevalent today.

Warhol's fascination with technology and mass production was not limited to traditional media. In the 1980s, he began experimenting with computers, using an Amiga to create digital art. This pioneering work placed him at the forefront of the digital art movement, highlighting his perpetual curiosity and willingness to explore new mediums.

Warhol's computer-generated art, much like his silkscreen prints, played with the themes of replication and mass production, anticipating the digital revolution that would transform the art world in the decades to come.

In the context of consumer culture, Warhol's work can be seen as both a reflection and a critique. His fascination with consumer goods and celebrity culture mirrored the increasing commercialization of American society in the post-war era. Yet, through his art, Warhol also offered a critical lens on the commodification of culture and the homogenization of individual identities. His work invites viewers to question the values and assumptions underpinning consumer culture and to reflect on the ways in which mass media shapes perceptions and desires.

In the digital age, Warhol's exploration of repetition and seriality takes on new significance. The proliferation of digital media and the rise of social networks echo Warhol's insights into the mass production and dissemination of images. Today, images are reproduced and shared at an unprecedented scale, creating a visual landscape where the boundaries between original and copy, art and commodity, are increasingly blurred. Warhol's work anticipates these developments, offering a prescient commentary on the dynamics of visual culture in the 21st century.

The concept of a "computer time vault" aligns intriguingly with Warhol's legacy and the enduring relevance of his work. If we imagine a repository where digital artifacts are preserved for future generations, Warhol's oeuvre would undoubtedly occupy a central place. His art encapsulates a pivotal moment in cultural history, reflecting the anxieties and aspirations of a society in the throes of rapid transformation. By preserving his work in such a vault, we acknowledge not only Warhol's influence on contemporary art but also his foresight in recognizing the ways in which technology and media shape human experience.

Warhol's legacy continues to resonate, influencing contemporary artists and shaping the discourse on art and culture. His exploration of the intersections between art, commerce, and technology remains relevant in an era defined by digital media and global consumerism. Artists such as Jeff Koons, Damien Hirst, and Takashi Murakami have drawn inspiration from Warhol's techniques and themes, further cementing his status as a pivotal figure in the history of art.

Moreover, Warhol's prescient understanding of the interplay between celebrity and media has become even more pertinent in the age of social media. The self-curated personas and commodified identities that proliferate on platforms like Instagram and TikTok echo Warhol's insights into the construction and consumption of celebrity. In this context, Warhol's work serves as both a mirror and a lens, reflecting contemporary cultural dynamics while offering a framework for understanding the pervasive influence of media and technology on identity and culture.

Warhol's Factory, often described as a 'factory' for art, was a precursor to the digital workspaces that would follow. Here, Warhol and his collaborators produced art in a manner akin to a production line, blurring the lines between the artist and the machine. This approach was revolutionary, challenging traditional notions of artistic creation and setting the stage for the integration of technology in art-making processes.

In conclusion, Andy Warhol's contribution to art and culture is profound and multifaceted. Through his innovative use of techniques and his incisive commentary on consumer culture, Warhol reshaped the boundaries of art and influenced a generation of artists and thinkers. His work continues to resonate, offering a critical lens on the dynamics of mass production, media, and celebrity. As we navigate an increasingly digital and interconnected world, Warhol's legacy provides valuable insights into the ways in which technology and culture intersect, reminding us of the enduring power of art to reflect and shape human experience. The Factory, with its pioneering use of technology and collaborative ethos, stands as a testament to Warhol's visionary approach, bridging the gap between the industrial age and the digital era.

27 POP ART AND COMIC AESTHETICS

Roy Lichtenstein, an iconic figure in the Pop Art movement, is celebrated for his distinctive style that drew heavily from comic strips and advertising imagery. His work encapsulated the essence of popular culture and challenged the boundaries between high art and mass media. Lichtenstein's art, characterized by bold colors, dramatic compositions, and Ben-Day dots, became a visual shorthand for the Pop Art era and continues to influence artists and designers to this day.

Lichtenstein was born in New York City in 1923 and developed an early interest in art. After serving in the army during World War II, he pursued his studies in art at Ohio State University, where he later taught. His early works were more traditional, but it wasn't until the 1960s that he found his unique voice and style. During this period, he began experimenting with imagery from comic books, which led to the creation of some of his most famous works.

The decision to use comic book imagery was both innovative and controversial. At a time when Abstract Expressionism, with its emphasis on individual emotion and spontaneity, was the dominant art movement, Lichtenstein's use of commercial and mass-produced sources seemed almost heretical. However, it was precisely this choice that positioned him at the forefront of Pop Art, a movement that sought to blur the lines between fine art and popular culture.

Lichtenstein's technique involved meticulous planning and execution. He would start with a drawing, often based on a panel from a comic book, which he would then project onto a canvas. This projection was then traced and painted, with Lichtenstein adding his characteristic Ben-Day dots, thick outlines, and vibrant primary colors. The use of Ben-Day dots, a printing process common in comic books and newspapers, became one of Lichtenstein's most recognizable trademarks. These dots, applied meticulously by hand or with the aid of stencils, gave his paintings a mass-produced look that both celebrated and critiqued the culture of mechanical reproduction.

One of Lichtenstein's most famous works, "Whaam!" (1963), exemplifies his approach. Based on an image from a 1962 issue of DC Comics' "All-American Men of War," the painting depicts a fighter plane firing a rocket that explodes in a vivid burst of flames and debris. The dramatic composition, complete with onomatopoeic text, captures the dynamism and immediacy of comic book art. Yet, by rendering the image on a large canvas and through a painstaking process, Lichtenstein elevates the ephemeral, disposable nature of comic strips to the status of fine art.

Lichtenstein's fascination with comic aesthetics was not merely about borrowing imagery but also about exploring the visual language and narrative techniques of the medium. His paintings often isolated and magnified individual panels, focusing on moments of heightened drama and emotion. In doing so, he invited viewers to reconsider the artistic merit and cultural significance of comic art, which had traditionally been dismissed as lowbrow or juvenile.

Another significant aspect of Lichtenstein's work was his engagement with themes of romance and heroism, common tropes in comic books. His paintings frequently depicted stereotypical scenes of lovers in moments of passion or conflict, often accompanied by melodramatic captions. These works, such as "Drowning Girl" (1963) and "Hopeless" (1963), both celebrated and parodied the exaggerated emotions and simplified narratives of romance comics. The juxtaposition of high drama and flat, mechanical rendering created a sense of irony and distance, prompting viewers to question the nature of sentimentality and the portrayal of gender roles in popular media.

Lichtenstein's exploration of comic aesthetics also extended to the realm of advertising and consumer culture. In works like "Oh, Jeff...I Love You, Too...But..." (1964), he mimicked the visual style of advertisements, with their clean lines, bold colors, and persuasive imagery. By appropriating the language of advertising, Lichtenstein highlighted the pervasive influence of commercial imagery on everyday life and its role in shaping desires and identities. His paintings thus served as a critique of the commodification of culture and the manipulation of consumer behavior through visual media.

Despite the apparent simplicity and reproducibility of his style, Lichtenstein's work involved a high degree of technical skill and conceptual rigor. His paintings required careful planning and execution, with each dot and line meticulously placed to achieve the desired effect. This painstaking process stood in stark contrast to the spontaneous, gestural techniques of Abstract Expressionism, positioning Lichtenstein's art as a deliberate and calculated commentary on the nature of artistic creation and originality.

Lichtenstein's influence extended beyond the boundaries of Pop Art, impacting various fields of visual culture, including graphic design, fashion, and advertising. His bold, graphic style and use of comic book aesthetics have inspired generations of artists and designers, contributing to the ongoing dialogue between high art and popular culture. In many ways, Lichtenstein's work anticipated the postmodern fascination with appropriation, pastiche, and the blending of high and low cultural forms.

Moreover, Lichtenstein's legacy can be seen in the broader cultural acceptance and appreciation of comic art. Today, comic books and graphic novels are recognized as legitimate forms of artistic and literary expression, with works by artists like Art Spiegelman, Alison Bechdel, and Chris Ware receiving critical acclaim and scholarly attention. Lichtenstein's pioneering use of comic aesthetics played a crucial role in challenging the hierarchical distinctions between fine art and popular culture, paving the way for a more inclusive and diverse understanding of artistic value.

In addition to his iconic paintings, Lichtenstein also explored other media, including sculpture, printmaking, and murals. His sculptures, often large-scale and brightly colored, translated his two-dimensional comic book style into three-dimensional forms. Works like "Brushstroke" (1996) and "House I" (1996) playfully manipulated perspective and scale, further blurring the boundaries between art and everyday life. His murals, such as the massive "Mural with Blue Brushstroke" (1984) at the Equitable Tower in New York City, brought his comic-inspired imagery into public spaces, making art accessible to a wider audience.

Lichtenstein's work also engaged with the history of art, appropriating and reinterpreting images from classical and modern art. In his "Art History" series, he reimagined works by artists like Picasso, Mondrian, and Monet in his signature comic book style. These works not only paid homage to the great masters of art but also questioned the conventions of art history and the processes of canonization and interpretation. By placing his own work in dialogue with that of earlier artists, Lichtenstein underscored the interconnectedness of artistic traditions and the ongoing evolution of visual language.

Throughout his career, Lichtenstein remained committed to exploring the intersections of art, commerce, and popular culture. His work challenged the elitism of the art world and expanded the possibilities of artistic expression by incorporating elements of everyday life and mass media. In doing so, he helped to democratize art, making it more relevant and accessible to a broader audience.

Lichtenstein's impact on the art world and popular culture is profound and enduring. His distinctive style, characterized by bold colors, dramatic compositions, and Ben-Day dots, continues to captivate viewers and inspire artists. His work serves as a reminder of the power of visual culture to shape our perceptions and experiences, and of the potential for art to challenge and transform our understanding of the world.

In conclusion, Roy Lichtenstein's contribution to the Pop Art movement and his use of comic aesthetics represent a significant chapter in the history of modern art. Through his innovative techniques and thoughtful engagement with popular culture, Lichtenstein challenged traditional notions of artistic value and expanded the possibilities of visual expression. His work continues to resonate with audiences and artists alike, offering a vibrant and critical commentary on the interplay between art, commerce, and everyday life. As we navigate an increasingly mediated and image-saturated world, Lichtenstein's legacy serves as a testament to the enduring relevance and power of art to reflect, critique, and shape our cultural landscape.

28 INSTALLATION AND CONTEMPORARY ART

Allan Kaprow is a pivotal figure in the history of contemporary art, best known for his development of "happenings" and his innovative approach to installations. His work played a crucial role in shifting the boundaries of art, challenging traditional forms, and exploring new modes of expression that emphasized the experiential and the ephemeral.

Born in 1927 in Atlantic City, New Jersey, Kaprow's early life and education were marked by a keen interest in the arts. He studied under Hans Hofmann, a prominent Abstract Expressionist, and later earned degrees in philosophy and art history. This academic background, combined with his practical training, influenced his approach to art, blending rigorous conceptual thinking with experimental practices.

Kaprow's contribution to contemporary art is perhaps best exemplified by his creation of happenings. These events, which emerged in the late 1950s and early 1960s, were a radical departure from traditional art forms. Happenings were not conventional performances with a clear narrative or a passive audience. Instead, they were immersive environments where the distinction between the artist, the artwork, and the audience was blurred. Participants were often given roles to play or tasks to perform, making them active contributors to the creation of the work.

The concept of the happening was revolutionary because it challenged the static nature of traditional art. Unlike a painting or sculpture, which is fixed in time and space, a happening was dynamic and temporal. It could not be easily commodified or preserved; its essence lay in the moment of its occurrence and the interactions it engendered. This emphasis on the ephemeral nature of art was a direct challenge to the art market and the notion of art as a collectible commodity.

One of Kaprow's most famous happenings was "18 Happenings in 6 Parts," first performed in 1959 at the Reuben Gallery in New York City. The piece consisted of a series of loosely scripted activities taking place in different rooms, involving sounds, movements, and interactions among the participants. The audience was given instructions on where to go and what to do, creating a sense of participation and unpredictability. This event set the stage for numerous other happenings, each designed to explore new ways of engaging with art and life.

Kaprow's happenings were influenced by a variety of sources, including the Dada movement, John Cage's experimental music, and Jackson Pollock's action painting. The Dadaists' embrace of chance and absurdity resonated with Kaprow's desire to break down conventional artistic boundaries. Cage's use of indeterminacy and his emphasis on the process over the final product provided a model for the open-ended structure of happenings. Pollock's physical engagement with his materials, famously captured in his drip paintings, inspired Kaprow to consider the act of creation as a form of performance.

In addition to happenings, Kaprow was a pioneer in the field of installation art. His installations were designed to transform the viewer's perception of space and to create immersive environments that challenged the conventions of gallery presentation. Unlike traditional artworks, which are often displayed on walls or pedestals, installations envelop the viewer, engaging multiple senses and creating a more holistic experience.

One of Kaprow's notable installations is "Yard," first created in 1961 at the Martha Jackson Gallery in New York. For this piece, Kaprow filled the gallery's courtyard with hundreds of used tires, creating a landscape that viewers were invited to navigate. The installation transformed the gallery space into an environment that was both playful and disorienting, encouraging viewers to interact physically with the artwork. This emphasis on viewer participation and the creation of a sensory-rich environment became hallmarks of Kaprow's installation work.

Kaprow's approach to installation art was informed by his interest in everyday life and his desire to break down the barriers between art and life. He often used commonplace materials and settings, such as tires, newspapers, or household objects, to create his installations. This use of everyday materials not only challenged traditional notions of what constituted art but also invited viewers to reconsider their relationship to their surroundings. By transforming familiar objects and spaces into sites of artistic engagement, Kaprow sought to make art more accessible and relevant to everyday experience.

The influence of Kaprow's happenings and installations on contemporary art cannot be overstated. His work paved the way for subsequent generations of artists who have continued to explore the boundaries of performance, participation, and site-specificity. Artists such as Yoko Ono, Marina Abramović, and Olafur Eliasson have drawn on Kaprow's legacy in their own explorations of immersive environments and audience interaction.

Yoko Ono's "Cut Piece," first performed in 1964, is a direct descendant of Kaprow's happenings. In this performance, Ono invited audience members to come on stage and cut pieces of her clothing, creating a powerful commentary on vulnerability, participation, and the relationship between the artist and the audience. Marina Abramović's endurance performances, such as "The Artist Is Present," also echo Kaprow's emphasis on the experiential and the ephemeral. Abramović's work often involves prolonged engagement with the audience, challenging viewers to confront their own physical and emotional responses.

Olafur Eliasson's large-scale installations, such as "The Weather Project" at Tate Modern in 2003, similarly draw on Kaprow's legacy. Eliasson's work transforms architectural spaces into immersive environments that engage multiple senses and encourage viewer interaction. "The Weather Project," which filled the museum's Turbine Hall with a glowing sun and mist, invited viewers to contemplate their relationship to nature and to each other, much like Kaprow's installations sought to transform everyday experiences into sites of artistic engagement.

Kaprow's influence extends beyond individual artists to broader movements in contemporary art. The rise of relational aesthetics in the 1990s and 2000s, exemplified by artists like Rirkrit Tiravanija and Thomas Hirschhorn, owes a significant debt to Kaprow's emphasis on participation and the social dimensions of art. Relational aesthetics focuses on the creation of social environments and the interactions that take place within them, reflecting Kaprow's belief in the potential of art to transform everyday life.

Kaprow's work also anticipated many of the concerns of contemporary installation art, particularly its emphasis on site-specificity and the transformation of space. Artists like Christo and Jeanne-Claude, whose large-scale environmental works alter landscapes and urban environments, share Kaprow's interest in the relationship between art and its surroundings. Their projects, such as "The Gates" in Central Park, create temporary, immersive experiences that engage viewers in new ways, much like Kaprow's installations sought to do.

In reflecting on Kaprow's legacy, it is important to recognize his commitment to the idea that art should be an integral part of life, not separate from it. This philosophy is evident in his later work, which often involved instructions for activities that viewers could perform on their own, outside of a gallery or performance space. These "Activities," as Kaprow called them, were designed to be simple, everyday tasks that encouraged participants to engage with their surroundings in new and mindful ways. By decentralizing the role of the artist and emphasizing the creative potential of the viewer, Kaprow sought to democratize art and make it a more inclusive and participatory practice.

Allan Kaprow's contributions to contemporary art through his happenings and installations have left an indelible mark on the field. His work challenged traditional notions of art, emphasizing the experiential, the ephemeral, and the participatory. By breaking down the boundaries between art and life, Kaprow paved the way for new modes of artistic expression that continue to influence and inspire artists today. His legacy serves as a reminder of the transformative potential of art and its ability to engage, challenge, and enrich our everyday experiences.

29 INSTALLATION AND SITE SPECIFICITY

Robert Smithson, an influential figure in the realm of contemporary art, is widely known for his pioneering work in land art and his innovative approach to site specificity. His installations challenge conventional notions of art by engaging directly with the environment and creating works that exist in harmony with, and are often inseparable from, their surroundings. Smithson's practice delves into the interplay between art, nature, and time, transforming landscapes into immersive experiences that provoke reflection on the relationship between humanity and the natural world.

Smithson's most famous work, "Spiral Jetty," epitomizes his approach to site-specific art. Created in 1970 at the Great Salt Lake in Utah, this monumental earthwork consists of a 1,500-foot-long, 15-foot-wide coil of basalt rock and earth extending into the lake. The choice of location was crucial; the lake's saline environment, fluctuating water levels, and the remote, almost otherworldly landscape all contribute to the work's dynamic and evolving nature. "Spiral Jetty" is not merely an object placed in a landscape but an integral part of it, interacting with the environment in a way that highlights natural processes such as erosion, sedimentation, and the passage of time.

The concept of site specificity is central to understanding Smithson's work. Unlike traditional sculptures or paintings that can be displayed in any location, site-specific works are created for a particular place and derive their meaning from their context. For Smithson, the site is not just a backdrop but an active participant in the artwork. He believed that art should engage with its environment in a way that is both physical and conceptual, blurring the boundaries between art and nature.

Smithson's fascination with entropy, the gradual decline into disorder, also plays a significant role in his site-specific installations. He saw entropy as a natural and inevitable process and incorporated this idea into his art. "Spiral Jetty," for instance, is subject to the forces of nature that cause it to change over time. The salt crystals that accumulate on the rocks, the fluctuating water levels that sometimes submerge the jetty entirely, and the varying hues of the lake all contribute to the artwork's continual transformation. This embrace of change and decay challenges the traditional notion of art as something permanent and unchanging, instead presenting it as an ever-evolving process.

In addition to "Spiral Jetty," Smithson's "Broken Circle/Spiral Hill," created in 1971 in Emmen, the Netherlands, further explores the concept of site-specificity. This work consists of two interconnected earthworks: "Broken Circle," a semicircular jetty extending into a quarry lake, and "Spiral Hill," a spiral ramp built from the excavated earth. The site, a disused sand quarry, was chosen for its unique geological and industrial history. By incorporating the site's characteristics into the work, Smithson transformed a place of industrial exploitation into a space of contemplation and aesthetic appreciation. "Broken Circle/Spiral Hill" invites viewers to consider the impact of human activity on the landscape and the potential for reclamation and renewal.

Smithson's theoretical writings also provide valuable insights into his approach to site-specificity. In his essay "A Sedimentation of the Mind: Earth Projects," he discusses the idea of "site" and "nonsite." A "site" is a location in the natural environment where an artwork is created, while a "nonsite" is an indoor gallery representation of that site, often consisting of maps, photographs, and materials from the original location. This concept highlights the tension between the actual experience of a place and its representation, emphasizing the importance of direct engagement with the environment. By bringing elements of the landscape into the gallery space, Smithson sought to bridge the gap between art and nature, encouraging viewers to consider the interconnectedness of different environments.

Another significant work, "Partially Buried Woodshed" (1970), demonstrates Smithson's interest in the transformative power of natural processes. Created on the campus of Kent State University, this installation involved partially burying an old woodshed under a pile of earth, causing the structure to collapse over time. This work, like "Spiral Jetty," is subject to the forces of entropy, with the gradual decay of the woodshed serving as a metaphor for the impermanence of human constructs. The choice of site—a university campus with its own historical and social context—adds another layer of meaning, inviting viewers to reflect on themes of memory, loss, and the passage of time.

Smithson's approach to site-specificity was also influenced by his interest in science fiction and the idea of the "alien" landscape. He often sought out locations that appeared otherworldly or surreal, such as the industrial wastelands and remote natural environments where he created many of his works. These landscapes, with their sense of desolation and decay, evoke a sense of timelessness and transcendence, challenging viewers to reconsider their relationship with the natural world. By situating his art in these contexts, Smithson created works that are both grounded in their specific locations and suggestive of broader, universal themes.

The legacy of Smithson's work can be seen in the practices of many contemporary artists who continue to explore the possibilities of site-specific art. His emphasis on the integration of art and environment, as well as his acceptance of change and decay as fundamental aspects of the creative process, has had a profound influence on the field. Artists such as Andy Goldsworthy, who creates ephemeral sculptures from natural materials, and Christo and Jeanne-Claude, known for their large-scale environmental interventions, have built on Smithson's ideas, further expanding the boundaries of site-specific art.

Smithson's work also raises important questions about the role of the artist in addressing environmental issues. By engaging directly with the landscape and highlighting the processes of change and decay, his installations encourage viewers to consider the impact of human activity on the environment and the need for sustainable practices. This ecological awareness is particularly relevant in today's context, as artists and audiences alike grapple with the challenges of climate change and environmental degradation.

In conclusion, Robert Smithson's installations and his approach to site specificity have left an indelible mark on the field of contemporary art. By creating works that are deeply rooted in their specific locations and responsive to the natural environment, Smithson challenged traditional notions of art and expanded the possibilities of artistic practice. His emphasis on the integration of art and nature, the acceptance of change and decay, and the importance of direct engagement with the environment continue to inspire and influence artists today. Through his innovative and thought-provoking works, Smithson has helped to redefine the relationship between art and the world around us, encouraging a deeper appreciation of the interconnectedness of all things.

30 NEO-POP AND KITSCH

Jeff Koons is an artist whose work has left a significant mark on contemporary art, particularly through his exploration of Neo-pop and kitsch aesthetics. His pieces often challenge the boundaries between high and low art, drawing on popular culture and everyday objects to create works that are both visually striking and thought-provoking.

Koons emerged in the art world during the 1980s, a period marked by a resurgence of interest in figurative art and a growing fascination with consumer culture. This era saw the rise of Neo-pop, a movement that took inspiration from the Pop Art of the 1960s but with a renewed focus on the commodification of art and the blurring of distinctions between art and commerce. Koons' work epitomizes these themes, often featuring bright, glossy surfaces and references to mass-produced items.

One of Koons' most famous series is "Celebration," which includes works like "Balloon Dog" and "Hanging Heart." These sculptures are notable for their immense size and reflective surfaces, which give them a playful yet monumental presence. The "Balloon Dog," in particular, has become an iconic symbol of Koons' style, embodying his fascination with childhood nostalgia and the aesthetics of consumerism. The piece resembles a balloon animal, something typically associated with children's parties, yet it is rendered in polished stainless steel and coated in a vibrant color, transforming it into a high-art object.

The concept of kitsch is central to Koons' work. Kitsch refers to art, objects, or design considered to be in poor taste because of excessive garishness or sentimentality, but sometimes appreciated in an ironic or knowing way. Koons embraces kitsch wholeheartedly, using it as a tool to question cultural hierarchies and the value judgments placed on art. His work often incorporates elements that might be dismissed as tacky or vulgar, such as inflatable toys, porcelain figurines, and advertising imagery. By elevating these elements to the status of fine art, Koons forces viewers to reconsider their preconceptions and biases.

Koons' use of kitsch is not merely for shock value; it also serves to democratize art. By referencing objects and images that are widely recognizable and often mass-produced, Koons makes his work accessible to a broad audience. This approach challenges the exclusivity of the art world, inviting people from diverse backgrounds to engage with his work. At the same time, it raises questions about the nature of artistic value and the role of the artist in contemporary society.

Another key aspect of Koons' work is his engagement with the concept of Neo-geo, or Neo-Geometric Conceptualism. This movement emerged in the 1980s and is characterized by the use of geometric shapes and forms, often in a way that critiques or reflects on contemporary society. While Koons' work is not strictly geometric, it shares with Neo-geo an interest in the visual language of modernity and the impact of technology and mass production on culture. His sculptures often feature clean lines, smooth surfaces, and a sense of precision that aligns with the aesthetic of Neo-geo artists.

In addition to his sculptural work, Koons has also made significant contributions to the field of painting. His "Luxury and Degradation" series, for example, explores themes of advertising and consumerism through a series of photorealistic paintings and sculptures. These works depict liquor advertisements, juxtaposing images of glamour and luxury with more troubling aspects of alcohol consumption. Through these pieces, Koons examines the seductive power of advertising and the ways in which it shapes our desires and perceptions.

Koons' work is deeply intertwined with contemporary technologies and the processes of mass production. He often employs advanced manufacturing techniques to realize his sculptures, working with teams of fabricators to produce pieces that are meticulously crafted and finished to a high degree of perfection. This approach reflects his interest in the intersection of art and commerce, as well as his belief in the potential of technology to create new forms of artistic expression.

Despite the commercial success and widespread recognition that Koons has achieved, his work has also been the subject of considerable controversy and criticism. Some critics argue that his embrace of kitsch and commercialism undermines the integrity of art, reducing it to mere spectacle or commodity. Others contend that his work is overly simplistic, relying on surface appeal rather than deeper intellectual or emotional engagement. However, Koons himself has consistently defended his approach, arguing that his work is intended to provoke thought and conversation about the nature of art and its role in society.

Koons' personal life and public persona have also contributed to his controversial reputation. He is known for his meticulous attention to detail and his insistence on perfection in his work, qualities that have earned him both admiration and criticism from colleagues and collaborators. His high-profile marriage to Italian porn star Ilona Staller, also known as Cicciolina, in the early 1990s further fueled public fascination with his life and work. The couple collaborated on a series of explicit sculptures and photographs, which explored themes of sexuality, celebrity, and the human body. These works, while provocative, also highlighted Koons' willingness to push boundaries and challenge societal norms.

In reflecting on Jeff Koons' career, it is clear that his work embodies a complex and often contradictory relationship with contemporary culture. On one hand, his sculptures and paintings celebrate the aesthetics of consumerism and popular culture, embracing the visual language of advertising, entertainment, and mass production. On the other hand, his work invites critical reflection on the values and assumptions that underpin our engagement with these cultural forms. Through his use of kitsch and Neo-pop aesthetics, Koons challenges us to reconsider our notions of taste, value, and the role of art in a commodified world.

Koons' influence on the art world extends beyond his own work, as he has also played a significant role in shaping contemporary art discourse. His exploration of the boundaries between high and low art, his engagement with mass production and technology, and his provocative use of kitsch have all contributed to ongoing debates about the nature and purpose of art in the 21st century. Whether celebrated or criticized, Koons' work remains a powerful force in contemporary art, prompting viewers to question and re-evaluate their own perceptions and assumptions.

As we continue to navigate a world increasingly shaped by digital technologies and consumer culture, the themes and questions raised by Koons' work become ever more relevant. His sculptures and paintings serve as a mirror to our own desires and anxieties, reflecting the complexities and contradictions of modern life. In this way, Koons' work not only entertains and provokes but also offers a space for critical engagement and reflection on the cultural forces that shape our world.

Ultimately, the legacy of Jeff Koons lies in his ability to fuse the aesthetic and the conceptual, creating works that are both visually captivating and intellectually challenging. His embrace of Neo-pop and kitsch, his engagement with Neo-geo concepts, and his use of contemporary technologies all contribute to a body of work that is as multifaceted and dynamic as the culture it reflects. Jeff Koonz uses AI too. Through his art, Koons continues to push the boundaries of what is possible, inviting us to see the world through a lens that is both playful and profound.

31 STREET ART AND SOCIAL ACTIVISM

Keith Haring was an artist whose vibrant, energetic work not only defined the visual culture of the 1980s but also served as a powerful vehicle for social activism. His journey began on the streets of New York City, where his bold, graffiti-inspired art quickly gained recognition and became a staple of urban life. Haring's art, characterized by its simple lines, vivid colors, and repetitive motifs, was accessible to the masses, often featuring themes of love, birth, death, and war. These universal subjects, combined with his commitment to social justice, made his work resonate deeply with people from all walks of life.

Haring's early life in Pennsylvania exposed him to the world of art and graphic design, but it was his move to New York City in 1978 that truly ignited his creative spirit. The city, bustling with energy and brimming with artistic potential, became Haring's canvas. He was drawn to the graffiti art movement, which at the time was burgeoning in the subways and streets. Haring began his artistic career with chalk drawings on empty advertising panels in subway stations, creating spontaneous pieces that were seen by thousands of commuters daily. This immediacy and public visibility were crucial to Haring's philosophy of art; he believed art should be for everyone, not confined to galleries and museums.

As his popularity grew, Haring's work began to appear in more formal settings. However, he remained committed to his roots in street art, frequently engaging in public art projects that retained the accessibility and raw energy of his subway drawings. One of his most famous public pieces is the mural "Crack is Wack," painted on a handball court in Harlem in 1986. This mural was not only a striking visual statement but also a poignant commentary on the crack cocaine epidemic that was ravaging communities at the time. Haring's ability to combine artistic expression with social activism made his work both impactful and relevant.

Haring's art was also deeply intertwined with his personal life and experiences, particularly his identity as a gay man and his activism in the fight against AIDS. In the 1980s, the AIDS crisis was devastating the LGBTQ+ community, and Haring used his art to raise awareness and promote safe sex practices. He created numerous works that directly addressed the epidemic, including posters, murals, and paintings that depicted the disease's impact and the importance of prevention. One of his most iconic pieces from this period is "Silence = Death," a powerful image featuring the pink triangle, a symbol reclaimed from its use during the Holocaust to denote gay men, with the stark, urgent message beneath it.

Beyond his work on AIDS awareness, Haring was passionate about a range of social issues, including apartheid, nuclear disarmament, and children's rights. His activism extended to his involvement with various charitable organizations and initiatives. In 1989, he established the Keith Haring Foundation, which continues to support programs and organizations that assist children, as well as those engaged in education, research, and care related to AIDS. Through his foundation, Haring ensured that his legacy would continue to make a difference long after his untimely death from AIDS-related complications in 1990.

Haring's artistic style, characterized by its simplicity and immediacy, also lent itself to a broader exploration of the intersection between art, technology, and society. Although he passed away before the digital revolution truly took hold, his work presaged many of the themes that would come to dominate discussions around art and technology in the decades to follow. His use of bold, graphic lines and repetitive patterns bears a striking resemblance to the aesthetic of early computer graphics and digital art. Haring's interest in the universality of symbols and the communicative power of visual language can be seen as a precursor to the iconography that has become ubiquitous in the digital age.

As computers and artificial intelligence (AI) have become more integrated into the creation and consumption of art, the questions raised by Haring's work remain relevant. How can art maintain its accessibility and immediacy in a world increasingly mediated by technology? How can artists leverage new tools to address social issues and engage with audiences in meaningful ways? Haring's emphasis on public art and social activism provides a valuable framework for considering these questions. His work demonstrates that art can be a powerful tool for communication and change, regardless of the medium through which it is created.

The rise of AI in the art world has opened up new possibilities for creativity and expression, challenging traditional notions of authorship and originality. AI algorithms can analyze vast amounts of data, identifying patterns and generating new images, music, and texts that push the boundaries of human imagination. This technology has the potential to democratize art, making it more accessible and inclusive. However, it also raises ethical and philosophical questions about the role of the artist and the nature of creativity. In this context, Haring's legacy serves as a reminder of the importance of human intention and social engagement in the creation of art.

Haring's approach to art was inherently collaborative, often involving the participation of communities and other artists. This spirit of collaboration is echoed in contemporary AI art practices, where artists work alongside programmers, data scientists, and other technologists to create new works. The fusion of human creativity and machine intelligence can result in innovative, boundary-pushing art that challenges our perceptions and broadens our understanding of what is possible. Yet, it is crucial to ensure that the human element—empathy, intention, and social awareness—remains at the forefront of these endeavors.

The integration of AI into artistic practice also necessitates a consideration of the social and ethical implications of technology. As AI becomes more prevalent in our lives, it is essential to critically examine its impact on society, particularly in terms of equity, privacy, and agency. Haring's work, with its focus on social justice and activism, provides a valuable lens through which to explore these issues. His commitment to using art as a tool for positive change can inspire contemporary artists and technologists to harness AI in ways that promote inclusivity, empowerment, and social good.

Moreover, the use of AI in art prompts a reevaluation of the relationship between artist and audience. Haring's street art was inherently interactive, engaging viewers directly and inviting them to participate in the artistic experience. Similarly, AI art can create dynamic, interactive works that respond to audience input and evolve over time. This interactivity can foster a deeper connection between the artwork and the viewer, making art a more participatory and communal experience.

Haring's influence extends beyond the visual arts, permeating popular culture, fashion, and design. His distinctive imagery has been featured on everything from clothing and accessories to album covers and advertising campaigns. This widespread adoption of his aesthetic underscores the enduring appeal and versatility of his work. As AI continues to shape the creative landscape, it will be interesting to see how Haring's legacy evolves and how contemporary artists draw on his pioneering spirit to navigate the challenges and opportunities of the digital age.

In reflecting on Keith Haring's life and work, it becomes clear that his impact was not only artistic but also deeply social and political. His art was a vehicle for communication, education, and activism, addressing some of the most pressing issues of his time. In today's world, where technology is transforming every aspect of our lives, Haring's legacy offers a powerful reminder of the potential for art to drive social change and foster human connection. As we continue to explore the intersections of art, technology, and society, the lessons of Haring's work remain as relevant and inspiring as ever.

Keith Haring's commitment to social activism and his innovative approach to art continue to resonate with audiences today. His work serves as a testament to the power of creativity to transcend boundaries, challenge norms, and inspire change. By embracing new technologies and maintaining a focus on social justice, contemporary artists can carry forward Haring's legacy, creating work that is not only visually compelling but also deeply meaningful and impactful. Through the lens of Haring's art, we are reminded of the enduring capacity of art to reflect and shape the world around us, fostering a more just, inclusive, and vibrant society.

SECTION FOUR

CULTURAL PHENOMENA AND MEDIA

The interplay between cultural phenomena and media has always been a dynamic and evolving field, continuously reshaped by technological advancements and societal shifts. In recent years, the rise of artificial intelligence (AI) has profoundly influenced this landscape, with tools like ChatGPT and DALL-E 3 spearheading new ways of creating and interacting with media.

ChatGPT, a language model developed by OpenAI, represents a significant leap in natural language processing. It can understand and generate human-like text based on the input it receives, making it a versatile tool for a range of applications, from customer service to creative writing. ChatGPT's ability to generate coherent and contextually relevant responses has revolutionized the way we interact with machines, providing a more seamless and intuitive user experience. This technology has also opened up new possibilities for content creation, enabling writers and artists to collaborate with AI in innovative ways. For instance, authors can use ChatGPT to brainstorm ideas, generate dialogue, or even write entire sections of text, while maintaining creative control over the final output.

Another groundbreaking development in the realm of AI and media is text-to-image generation, exemplified by DALL-E 3. This AI model can create detailed and imaginative images from textual descriptions, bridging the gap between verbal and visual creativity. DALL-E 3's ability to generate diverse and high-quality images based on user prompts has a wide range of applications, from advertising and design to education and entertainment. Artists and designers can leverage this technology to quickly visualize concepts, experiment with different styles, or generate unique artwork. The implications for industries such as gaming, animation, and virtual reality are particularly exciting, as DALL-E 3 can help create richly detailed and immersive environments based on simple textual inputs.

The broader impact of AI on cultural phenomena and media is further underscored by the emergence of new wave technologies. These include advancements in machine learning, computer vision, and natural language understanding, which are transforming how we create, consume, and interact with media. The new wave movement in technology is characterized by its focus on integrating AI into everyday applications, making it more accessible and user-friendly. This movement is driving innovation across various sectors, from healthcare and finance to entertainment and education, highlighting the versatility and transformative potential of AI.

Large Language Models (LLMs), like ChatGPT, are at the forefront of this new wave, offering unprecedented capabilities in understanding and generating human language. LLMs are trained on vast datasets and can perform a wide array of tasks, including translation, summarization, and sentiment analysis. Their ability to process and generate text with high accuracy and fluency makes them invaluable tools for businesses, researchers, and content creators. The development of LLMs has also sparked important discussions about ethics, bias, and the societal impact of AI, prompting a deeper examination of how these technologies should be developed and deployed.

The integration of AI in media has also led to the rise of cyber art, where digital technologies and AI are used to create new forms of artistic expression. Cyber art encompasses a wide range of practices, from digital painting and 3D modeling to interactive installations and virtual reality experiences. Artists working in this field are exploring the intersection of technology and creativity, pushing the boundaries of traditional art forms and engaging with contemporary issues in innovative ways. AI tools like DALL-E 3 are enabling artists to experiment with new techniques and mediums, creating works that are not only visually striking but also conceptually rich and thought-provoking.

The impact of AI on cultural phenomena is also evident in the way we consume media. Streaming platforms, social media, and digital content distribution have transformed the media landscape, offering new ways for audiences to access and engage with content. AI algorithms play a crucial role in personalizing recommendations, optimizing content delivery, and enhancing user experiences. These advancements are changing the dynamics of media consumption, making it more interactive, personalized, and immersive.

As we continue to explore the potential of AI in media, it is important to consider the broader societal implications of these technologies. Issues such as data privacy, algorithmic bias, and the digital divide need to be addressed to ensure that the benefits of AI are equitably distributed. The development of ethical guidelines and regulatory frameworks is crucial to navigating the complex landscape of AI and media, ensuring that these technologies are used responsibly and for the greater good.

In conclusion, the convergence of cultural phenomena and media in the age of AI is driving a new era of creativity, innovation, and interaction. Technologies like ChatGPT, DALL-E 3, and LLMs are transforming how we create, consume, and engage with media, offering new possibilities for artistic expression and content creation. As we embrace the potential of AI, it is essential to remain mindful of the ethical and societal challenges that accompany these advancements, fostering a responsible and inclusive approach to the future of media and technology.

32 ANALYSIS OF AMERICAN CULTURE

Joseph Beuys was a German artist whose works often combined performance, sculpture, and social theory, and whose 1974 piece "I Love America and America Loves Me" serves as a profound exploration and critique of American culture. This work, which is as much a statement as it is an art piece, reflects Beuys' complex relationship with the United States and delves into themes of identity, politics, and the nature of human interaction.

"I Love America and America Loves Me" is a performance art piece that took place in May 1974 at the René Block Gallery in New York. The performance involved Beuys being transported from the airport to the gallery wrapped in felt, ensuring he did not directly touch American soil. Once at the gallery, he spent three days in a room with a wild coyote, a powerful symbol in Native American culture and American wilderness mythology. Beuys' interaction with the coyote was meticulously documented, both in video and through photographs, creating a lasting record of this intense and symbolic encounter.

The choice of the coyote is crucial for understanding the work's deeper meanings. Coyotes are often seen as tricksters and symbols of survival in harsh environments, embodying both the wild spirit of America and the plight of Native American cultures. By choosing to spend time with a coyote, Beuys was engaging directly with these layers of symbolism. His interactions with the coyote, which included offering felt and other objects to the animal, can be seen as an attempt to communicate and bridge a cultural and existential gap. This act was not just about taming or confronting a wild animal, but about acknowledging and respecting a presence that is deeply intertwined with the land and its original inhabitants.

The performance was recorded on video, adding a layer of documentation that has allowed the piece to endure far beyond its original execution. The video captures the evolving relationship between Beuys and the coyote, showing moments of tension, curiosity, and a tentative understanding. This visual record transforms the performance into a shared experience that can be revisited and reinterpreted by audiences, contributing to the piece's legacy as a seminal work of postmodern art.

Postmodernism, a movement characterized by its skepticism of grand narratives and its embrace of irony, pastiche, and fragmented realities, provides a critical framework for understanding "I Love America and America Loves Me." Beuys' work disrupts conventional categories of art, merging performance, installation, and political commentary. It challenges viewers to reconsider the nature of artistic expression and the role of the artist in society. The piece's very title, with its ambiguous claim of mutual affection, invites reflection on the complexities and contradictions inherent in the relationship between Europe and America, as well as between colonizers and indigenous peoples.

Beuys' performance is also a powerful example of storytelling through art. By creating a narrative around his journey to America, his isolation from direct contact with American soil, and his interactions with the coyote, Beuys crafts a story that is rich in metaphor and open to multiple interpretations. This narrative aspect is enhanced by the installation elements within the gallery space, which included various objects and materials that Beuys used in his interaction with the coyote. These objects serve as both props in the performance and as symbols within the broader story that Beuys is telling.

The installation component of "I Love America and America Loves Me" is integral to the work's impact. The gallery space was transformed into a kind of stage, with the coyote as a co-performer and the objects as part of the set. This transformation of space underscores the theatricality of the piece, blurring the lines between art and life, and between performance and reality. The felt, a material often used by Beuys, serves as a protective and symbolic element, representing warmth, healing, and insulation. Its use in the installation highlights Beuys' interest in materials that have both functional and symbolic meanings.

Beuys' work often engaged with themes of healing and transformation, and "I Love America and America Loves Me" is no exception. The performance can be seen as a ritualistic attempt to heal the rifts between different cultures and histories. By isolating himself from direct contact with American society and instead engaging with a symbol of its wild and untamed nature, Beuys creates a space for reflection and potential reconciliation. This aspect of the work aligns with his broader belief in art as a transformative force, capable of fostering social change and personal enlightenment.

The political dimensions of Beuys' performance are also significant. By choosing America as the setting for this piece, Beuys was engaging with the political and cultural dynamics of the time. The 1970s were a period of significant upheaval in the United States, marked by the aftermath of the Vietnam War, the Watergate scandal, and ongoing civil rights struggles. In this context, Beuys' performance can be seen as a critique of American imperialism and a call for a deeper understanding of the country's complex cultural and historical landscape. His isolation from direct contact with American society can be interpreted as a commentary on the alienation and fragmentation that many felt during this period.

The use of video to document the performance adds a crucial dimension to the work. Video as a medium allows for the preservation and dissemination of ephemeral art forms like performance, ensuring that they can be experienced by a wider audience. The video's role in "I Love America and America Loves Me" is not just to document the event, but to extend its reach and impact. It transforms the performance into a piece of media that can be analyzed, interpreted, and recontextualized, contributing to its status as a landmark in postmodern art.

Joseph Beuys' "I Love America and America Loves Me" is a profound exploration of American culture, identity, and the potential for art to foster dialogue and transformation. Through its combination of performance, installation, and video, the piece challenges conventional notions of art and engages deeply with the social and political issues of its time. It is a testament to Beuys' belief in the power of art to address complex cultural dynamics and to inspire reflection and change.

The narrative structure of the piece, with its clear beginning, middle, and end, enhances its impact as a form of storytelling. Beuys' journey from Germany to New York, his isolation from American soil, and his subsequent interactions with the coyote create a compelling story that resonates on multiple levels. This narrative invites viewers to consider their own relationships with cultural identity, history, and the natural world, making the piece both personal and universal.

In conclusion, "I Love America and America Loves Me" is a multifaceted work that encapsulates Joseph Beuys' approach to art as a vehicle for social and cultural commentary. Its use of performance, installation, and video creates a rich, immersive experience that continues to inspire and provoke discussion. Through this piece, Beuys offers a powerful critique of American culture while also exploring broader themes of identity, healing, and transformation. The work's enduring relevance is a testament to Beuys' vision and his ability to use art to address some of the most pressing issues of his time and ours.

33 INTERNET CULTURE AND VIRAL PHENOMENA

The phenomenon of Keyboard Cat, is one of the most iconic and enduring memes to emerge from internet culture. It encapsulates the whimsical, humorous, and often unpredictable nature of viral content that defines the digital age. The journey of Keyboard Cat from a simple video to a widespread cultural touchstone provides insight into how memes propagate and influence popular culture.

Keyboard Cat originated from a video recorded by Charlie Schmidt in 1984, featuring his cat, Fatso, seemingly playing an upbeat tune on an electric keyboard. The video, charmingly low-tech and endearingly quirky, lay dormant for over two decades before it found its way to the internet. It wasn't until 2007, when Schmidt uploaded the video to YouTube, that Keyboard Cat began its ascent into viral fame.

The video's premise is simple yet universally amusing: a cat, with a stoic and almost disinterested expression, appears to be playing a catchy melody on a keyboard. This combination of the familiar and the absurd—an animal engaging in a human-like activity—struck a chord with viewers. The internet, with its penchant for quirky and unexpected humor, embraced Keyboard Cat wholeheartedly.

As with many viral phenomena, the appeal of Keyboard Cat lies in its blend of humor, surprise, and relatability. The video taps into the internet's love for animals, especially cats, which have long been a staple of online content. Cats are seen as independent, mysterious, and often humorous creatures, making them perfect subjects for internet entertainment. The juxtaposition of Fatso's nonchalant demeanor with the lively music creates a comedic effect that is both endearing and memorable.

Memes thrive on repetition and adaptation, and Keyboard Cat was no exception. The original video inspired countless remixes, parodies, and mashups, spreading across various platforms and reaching a global audience. People began using the clip to create their own versions, often setting the video to different songs or integrating it into other media. This adaptability allowed Keyboard Cat to remain relevant and engaging, as each new iteration offered a fresh take on the familiar theme.

One of the key elements in the viral spread of Keyboard Cat was its integration into other contexts and formats. The video was often used as a humorous coda to other videos, particularly those featuring fail scenarios or awkward moments. By juxtaposing the playful and cheerful image of Keyboard Cat with moments of human error or discomfort, creators were able to inject humor and lighten the mood. This use of Keyboard Cat as a comedic device helped cement its place in internet culture, turning it into a versatile and widely recognized meme.

The virality of Keyboard Cat also highlights the role of community and collaboration in meme culture. The internet is a space where users constantly interact, share, and build upon each other's ideas. Keyboard Cat became a shared cultural reference point, a piece of collective digital folklore that users could modify and repurpose in endless ways. This collaborative aspect of meme culture fosters a sense of participation and creativity, allowing individuals to contribute to the ongoing evolution of the meme.

The impact of Keyboard Cat extends beyond its immediate popularity. It serves as a case study in how digital content can achieve widespread recognition and influence. The meme's success illustrates several principles of virality: the importance of humor, the appeal of animals, the power of remix culture, and the role of community engagement. These elements, when combined, create a fertile environment for content to spread rapidly and gain cultural significance.

Moreover, Keyboard Cat exemplifies the democratizing nature of the internet. In the digital age, anyone with a camera and an internet connection can create content that has the potential to reach millions. This accessibility allows for a diverse range of voices and perspectives to be heard, breaking down traditional barriers to entry in the media landscape. Keyboard Cat is a prime example of how a simple, home-recorded video can become a global sensation, demonstrating the transformative power of digital platforms.

The legacy of Keyboard Cat continues to influence internet culture and the way we understand and interact with viral content. Its success paved the way for other animal-related memes and videos, contributing to the ongoing popularity of pet content online. The meme also underscored the importance of humor and relatability in digital media, highlighting how simple, everyday moments can resonate with a broad audience.

In reflecting on the phenomenon of Keyboard Cat, it's important to recognize the broader implications of viral culture. Memes like Keyboard Cat are not just fleeting trends; they are part of a larger narrative about how we communicate, share, and find joy in the digital age. They bring people together, create shared experiences, and offer a form of entertainment that is uniquely suited to the fast-paced, interconnected world we live in.

Keyboard Cat also serves as a reminder of the unpredictability of viral success. While there are certain strategies and elements that can increase the likelihood of content going viral, there is no guaranteed formula. The internet is a dynamic and ever-changing space, where trends can emerge spontaneously and spread with astonishing speed. This unpredictability is part of what makes viral phenomena so fascinating and compelling.

The story of Keyboard Cat is a testament to the power of simplicity and authenticity. In an era where highly produced and polished content often dominates, the charm of a straightforward, unpretentious video can cut through the noise and capture the hearts of viewers. Keyboard Cat embodies the idea that sometimes the most memorable and impactful content is that which is genuine and unrefined.

In conclusion, Keyboard Cat is more than just a viral video; it is a cultural landmark that encapsulates the essence of internet humor and the dynamics of meme culture. Its journey from a forgotten home video to a beloved internet icon illustrates the power of digital platforms to amplify and celebrate the whimsical and the absurd. As we continue to navigate the ever-evolving landscape of online content, Keyboard Cat stands as a reminder of the joy and creativity that define the digital age, inviting us to find delight in the unexpected and to embrace the playful spirit of the internet.

34 ETERNAL ECHOES AND THE SPECULATIVE JOURNEY THROUGH TIME

Wong Kar-wai's film "2046" is a tantalizing and enigmatic piece of cinema that delves deep into the realms of memory, love, and the futuristic speculative imagination. Set in the years leading up to and around the titular year, the film interweaves multiple storylines and characters, creating a rich tapestry that explores the nature of time, the persistence of the past, and the elusive nature of the future.

"2046" functions on several levels, merging science fiction with a deeply personal and emotional narrative. The central character, Chow Mo-wan, portrayed by Tony Leung Chiu-wai, is a writer struggling with his memories and emotions following a series of failed relationships. Chow's story is set against the backdrop of 1960s Hong Kong, a time of rapid change and uncertainty. His personal journey becomes a reflection of the broader societal shifts, capturing the anxieties and hopes of a city and its people on the brink of transformation.

In Chow's fictional narrative, 2046 is a mysterious place where people go to recover lost memories. It's a futuristic train journey to a destination where nothing ever changes, and passengers can reclaim the past. However, no one has ever returned from 2046, making it a place of both promise and peril. This speculative aspect of the film serves as a metaphor for the characters' struggles with their own pasts and the pain of unresolved emotions.

The film's title, "2046," also refers to the year 2046, which has significant political implications for Hong Kong. The year marks fifty years after the 1997 handover of Hong Kong from Britain to China, a period during which Hong Kong was promised a high degree of autonomy under the "one country, two systems" framework. Wong Kar-wai uses this temporal marker to subtly comment on the uncertain future of the city and its people, blending personal narratives with broader social and political concerns.

Chow Mo-wan's interactions with various women, each representing different aspects of love and loss, form the emotional core of the film. There is Su Li-zhen, played by Maggie Cheung, a ghostly figure from Chow's past who haunts his memories. Their brief and poignant relationship in "In the Mood for Love," the film's predecessor, casts a long shadow over "2046," influencing Chow's actions and decisions. In his search for meaning and closure, Chow engages in a series of relationships, each marked by its own complexity and poignancy.

One of the central relationships in "2046" is between Chow and Bai Ling, portrayed by Zhang Ziyi. Bai Ling is a seductive and lonely woman who becomes emotionally entangled with Chow. Their relationship is intense and passionate but ultimately doomed by Chow's inability to commit and his lingering attachment to the past. Bai Ling's vulnerability and desire for genuine connection stand in stark contrast to Chow's emotional detachment, highlighting the pain and disillusionment that often accompany love.

Another significant relationship is with Jing Wen, played by Faye Wong. Jing Wen is a young woman who dreams of escaping to Japan to be with her lover, a Japanese man her father disapproves of. Chow helps her by ghostwriting love letters, and in the process, they form a deep but platonic bond. Jing Wen's story parallels Chow's own journey, as both characters grapple with unfulfilled desires and the constraints of their circumstances.

The speculative elements of "2046" are brought to life through the visual and stylistic choices of Wong Kar-wai. The film's cinematography, by Christopher Doyle and Kwan Pun-leung, is lush and evocative, capturing the notion no one has ever returned from 2046. This fictional concept serves as a metaphor for Chow's own emotional stasis and his inability to move on from his past loves. The train to 2046 represents a journey into the depths of memory and nostalgia, a place where time stands still and the past can be relived indefinitely.

Chow's life in the 1960s is filled with a series of intense yet fleeting relationships, each one leaving an indelible mark on his psyche. These relationships are portrayed with Wong Kar-wai's characteristic visual style, rich in color and texture, capturing the intimacy and ephemerality of human connections. The women in Chow's life, including Su Li-zhen (played by Gong Li) and Bai Ling (played by Zhang Ziyi), are portrayed with depth and complexity, their interactions with Chow revealing his vulnerabilities and emotional scars.

The speculative elements of "2046" are intertwined with Chow's real-life experiences, blurring the lines between reality and fiction. In his futuristic story, Chow imagines androids and futuristic landscapes, reflecting his own sense of alienation and desire for permanence in a world that is constantly changing. These speculative elements are not just a backdrop but are integral to understanding Chow's inner world. The androids in his stories, unable to feel or change, mirror his own emotional paralysis and the unresolved grief he carries.

The year 2046 also holds significance as a marker of time and change, particularly in the context of Hong Kong's political future. The film subtly alludes to the handover of Hong Kong to China in 1997 and the 50-year period of promised autonomy, set to end in 2047. This looming date adds another layer of speculative tension to the narrative, as characters grapple with their personal futures and the uncertain destiny of their city.

Wong Kar-wai's use of non-linear storytelling and fragmented narrative structures heightens the film's dreamlike quality. The past, present, and future are interwoven seamlessly, reflecting the fluidity of memory and time. Chow's reflections on his past loves are interspersed with scenes from his speculative fiction, creating a complex and layered narrative that invites multiple interpretations.

The cinematography of "2046" is striking and evocative, with Christopher Doyle and Kwan Pun-leung capturing the neon-lit streets of Hong Kong and the imagined futuristic worlds with equal beauty. The use of color, light, and shadow enhances the emotional depth of the film, creating a visual poetry that complements the intricate narrative. The film's soundtrack, featuring lush orchestral pieces and haunting melodies, further immerses the audience in its melancholic and nostalgic atmosphere.

"2046" is not just a film about the future but a meditation on the nature of time itself. It explores how the past shapes the present and how the future is imagined through the lens of memory and desire. Wong Kar-wai's characters are often caught between longing and loss, seeking solace in their memories while struggling to face the unknown. This tension between past and future, memory and reality, gives "2046" its profound emotional resonance.

Chow's journey is ultimately one of self-discovery and acceptance. Through his writing and his interactions with the people around him, he begins to confront his own fears and regrets. The speculative elements of his stories serve as a means of processing his experiences and coming to terms with his emotions. By the end of the film, there is a sense of catharsis and a tentative step towards the future, even if it remains uncertain and unresolved.

"2046" stands as a testament to Wong Kar-wai's mastery of blending genres and creating films that are both visually stunning and emotionally rich. It challenges the audience to reflect on their own memories and aspirations, to consider how the past influences their perception of the future. The film's speculative aspects are not merely a narrative device but a profound exploration of human consciousness and the enduring quest for meaning in an ever-changing world.

In essence, "2046" is a film that transcends time, inviting viewers to embark on their own journey of introspection and discovery. It is a cinematic experience that lingers long after the credits roll, a poignant reminder of the fragility of human connections and the enduring power of love and memory. Through its speculative lens, "2046" captures the essence of what it means to be human, navigating the complexities of time, desire, and identity in a world that is perpetually on the cusp of transformation.

35 A CINEMATIC EXPLORATION OF TRANSGRESSION AND EROTICISM

Georges Bataille, a French intellectual and writer known for his provocative and often controversial works, authored "Story of the Eye" ("Histoire de l'œil") in 1928. This novella has since become a classic in the realm of erotic literature, known for its explicit content and surreal narrative. Bataille's work delves into themes of transgression, eroticism, and the limits of experience, challenging societal norms and taboos through its vivid and unsettling imagery.

"Story of the Eye" centers on a young couple, referred to as the Narrator and Simone, who embark on a series of increasingly bizarre and erotic adventures. Their journey is marked by a fixation on eyes, which serves as a recurring motif throughout the narrative. This obsession with eyes symbolizes various aspects of human experience, from voyeurism to the quest for deeper knowledge and understanding. Bataille's prose is both poetic and disturbing, blending the sublime with the grotesque in a way that forces readers to confront their own boundaries and discomforts.

The novella's influence has extended beyond literature, inspiring various adaptations and reinterpretations across different media. One notable adaptation is a DVD film that brings Bataille's controversial work to the screen. This adaptation, directed by Albert Maurice, captures the essence of the original text while adding new dimensions through visual storytelling. Maurice, known for his avant-garde approach to filmmaking, employs a mix of surreal imagery and stark realism to convey the novella's intense and often disconcerting themes.

The "Story of the Eye" DVD adaptation is not a straightforward narrative but rather a visual and sensory experience that mirrors the fragmented and dreamlike structure of Bataille's prose. The film's cinematography is marked by stark contrasts, with scenes of stark beauty juxtaposed against moments of visceral horror. Maurice's direction emphasizes the novella's exploration of the body and its limits, using close-ups and lingering shots to highlight the physicality of the characters' experiences.

One of the challenges in adapting "Story of the Eye" to film is capturing the internal, almost hallucinatory quality of Bataille's writing. Maurice achieves this through a combination of innovative camera work and experimental sound design. The film's soundtrack, a blend of dissonant music and ambient noise, enhances the unsettling atmosphere and draws viewers into the characters' increasingly unhinged world. The result is a film that is as much about evoking a mood and psychological state as it is about telling a story.

The "Story of the Eye" DVD has been made available through various distribution channels, reflecting the evolving landscape of media consumption. Initially released as a direct-to-video offering, it bypassed traditional theatrical distribution in favor of reaching audiences through home viewing. This approach aligns with the novella's status as a cult classic, appealing to a niche audience that seeks out unconventional and challenging works.

In addition to its physical release, the "Story of the Eye" DVD has also been made available for digital download and on-demand streaming. These options cater to modern viewing habits, allowing audiences to access the film on their own terms and at their convenience. The availability of the film through multiple platforms ensures that Bataille's provocative vision continues to reach new audiences, fostering ongoing discussion and analysis.

Albert Maurice's adaptation of "Story of the Eye" is notable for its fidelity to the source material while also introducing new elements that enhance the viewer's experience. The film's use of visual symbolism, such as the recurring motif of the eye, mirrors Bataille's own use of symbolism in the novella. This attention to detail underscores the director's deep understanding of the original text and his ability to translate its complex themes into a visual medium.

The film's reception has been mixed, reflecting the polarizing nature of Bataille's work. Some critics have praised Maurice's bold and uncompromising vision, noting the film's ability to capture the raw intensity of the novella. Others, however, have found the film's explicit content and unsettling imagery difficult to stomach, echoing the controversy that surrounded the original publication of "Story of the Eye." Despite this, the film has garnered a dedicated following among fans of avant-garde cinema and erotic literature, cementing its place as a noteworthy adaptation of Bataille's work.

In the context of direct-to-video releases, "Story of the Eye" stands out for its artistic ambition and willingness to push boundaries. While many direct-to-video films are produced with modest budgets and target mainstream audiences, Maurice's adaptation is a testament to the potential for this distribution model to support experimental and high-concept projects. The film's success in reaching its intended audience through digital downloads and on-demand streaming further highlights the flexibility and reach of modern media distribution.

The intersection of literature and film in the adaptation of "Story of the Eye" also speaks to the broader cultural impact of Bataille's work. By bringing the novella to a new medium, Maurice has expanded the ways in which audiences can engage with Bataille's provocative ideas. The film serves as both a standalone work of art and a companion piece to the original text, inviting viewers to explore the connections between the two and to consider the unique ways in which each medium can convey complex themes.

In conclusion, Georges Bataille's "Story of the Eye" remains a powerful and challenging work, both in its original literary form and in its film adaptation directed by Albert Maurice. The DVD release, along with its availability through digital downloads and on-demand streaming, ensures that this provocative tale continues to provoke and inspire audiences. Maurice's adaptation captures the essence of Bataille's vision while leveraging the unique strengths of the film medium to create a deeply immersive and unsettling experience. As the landscape of media consumption continues to evolve, works like "Story of the Eye" demonstrate the enduring power of boundary-pushing art to challenge and captivate audiences across different formats and generations.

36 DYSTOPIAN FUTURES IN FILM

In the expansive universe of dystopian films, "Code 46" stands out as a unique exploration of future societies shaped by stringent regulations and profound ethical dilemmas. Directed by Michael Winterbottom and released in 2003, "Code 46" presents a world where genetic compatibility laws govern human interactions, reflecting deeper anxieties about identity, freedom, and the consequences of technological advancements.

Set in a near-future society, "Code 46" envisions a world where cities are heavily controlled and regulated, and movement between them is restricted. The title refers to a law that prohibits genetically incompatible individuals from conceiving children. This law aims to prevent genetic diseases and maintain the purity of human DNA, a theme that resonates with contemporary debates on genetic engineering and reproductive rights. The film's protagonists, William Geld and Maria Gonzales, become entangled in a forbidden romance that challenges these societal norms, leading to a poignant exploration of human emotions against a backdrop of surveillance and control.

The visual and thematic elements of "Code 46" are strikingly distinctive. The film's aesthetic, characterized by its use of real-world locations such as Shanghai and Dubai, creates a sense of realism within its futuristic setting. This approach grounds the narrative, making the dystopian aspects more relatable and immediate. The blending of languages—where characters speak a mix of English, Spanish, French, and Mandarin—further emphasizes the globalized yet fragmented nature of the world depicted in the film. This linguistic melting pot reflects the interconnectedness of contemporary societies while highlighting the barriers that still exist between different cultures and classes.

At its core, "Code 46" is a love story complicated by the oppressive structures of its setting. William, played by Tim Robbins, is an insurance fraud investigator who uses an empathy virus to detect lies and uncover illegal activities. Maria, portrayed by Samantha Morton, is a factory worker involved in producing counterfeit travel permits. Their illicit relationship unfolds within the constraints of Code 46, illustrating the tension between personal desires and societal obligations. This dynamic mirrors the larger conflict between individual autonomy and collective control that defines many dystopian narratives.

The film's depiction of a highly regulated society raises questions about the nature of freedom and the extent to which governments should intervene in the lives of citizens. In "Code 46," the state's control over genetic information and reproduction is a means of maintaining order, but it also strips individuals of their agency. This tension is evident in the characters' struggles to navigate their emotions and relationships within the confines of the law. The film suggests that while regulations may be intended to protect society, they can also dehumanize and oppress those they are meant to serve.

Winterbottom's direction and Frank Cottrell Boyce's screenplay imbue "Code 46" with a sense of melancholy and introspection. The film's pacing is deliberate, allowing viewers to absorb the nuances of its world and the emotional weight of the characters' experiences. The cinematography, with its use of natural light and urban landscapes, enhances the film's atmosphere, creating a visual representation of the themes of isolation and surveillance.

One of the most compelling aspects of "Code 46" is its exploration of memory and identity. The use of the empathy virus by William highlights the invasive nature of technology and its impact on personal privacy. This technology allows him to access the innermost thoughts and feelings of others, blurring the line between self and other. Maria's amnesia, induced by the state to erase her memories of their relationship, underscores the fragility of identity and the power of the state to reshape reality. The film raises important questions about the ethics of such interventions and the extent to which technology should be used to control human behavior.

"Code 46" also delves into the concept of love in a world where genetic compatibility dictates relationships. The film challenges the notion that love can be regulated or controlled, portraying it as a fundamental human experience that transcends societal boundaries. William and Maria's relationship, though illicit and ultimately tragic, represents a form of resistance against the dehumanizing forces of the state. Their love defies the constraints of Code 46, illustrating the enduring power of human connection in the face of oppression.

In the broader context of dystopian cinema, "Code 46" shares thematic similarities with other films that explore the consequences of technological advancements and state control. Movies like "Blade Runner," "Gattaca," and "Children of Men" also examine the ethical and societal implications of scientific progress and the tension between individual freedom and collective security. However, "Code 46" distinguishes itself through its intimate focus on personal relationships and its realistic portrayal of a globalized yet divided world.

The film's relevance extends beyond its fictional setting, reflecting contemporary concerns about privacy, genetic engineering, and government surveillance. In an age where technology increasingly pervades every aspect of life, "Code 46" serves as a cautionary tale about the potential dangers of unchecked state power and the erosion of individual rights. It encourages viewers to consider the ethical implications of scientific advancements and to question the balance between security and freedom in their own societies.

"Code 46" received mixed reviews upon its release, with some critics praising its thought-provoking themes and atmospheric visuals, while others found its pacing slow and its narrative disjointed. Despite these criticisms, the film has garnered a cult following and is appreciated for its ambitious exploration of complex issues. Its understated and contemplative approach sets it apart from more action-oriented dystopian films, offering a reflective and nuanced perspective on the future.

In conclusion, "Code 46" is a compelling addition to the genre of dystopian cinema, offering a unique and thought-provoking exploration of a future shaped by genetic compatibility laws and state control. Through its intimate portrayal of a forbidden romance, the film delves into profound questions about identity, freedom, and the ethics of technological advancements. Its realistic aesthetic and globalized setting create a relatable and immediate vision of the future, while its focus on personal relationships adds emotional depth to its themes. "Code 46" serves as a poignant reminder of the enduring power of human connection and the importance of safeguarding individual rights in an increasingly regulated world.

37 TELEVISION AND POST-9/11 CULTURE

The advent of television in the 20th century revolutionized the way people consumed information and entertainment. However, the role of television evolved significantly in the wake of the September 11, 2001, terrorist attacks. Post-9/11 culture, marked by heightened security concerns, political shifts, and a new societal consciousness, saw television adapting to reflect and shape the changing world.

In the immediate aftermath of the 9/11 attacks, television served as the primary medium through which people experienced and understood the event. News channels provided continuous coverage, showing harrowing footage of the towers collapsing, interviews with survivors, and updates on the unfolding investigation. This non-stop news cycle was unprecedented, setting a new standard for real-time broadcasting. The constant replaying of the attacks and their aftermath created a shared, collective experience that was deeply ingrained in the public consciousness.

Television also played a crucial role in shaping the narrative of 9/11 and its aftermath. Networks framed the events within a context of patriotism and resilience, often emphasizing themes of unity and national strength. This was evident in the speeches of political leaders, particularly President George W. Bush, whose addresses were broadcast live and repeatedly analyzed. Television became a platform for these messages, reinforcing a sense of national identity and purpose.

In the years following 9/11, the influence of the attacks was evident in the content and tone of television programming. Dramas, comedies, and reality TV all began to reflect the anxieties and issues prevalent in post-9/11 America. Shows like "24" and "Homeland" delved into themes of terrorism, national security, and the moral ambiguities of the war on terror. These programs depicted the complexities of intelligence work and counterterrorism, often featuring protagonists who operated in morally gray areas, reflecting the real-world challenges faced by governments and security agencies.

"24" particularly stood out as a cultural phenomenon. Premiering shortly after the attacks, it captured the zeitgeist with its real-time format and intense focus on the threat of terrorism. The show's protagonist, Jack Bauer, became a symbol of the post-9/11 hero – tough, relentless, and willing to cross ethical lines to protect his country. The show's portrayal of torture and the ticking time-bomb scenario sparked significant debate about the ethics of counterterrorism tactics, mirroring real-world discussions about the balance between security and civil liberties.

The impact of 9/11 on television wasn't limited to dramas. Comedies like "The Daily Show" with Jon Stewart and "The Colbert Report" emerged as influential platforms for political satire and commentary. These shows provided a space for critical reflection on the government's actions and media coverage, offering a blend of humor and insight that resonated with audiences. They became essential viewing for many Americans seeking to make sense of the complex political landscape post-9/11.

Reality television also saw a shift in the post-9/11 era. Shows like "Survivor" and "The Amazing Race" gained popularity, perhaps reflecting a collective fascination with resilience, competition, and global adventure. These programs offered escapism but also subtly reinforced themes of endurance and adaptability in challenging times.

Television news continued to evolve, with cable news networks like CNN, Fox News, and MSNBC expanding their influence. The post-9/11 period saw a significant rise in opinion-driven news programming, where commentary and analysis often took precedence over straightforward reporting. This shift contributed to the polarization of American media, with different networks catering to specific political viewpoints. Fox News, for instance, adopted a more conservative stance, while MSNBC leaned liberal. This division mirrored the broader political polarization in the country and influenced how audiences perceived and understood national and global events.

Documentaries and special reports on 9/11 and its consequences became staples of television programming. Channels like the History Channel and National Geographic produced in-depth documentaries that examined the attacks from various angles – from personal stories of survival to detailed analyses of the geopolitical ramifications.

These documentaries served both as educational tools and as a means of memorializing the events, ensuring that the impact of 9/11 remained a significant part of public discourse.

The representation of Muslims and Middle Eastern cultures on television also underwent notable changes post-9/11. Initially, there was an increase in stereotypical portrayals of Muslims as terrorists or extremists, reflecting widespread fears and prejudices. However, over time, there was a gradual shift towards more nuanced and diverse representations. Shows like "Ramy" and "Little Mosque on the Prairie" sought to present more authentic and multifaceted portrayals of Muslim life, challenging stereotypes and fostering greater understanding.

The entertainment industry's response to 9/11 extended beyond television shows to include special events and tributes. Benefit concerts, telethons, and memorial services were broadcast widely, bringing together celebrities, politicians, and ordinary citizens in expressions of solidarity and remembrance. These events highlighted the role of television as a unifying force, capable of bringing people together in times of crisis.

Furthermore, the technological advancements in television production and broadcasting played a significant role in shaping post-9/11 culture. The rise of digital television and the internet expanded access to information and entertainment, allowing for more diverse voices and perspectives to be heard. Online streaming platforms like Netflix, Hulu, and Amazon Prime emerged, offering new ways to consume television content and giving rise to a more fragmented but richly diverse media landscape.

The interplay between television and post-9/11 culture is also evident in the way societal issues and political themes were addressed in family-oriented programming. Shows like "The West Wing" tackled the complexities of governance and national security in a post-9/11 world, providing viewers with a more in-depth look at the inner workings of the government. "The West Wing," in particular, addressed the ethical and moral dilemmas faced by leaders in times of crisis, emphasizing themes of integrity and public service.

Children's programming also adapted to the new reality. Shows like "Sesame Street" and "Mister Rogers' Neighborhood" provided gentle yet effective ways of helping children understand and process the events of 9/11. These programs offered messages of reassurance, safety, and community, aiming to soothe the fears of young viewers and their families.

In the realm of sports, television played a crucial role in the nation's healing process. The return of major sporting events, such as NFL games and the World Series, was televised as symbols of resilience and normalcy. The iconic moment when President Bush threw the first pitch at the World Series game at Yankee Stadium became an enduring image of post-9/11 patriotism and unity. Sports broadcasts frequently included tributes to the victims and heroes of 9/11, reinforcing themes of strength and community.

As television continued to evolve in the years following 9/11, it remained a powerful medium for reflecting and shaping public sentiment. The portrayal of heroism, sacrifice, and the complexities of the modern world in television programming provided viewers with both escapism and a deeper understanding of the issues facing society. The medium's ability to adapt and respond to cultural shifts ensured its continued relevance and influence.

In conclusion, the impact of 9/11 on television was profound and multifaceted. The medium not only served as a primary source of information during the immediate aftermath but also played a critical role in shaping the cultural and political landscape of the post-9/11 era. Through news coverage, dramas, comedies, reality shows, and documentaries, television reflected the anxieties, challenges, and resilience of a nation grappling with the aftermath of a seismic event. As society continues to evolve, television remains a vital tool for understanding and navigating the complexities of the modern world, demonstrating its enduring power to inform, entertain, and unite.

38 SUCCESS AND ETHICS IN CONTEMPORARY PHILOSOPHY

In contemporary society, the concept of winning is often intricately intertwined with success, ambition, and the ethical dimensions that govern our actions and decisions. The portrayal of winning and success in popular culture, particularly through media and television, serves as both a mirror and a mold for societal values and personal aspirations. One prominent example of this intersection is the character Charlie Harper from the television show "Two and a Half Men," portrayed by Charlie Sheen. Through Charlie Harper, the show explores themes of success, excess, and morality, often blurring the lines between them in a way that reflects broader societal attitudes.

Charlie Harper is the epitome of hedonistic success: a wealthy jingle writer living in a luxurious beachfront house in Malibu, enjoying a life of casual relationships, alcohol, and leisure. His character encapsulates a certain ideal of winning in contemporary society, where success is measured by material wealth, social status, and the ability to indulge in one's desires without constraint. This portrayal resonates with a broader cultural narrative that equates success with the accumulation of wealth and the freedom to live a life of pleasure.

However, the character of Charlie Harper also serves as a critique of this version of success. Despite his apparent winning in life, Charlie is often depicted as lonely, unfulfilled, and grappling with the consequences of his choices. His relationships are superficial, his health is frequently at risk due to his lifestyle, and his personal growth remains stunted by his refusal to confront deeper emotional and ethical issues. This dichotomy highlights a critical perspective on the philosophy of winning: while societal metrics of success might reward financial and social achievements, they often neglect the importance of ethical considerations and personal fulfillment.

The tension between success and ethics in "Two and a Half Men" can be seen as a microcosm of broader societal struggles. In many ways, contemporary society celebrates the Charlie Harpers of the world—those who achieve visible success and live flamboyantly. The cultural fascination with celebrities, influencers, and successful entrepreneurs often emphasizes their achievements and lifestyles while glossing over the ethical implications of their actions. This can lead to a skewed perception of success, where the ends are seen as justifying the means, and ethical lapses are overlooked in favor of financial or social gain.

Charlie Sheen's real-life persona further complicates this narrative. Known for his own tumultuous lifestyle and public controversies, Sheen's off-screen life mirrors the excesses and pitfalls of his on-screen character. His public battles with substance abuse, legal issues, and personal conflicts have been widely publicized, casting a shadow on his professional achievements. Sheen's story serves as a stark reminder of the fragility of success when ethical and personal dimensions are neglected. It also underscores the role of media in shaping and sometimes distorting public perceptions of winning and success.

The ethics of success in contemporary society are not merely a matter of personal conduct but also extend to broader systemic issues. Corporate scandals, political corruption, and social injustices often reflect a disconnect between societal values and ethical standards. In a world where success is frequently measured by financial metrics, there can be a tendency to overlook or rationalize unethical behavior. This is evident in various sectors, from business to politics to entertainment, where the pressure to succeed can lead individuals and organizations to engage in morally questionable actions.

For instance, corporate leaders who prioritize profits over ethical considerations can engage in practices that harm the environment, exploit workers, or mislead consumers. Political figures may pursue power at the expense of integrity, engaging in corruption or pandering to special interests. In the entertainment industry, the relentless pursuit of fame and fortune can lead to a culture of exploitation and abuse. These examples illustrate the broader societal implications of the philosophy of winning when it is divorced from ethical considerations.

The media plays a significant role in perpetuating and challenging these narratives. Television shows like "Two and a Half Men" can offer critical insights into societal values, even as they entertain. By presenting characters like Charlie Harper, who embody both the allure and the emptiness of material success, such shows invite viewers to reflect on their own definitions of winning and the ethical dimensions of their pursuits. At the same time, the media can also perpetuate problematic ideals by glamorizing excess and downplaying the consequences of unethical behavior.

One of the challenges in addressing the ethics of success is the pervasive influence of neoliberal ideologies that prioritize individualism and market-driven values. In such a framework, success is often seen as a zero-sum game, where individuals must compete against one another for limited resources and opportunities. This competitive ethos can undermine collective ethical standards, as the pressure to win can lead to cutthroat tactics and a disregard for the well-being of others. It also fosters a culture of envy and dissatisfaction, as individuals measure their self-worth against the achievements of others.

To counteract these tendencies, there is a need for a more holistic understanding of success that integrates ethical considerations and personal fulfillment. This involves redefining winning to include not only material and social achievements but also the cultivation of virtues such as integrity, empathy, and social responsibility. It requires recognizing the interconnectedness of individual and collective well-being and fostering a culture that values ethical conduct as much as, if not more than, financial or social success.

Education and mentorship can play a crucial role in promoting this more balanced perspective on success. By teaching ethical principles and encouraging critical reflection on societal values, educators and mentors can help individuals develop a more nuanced understanding of what it means to win in life. This involves not only imparting knowledge but also modeling ethical behavior and creating environments that support ethical decision-making. It also requires challenging the narratives that equate success with material wealth and social status, and instead highlighting examples of individuals and organizations that prioritize ethical conduct and contribute to the greater good.

In conclusion, the philosophy of winning in contemporary society is a complex interplay of success, ethics, and cultural narratives. Characters like Charlie Harper in "Two and a Half Men" and real-life figures like Charlie Sheen offer compelling case studies of the allure and pitfalls of material success. While society often celebrates visible achievements and the trappings of wealth, there is a growing recognition of the importance of ethical considerations and personal fulfillment in defining true success. By fostering a more holistic understanding of winning that integrates ethical principles and collective well-being, society can create a more just and fulfilling vision of success for individuals and communities alike.

39 TECHNOLOGY AND DYSTOPIAN NARRATIVES

"Black Mirror" is a critically acclaimed anthology series created by Charlie Brooker that explores the dark and often dystopian side of technology and its impact on society. Each standalone episode delves into a different aspect of contemporary or near-future life, presenting a thought-provoking narrative that often serves as a cautionary tale about our increasingly digital world.

One of the show's most compelling aspects is its ability to reflect current societal anxieties about technology. By taking existing technologies and extrapolating their potential consequences, "Black Mirror" creates scenarios that feel eerily plausible. This approach resonates with viewers because it taps into real fears and concerns about the direction in which our world is heading. The show forces us to confront the potential dark side of technological advancements that we often embrace without fully considering their long-term implications.

A recurring theme in "Black Mirror" is the loss of privacy. In episodes like "Nosedive" and "Shut Up and Dance," the series explores how social media and surveillance technologies can erode personal privacy and autonomy. "Nosedive" presents a world where people are constantly rated by others, and these ratings determine their social standing and opportunities. The protagonist, Lacie, becomes obsessed with improving her rating, only to find that this pursuit leads to her downfall. This episode highlights how the pressure to curate a perfect online persona can lead to a loss of authenticity and personal freedom.

"Shut Up and Dance" takes the invasion of privacy to a more sinister level. In this episode, a young man named Kenny is blackmailed by hackers who have recorded him in a compromising situation. The hackers manipulate Kenny and other victims into committing increasingly dangerous and immoral acts. This episode underscores the dangers of living in a world where our every move is potentially recorded and exploited. It raises questions about the erosion of privacy in the digital age and the power dynamics that arise when private information is used as leverage.

Another significant theme in "Black Mirror" is the dehumanizing effect of technology. In "Fifteen Million Merits," individuals are reduced to living in a highly controlled environment where they must generate currency by performing menial tasks. The protagonist, Bing, rebels against this system, but his act of defiance is ultimately co-opted and commodified. This episode critiques a society where human value is measured by productivity and entertainment, and where genuine rebellion is absorbed by the very system it seeks to challenge.

"White Christmas" is another episode that explores dehumanization through technology. It features a device called the "Cookie," which can create digital copies of individuals' consciousness. These copies are used for various purposes, including as personal assistants. The episode raises ethical questions about the treatment of sentient digital beings and the moral implications of creating consciousness solely to serve human needs. It forces viewers to consider what it means to be human and whether digital consciousness deserves the same rights and protections as biological life.

The theme of identity and its manipulation through technology is also prevalent in "Black Mirror." In "Be Right Back," a grieving woman named Martha uses a service that creates a digital replica of her deceased boyfriend, Ash, based on his online presence. While the replica initially provides comfort, Martha eventually realizes that it is a hollow imitation of the person she loved. This episode explores the limits of technology in replicating human relationships and the emotional complexities that arise when we attempt to use technology to cope with loss.

Similarly, "USS Callister" addresses identity manipulation through virtual reality. The episode follows Robert Daly, a software developer who creates a virtual world based on his favorite sci-fi show. Daly populates this world with digital clones of his coworkers, whom he can control and manipulate. This episode examines the ethics of creating digital replicas of real people and the psychological consequences of living in a virtual world where one's identity and agency are controlled by someone else. It also serves as a commentary on power dynamics and the potential for abuse in virtual environments.

"Black Mirror" often portrays a future where technology exacerbates social inequalities. In "Men Against Fire," soldiers are implanted with technology that alters their perception, making them see their enemies as monstrous creatures rather than human beings. This dehumanization makes it easier for soldiers to kill without remorse. The episode critiques the use of technology to desensitize individuals to violence and the moral implications of manipulating perception to serve military and political agendas.

In "Hated in the Nation," social media is weaponized to carry out public executions. The episode centers on a series of deaths caused by autonomous drone insects that are controlled by a hashtag-driven social media campaign. This narrative highlights the dangers of mob mentality and the potential for technology to amplify and enact collective aggression. It serves as a stark reminder of the power of social media to influence real-world actions and the ethical responsibilities that come with such power.

Despite its often bleak outlook, "Black Mirror" occasionally offers glimpses of hope and redemption. "San Junipero" is a standout episode that presents a more optimistic view of technology. It tells the story of two women, Yorkie and Kelly, who fall in love in a virtual reality afterlife. This episode explores themes of love, memory, and the possibility of eternal life through technology. It suggests that, while technology can be harmful, it also has the potential to create new and meaningful experiences.

In "Hang the DJ," another relatively hopeful episode, a dating app simulates entire relationships to find perfect matches for its users. The protagonists, Amy and Frank, navigate a series of relationships within the simulation, ultimately rebelling against the system to be together. This episode explores the complexities of love and compatibility in the digital age and suggests that genuine human connection can transcend technological manipulation.

"Black Mirror" succeeds in part because of its ability to blend speculative fiction with real-world issues. The series holds up a mirror to contemporary society, reflecting our deepest fears and anxieties about the ways technology is shaping our lives. It challenges viewers to think critically about the ethical implications of technological advancements and to consider how we can navigate a future that is increasingly influenced by digital innovation.

The show's impact extends beyond entertainment; it has sparked conversations about privacy, ethics, and the social consequences of technology. It serves as a reminder that, while technology has the potential to improve our lives, it also poses significant risks that must be carefully managed. By presenting dystopian scenarios that feel all too possible, "Black Mirror" encourages us to reflect on our relationship with technology and to consider how we can build a future that prioritizes human well-being and ethical considerations.

In conclusion, "Black Mirror" is a powerful and thought-provoking series that explores the dark side of technology and its impact on society. Through its compelling narratives and richly imagined worlds, the show challenges viewers to confront the potential consequences of technological advancements and to reflect on the ethical implications of our digital age. By blending speculative fiction with real-world issues, "Black Mirror" holds up a mirror to our society, encouraging us to think critically about the future we are creating and the values we want to uphold in an increasingly digital world.

SECTION FIVE

VISIONARIES AND FUTURISTS

The concept of visionaries and futurists has always been intertwined with the pursuit of progress, the yearning to break boundaries, and the ambition to shape a better world. These individuals often possess an extraordinary ability to foresee trends, innovate, and inspire others to join them in their quest for transformation. Among the myriad tools and technologies that have propelled visionaries forward, neural networks and advancements in artificial intelligence stand out as particularly influential.

Neural networks, a subset of machine learning, are designed to simulate the way the human brain processes information. These complex algorithms can recognize patterns, make decisions, and even predict outcomes by learning from vast amounts of data. As neural networks continue to evolve, their potential to enhance various aspects of life becomes increasingly apparent. From revolutionizing healthcare with predictive diagnostics to transforming the creative arts through generative design, the impact of these technologies is profound.

One area where neural networks are making significant strides is in the realm of aesthetics. Traditionally, aesthetics has been the domain of artists, designers, and creatives who rely on their intuition, experience, and a deep understanding of beauty and form. However, the advent of neural networks has introduced a new dimension to this field, allowing machines to not only mimic but also innovate in the creation of aesthetically pleasing and functionally superior designs.

The fusion of human creativity and machine intelligence has given rise to a new breed of tools that can augment the artistic process. These tools enable artists and designers to explore uncharted territories, push the boundaries of their creativity, and produce works that were previously unimaginable. By analyzing vast datasets of visual art, design principles, and user preferences, neural networks can suggest novel ideas, optimize design elements, and even create entirely new art forms.

For instance, generative adversarial networks (GANs) have become a popular tool in the hands of modern artists. GANs consist of two neural networks—the generator and the discriminator—that work in tandem to produce new data that closely resembles the training data. Artists can use GANs to generate unique artworks, experiment with different styles, and even collaborate with the machine in a sort of digital co-creation process. This collaboration between human and machine not only expands the artist's creative toolkit but also challenges our conventional notions of authorship and creativity.

In the realm of design, neural networks are being leveraged to create more user-centric and aesthetically pleasing products. By analyzing user feedback, market trends, and ergonomic principles, these systems can suggest improvements to existing designs or generate new concepts that are both beautiful and functional. For example, in the fashion industry, neural networks can predict upcoming trends, assist in fabric selection, and even design garments that cater to individual preferences and body types. This level of personalization and precision would be difficult, if not impossible, to achieve through traditional methods alone.

Moreover, the influence of neural networks extends beyond the visual arts and design into other areas such as music, literature, and architecture. In music, AI composers can generate original pieces by learning from the works of past masters and contemporary musicians alike. These compositions can range from classical symphonies to modern electronic music, offering composers new sources of inspiration and collaboration. In literature, neural networks can assist writers by suggesting plot twists, character developments, and even entire narratives, thus enhancing the storytelling process.

Architecture, too, has seen the integration of neural networks in the design and planning stages. By analyzing environmental data, historical building styles, and user needs, these systems can propose sustainable and innovative architectural solutions. From optimizing spatial layouts to designing energy-efficient buildings, the potential applications of neural networks in architecture are vast and transformative.

The enhancement of aesthetics through neural networks is not without its challenges and controversies. Questions about the role of the artist, the authenticity of AI-generated works, and the ethical implications of machine creativity are hotly debated. Some purists argue that true art must be the product of human experience and emotion, while others embrace the collaborative possibilities offered by AI.

Despite these debates, it is undeniable that neural networks have opened new avenues for exploration and expression in the arts. They have democratized access to sophisticated design tools, allowing more people to engage in creative pursuits. They have also introduced a level of objectivity in areas where subjective judgment has traditionally reigned, such as in the evaluation of beauty and quality.

As we look to the future, the role of visionaries and futurists will be crucial in guiding the ethical and responsible development of these technologies. It is essential to ensure that the integration of neural networks in creative fields enhances human potential rather than diminishes it. This involves fostering a symbiotic relationship between human intuition and machine intelligence, where each complements the other's strengths.

Education and collaboration will play key roles in achieving this balance. Artists, designers, and technologists must work together to understand the capabilities and limitations of neural networks. By sharing knowledge and insights, they can develop best practices and ethical guidelines that ensure the responsible use of AI in the arts. This collaborative approach will also help to dispel fears and misconceptions about AI, fostering a more inclusive and forward-thinking creative community.

In addition, public engagement and dialogue are vital in shaping the future of AI in aesthetics. By involving diverse voices and perspectives, we can ensure that the development of these technologies reflects a wide range of cultural values and artistic traditions. This inclusivity will help to create AI systems that are more attuned to the nuances of human creativity and more capable of enhancing rather than overshadowing it.

Ultimately, the integration of neural networks in aesthetics represents a significant step forward in our ongoing quest to explore and expand the boundaries of human creativity. By embracing these technologies, visionaries and futurists can unlock new possibilities for artistic expression and design, leading to a richer and more diverse cultural landscape. As we continue to navigate this exciting frontier, it is essential to remain mindful of the ethical considerations and to prioritize the human element in all creative endeavors. By doing so, we can ensure that the future of aesthetics is one where technology enhances rather than eclipses the beauty and wonder of human creativity.

40 THE PLAYFUL LIMITS OF LANGUAGE

Oulipo, short for "Ouvroir de littérature potentielle," is a French literary movement founded in 1960 by mathematician François Le Lionnais and writer Raymond Queneau. The group's name translates to "Workshop of Potential Literature," and its members are known for employing constrained writing techniques to explore the possibilities of language and storytelling. These constraints often involve mathematical and logical structures, transforming the act of writing into a playful and intellectually stimulating challenge.

Cryptography, the practice of secure communication, shares an intrinsic connection with the principles of Oulipo. Both fields involve encoding and decoding information, often through complex and seemingly obscure rules. In Oulipian literature, constraints function as a form of cryptographic cipher, where the underlying meaning is unlocked through the reader's engagement with the text. This interplay between restriction and creativity mirrors the dynamic of cryptography, where security is ensured through the careful application of constraints.

One prominent example of Oulipian technique is the lipogram, a work that deliberately avoids using one or more letters of the alphabet. Georges Perec, an illustrious member of Oulipo, famously wrote the novel "La Disparition" (1969), a 300-page lipogrammatic novel entirely devoid of the letter "e." This constraint not only posed a significant linguistic challenge but also added a layer of depth to the novel, as the missing letter became a metaphor for absence and loss. Perec's achievement demonstrated the potential of constraints to yield rich and innovative literary expressions.

Another fascinating constraint employed by Oulipo writers is the palindrome, a word, phrase, or sequence of characters that reads the same backward and forward. Palindromes require a high degree of linguistic dexterity and often result in playful, enigmatic texts. The crafting of palindromes can be seen as a form of linguistic cryptography, where symmetry and reversibility are key principles. By adhering to these constraints, Oulipian writers produce works that challenge conventional narrative structures and invite readers to engage with the text in novel ways.

Harry Mathews, an American writer and the only non-French member of Oulipo, contributed significantly to the group's body of work. His novel "Cigarettes" (1987) exemplifies the Oulipian ethos through its intricate structure and narrative complexity. Mathews often employed constraints such as the "circular" narrative, where the end of the story loops back to the beginning, creating a continuous and self-referential text. This technique not only reflects the recursive nature of palindromes but also underscores the potential for constraints to generate innovative and engaging narratives.

Raymond Queneau, a co-founder of Oulipo, was instrumental in establishing the group's foundational principles. His work "Exercises in Style" (1947) is a quintessential Oulipian text, comprising 99 retellings of a simple story, each in a different style or form. This exploration of narrative constraints illustrates the group's commitment to experimenting with the boundaries of literary form. Queneau's playful and inventive approach to writing set the tone for subsequent generations of Oulipian writers, who continue to push the limits of what literature can achieve.

The relationship between Oulipo and technology is epitomized by the group's use of computers to enhance their writing processes. "L'ordinateur," or "the computer," became an important tool for Oulipian writers, enabling them to explore more complex constraints and generate new forms of literature. The use of algorithms and computational methods allowed for the creation of texts that would have been impossible to produce manually. This integration of technology highlights Oulipo's forward-thinking approach and its embrace of modernity as a means of expanding the possibilities of literature.

Jacques Roubaud, a prominent Oulipian poet and mathematician, has extensively explored the interplay between mathematical structures and literary forms. His work often incorporates elements of combinatorics, algebra, and geometry, demonstrating the profound connections between mathematics and language. Roubaud's poetry exemplifies the Oulipian belief in the generative potential of constraints, where the imposition of rules and structures can lead to new and unexpected creative outcomes.

Hervé Le Tellier, a contemporary member of Oulipo, has continued the tradition of innovative and constrained writing. His novel "The Anomaly" (2020) employs a unique narrative structure, intertwining multiple storylines and perspectives to create a complex and engaging text. Le Tellier's work demonstrates the enduring relevance of Oulipian principles in contemporary literature, showcasing how constraints can be used to produce fresh and compelling narratives.

The influence of Oulipo extends beyond its immediate members, inspiring writers and artists across various disciplines. The group's emphasis on formal constraints and playful experimentation has resonated with creators seeking to explore the limits of their mediums. By demonstrating the creative potential of restrictions, Oulipo has challenged conventional notions of artistic freedom and opened up new avenues for innovation and expression.

Oulipo's legacy is marked by its commitment to the exploration of potentiality in literature. The group's use of constraints as a creative tool has yielded a rich and diverse body of work, showcasing the versatility and adaptability of language. Through their inventive and often playful approaches to writing, Oulipian writers have expanded the horizons of what literature can achieve, demonstrating that creativity thrives within the bounds of limitation.

In conclusion, Oulipo's contributions to literature are characterized by their innovative use of constraints, their exploration of the relationship between mathematics and language, and their embrace of technology as a means of enhancing creative processes. By challenging conventional narrative structures and pushing the boundaries of literary form, Oulipian writers have demonstrated the generative potential of constraints, inspiring new approaches to storytelling and expanding the possibilities of literature. Through the works of figures like Georges Perec, Raymond Queneau, Harry Mathews, Jacques Roubaud, and Hervé Le Tellier, Oulipo continues to influence and inspire writers and artists around the world, affirming the enduring relevance of constrained writing techniques in contemporary literature.

41 THE INFINITE LABYRINTH

Jorge Borges was a man of immense intellect and boundless curiosity, traits that shaped his lifelong pursuit of knowledge and understanding. His name was synonymous with the labyrinthine complexities of literature and thought, a fitting reflection of his own mind, which seemed to contain infinite twists and turns. Borges was not merely a collector of books but an accumulator of stories, ideas, and mysteries. His library was not just a room but a labyrinth, a sprawling network of shelves and corridors that seemed to extend infinitely in all directions.

This massive collection was his pride and joy, a testament to his relentless quest for wisdom. Each book was a doorway into another world, another dimension of thought and experience. Borges often found himself wandering through his labyrinthine library, running his fingers along the spines of the countless volumes that filled its shelves. Each touch seemed to conjure memories of the worlds contained within those pages, a cacophony of voices from the past and present, each whispering their secrets to him.

The labyrinth was not just physical but metaphorical. Borges reveled in the idea of a universe composed of endless possibilities, each decision branching off into new and unforeseen directions, creating an ever-expanding web of potential realities. This concept fascinated him and often found its way into his writing. His stories were riddles, puzzles designed to challenge the reader's perception of reality and truth. They were intricate constructions, each layer revealing deeper complexities, much like the labyrinth he had constructed in his home.

The mystery was at the heart of everything Borges did. He believed that the world was a vast enigma, a puzzle to be solved. His writing was his way of exploring this enigma, of delving into the hidden corners of human experience and uncovering the secrets that lay within. He wrote of infinite libraries, of books that contained all possible knowledge, of labyrinths that defied the constraints of time and space. Each story was a piece of the puzzle, a fragment of the larger mystery that he sought to understand.

Borges' fascination with the labyrinthine nature of existence was not merely intellectual but deeply personal. He often spoke of his own life as a labyrinth, a series of interconnected experiences and decisions that had led him to where he was. He saw himself as a wanderer, perpetually seeking the center of the maze, the ultimate truth that lay at its heart. This quest for understanding drove him, propelled him through the winding corridors of his own mind and the vast expanse of his library.

The labyrinth was also a symbol of his belief in the interconnectedness of all things. Borges saw the world as a complex network of relationships and influences, each part connected to the whole in ways that were often hidden from view. His stories reflected this belief, weaving together disparate elements into a cohesive and intricate tapestry. He reveled in the idea that everything was connected, that every action had repercussions that echoed through the labyrinth of existence.

His library was a physical manifestation of this belief. It was a place where the boundaries between past and present, reality and fiction, blurred and dissolved. Borges would lose himself for hours, sometimes days, wandering through its endless corridors, pulling books from the shelves at random, letting their stories intertwine with his own thoughts and experiences. Each book was a thread in the larger tapestry of his understanding, each story a piece of the puzzle he was trying to solve.

Borges was also a master of the paradox, delighting in the contradictions and complexities that lay at the heart of existence. His stories were often built around paradoxical concepts, exploring the ways in which seemingly opposing ideas could coexist and even enhance one another. He believed that the true nature of reality was far more complex and nuanced than it appeared on the surface, and his writing sought to capture this complexity, to delve into the heart of the paradox and reveal its hidden truths.

The labyrinth was a perfect symbol for this belief. It was a place of contradictions, where paths twisted back on themselves, leading to unexpected destinations, where the boundaries between inside and outside, beginning and end, were fluid and ever-changing. Borges saw his own mind as a labyrinth, a place where ideas and experiences interwove and overlapped in ways that were often surprising and unexpected. His writing was an attempt to map this labyrinth, to chart its complexities and reveal the hidden patterns that lay within.

Borges' fascination with the labyrinth and the mystery of existence was also deeply influenced by his love of literature. Each book represented a piece of the vast puzzle he spent his life trying to solve, a fragment of the infinite mystery that he believed was the universe itself.

Among these countless volumes, Borges discovered many rare and obscure texts that were unknown to most scholars. He would spend hours poring over ancient manuscripts, deciphering cryptic symbols, and unraveling the secrets hidden within their pages. It was not just the content of the books that fascinated him, but also their histories, the journeys they had taken through time and space to end up in his hands.

One evening, as Borges was exploring a particularly dusty and seldom-visited corner of his library, he stumbled upon a small, leather-bound book that he had never noticed before. It was nestled between two massive tomes, its cover worn and faded, its pages yellowed with age. Intrigued, he carefully pulled it from the shelf and carried it to his reading chair, the one place in the labyrinth where he felt most at home.

As he opened the book, he was struck by the beauty of its script. The letters were delicate and flowing, almost as if they were dancing across the page. The language was unfamiliar, yet there was something hauntingly familiar about it, as if he had encountered it in a dream. Borges felt a thrill of excitement as he began to read, the words pulling him deeper into their enigmatic embrace.

The book told the story of a mysterious labyrinth, much like his own library, but far more ancient and vast. It was said to be hidden somewhere in the heart of a great desert, guarded by a series of riddles and traps designed to deter all but the most determined seekers. According to the legend, the labyrinth contained a treasure of unimaginable value, a secret that could unlock the mysteries of the universe.

Borges was captivated by the tale, feeling a strange connection to the unknown author who had penned these words so many centuries ago. The labyrinth described in the book seemed to mirror his own inner world, a place where knowledge and mystery intertwined, where every answer only led to more questions. He spent the next several weeks completely absorbed in the book, deciphering its riddles and piecing together its clues.

As he delved deeper into the text, Borges began to experience strange and vivid dreams. In these dreams, he found himself wandering through a labyrinth that seemed to be an amalgamation of his library and the one described in the book. The corridors were lined with bookshelves that stretched up to the sky, and the walls were covered in cryptic symbols and ancient runes. He felt a sense of déjà vu, as if he had been there before, perhaps in another life or another dimension.

One night, in the midst of one of these dreams, Borges came across a door that he had never seen before. It was made of heavy, weathered wood, and it was adorned with intricate carvings that seemed to pulse with a strange, otherworldly energy. With a mixture of fear and curiosity, he reached out and turned the handle, feeling a jolt of electricity course through his body as the door creaked open.

On the other side of the door was a small, dimly lit room. At its center stood a pedestal, upon which rested a single, ancient-looking book. The air was thick with the scent of old parchment and ink, and the walls seemed to hum with a low, almost imperceptible vibration. Borges approached the pedestal with trepidation, his heart pounding in his chest.

As he reached out to touch the book, he was suddenly engulfed by a blinding light. When the light faded, he found himself standing in the middle of a vast, open desert, the sun blazing overhead. The labyrinth from his dreams and the ancient book had somehow become his reality. He was no longer just a reader of the tale but a participant in it.

Borges knew that he had to find the labyrinth and uncover its secrets. He felt an inexplicable sense of urgency, as if the fate of the world depended on his success. With nothing but the clothes on his back and the knowledge he had gleaned from the book, he set off into the desert, determined to find the entrance to the ancient maze.

Days turned into weeks as Borges wandered through the harsh, unforgiving landscape. The sun was merciless, and the nights were bitterly cold. He faced many trials and dangers along the way, but his resolve never wavered. He was driven by a force greater than himself, a deep, unshakable belief that the answers he sought were within his reach.

One evening, as the sun was setting and casting long shadows across the sand, Borges came upon a strange rock formation. It was unlike anything he had seen before, a series of towering stone pillars arranged in a perfect circle. At the center of the circle was a large, flat stone with an inscription carved into its surface.

Borges knelt down to read the inscription, his hands trembling with anticipation. The words were written in the same cryptic script as the book he had found in his library, and as he read them, he felt a surge of recognition. The inscription was a riddle, one that he had already solved in his dreams.

With newfound determination, Borges began to search the area around the rock formation. It wasn't long before he found what he was looking for: a narrow, hidden entrance that led down into the earth. Taking a deep breath, he descended into the darkness, his heart racing with a mixture of fear and excitement.

The passageway was long and winding, and it seemed to go on forever. The air was cool and damp, and the walls were lined with ancient, crumbling stone. Borges felt as if he were walking back through time, each step bringing him closer to the heart of the labyrinth. He followed the twists and turns of the tunnel, guided by an instinct he couldn't explain.

Eventually, the passageway opened up into a vast, underground chamber. The ceiling was so high that it was lost in shadow, and the walls were covered in intricate carvings that glowed with a faint, ethereal light. In the center of the chamber was a massive, circular door, adorned with the same strange symbols that had led him here.

Borges approached the door, his mind racing with thoughts of the mysteries that lay beyond. He knew that this was the final test, the last riddle he had to solve. As he stood before the door, he felt a sense of calm wash over him. He had been preparing for this moment his entire life, and now it was finally within his grasp.

With a steady hand, Borges reached out and traced the symbols on the door, his fingers moving with a confidence born of deep understanding. As he completed the sequence, the door began to tremble and slowly swing open. A brilliant light poured out from the chamber beyond, illuminating the darkness and revealing the true heart of the labyrinth.

Borges stepped through the doorway and into the light, feeling a profound sense of awe and wonder. The chamber was filled with books, more books than he had ever seen in his life. They were arranged in neat rows, stretching out in all directions, a seemingly infinite library that dwarfed even his own massive collection.

At the center of the chamber stood a pedestal, much like the one in his dream, and upon it rested a single, ancient book. Borges approached the pedestal with reverence, his heart filled with a sense of completion. He had finally found what he had been searching for, the ultimate source of knowledge and mystery.

As he opened the book, Borges felt a rush of understanding flood his mind. The words on the pages were not just a story, but a map, a guide to the infinite labyrinth of the universe. He realized that he had always been a part of this greater mystery, and that his life's work had been leading him to this moment.

In that instant, Jorge Borges understood the true nature of the labyrinth. It was not just a physical place, but a reflection of the mind, a symbol of the endless quest for knowledge and meaning. He knew that he would never truly leave the labyrinth, for it was a part of him, just as he was a part of it.

With this newfound understanding, Borges closed the book and looked around the chamber, feeling a deep sense of peace. He knew that his journey was far from over, and that there were still many mysteries to uncover and riddles to solve. But he also knew that he had found his place within the labyrinth, and that he would never again feel lost.

As he turned to leave the chamber, Borges felt a sense of lightness and freedom. He had become one with the labyrinth, and in doing so, had found the answers he had been seeking all his life. The infinite collection of books, the winding corridors, the ancient symbols – they were all a part of him now, a testament to his relentless pursuit of the ultimate mystery.

And so, Jorge Borges continued his journey, forever wandering the labyrinth, forever seeking, forever discovering. The labyrinth was his home, his sanctuary, and his greatest adventure.

42 CHAOS AND CYBER CULTURE

Timothy Leary was a seminal figure in the 20th century, whose work traversed various domains such as psychology, psychedelic research, and the burgeoning field of cyberculture. His multifaceted contributions have left an indelible mark on contemporary thought, particularly in how we understand the intersections between technology, consciousness, and societal structures.

Leary's exploration of AI computing was deeply intertwined with his broader philosophical perspectives on human consciousness and societal evolution. He foresaw the potential of artificial intelligence not merely as a tool for computational tasks but as a transformative force that could augment human cognition and expand the boundaries of human experience. In Leary's view, AI represented a kind of electronic extension of the human nervous system, capable of interfacing with our cognitive processes in profound ways.

His vision of AI was optimistic and utopian, suggesting that intelligent machines could help humanity achieve higher states of awareness and creativity. Leary believed that the integration of AI into human life could lead to what he called "cybernetic transcendence," a state where the fusion of human minds with advanced computational systems would open up new realms of thought and experience. This perspective was rooted in his broader philosophical framework that emphasized the potential for technology to catalyze evolutionary leaps in human consciousness.

Leary's work on chaos and cyberculture further exemplified his visionary approach to technology and society. He was fascinated by the concept of chaos theory, which posits that complex systems exhibit unpredictable and non-linear behavior. For Leary, chaos was not something to be feared but rather embraced as a fundamental aspect of the universe that could drive creativity and innovation. He saw parallels between chaos theory and the dynamic, decentralized nature of cyberculture, which was just beginning to emerge in the late 20th century.

In the realm of cyberculture, Leary envisioned a future where digital technologies would enable new forms of social organization and communication. He anticipated the rise of the internet and other digital networks as platforms for cultural and intellectual exchange, where individuals could connect and collaborate across geographical and cultural boundaries. Leary's enthusiasm for cyberculture was grounded in his belief that these technologies could democratize knowledge and empower individuals to explore new dimensions of consciousness and self-expression.

Psychedelics played a central role in Leary's exploration of consciousness, both in his personal experiences and his professional research. He is perhaps best known for his advocacy of psychedelic substances such as LSD, which he believed had the potential to unlock profound insights into the nature of the mind and reality. Leary's experiments with psychedelics were aimed at understanding how these substances could facilitate altered states of consciousness and enhance human creativity, empathy, and spiritual awareness.

Leary's approach to psychedelics was heavily influenced by his background in psychology and his interest in Eastern spiritual traditions. He often drew parallels between the effects of psychedelics and the practices of meditation and yoga, suggesting that these substances could serve as catalysts for achieving states of enlightenment and self-realization. This perspective was encapsulated in his famous slogan, "Turn on, tune in, drop out," which encouraged individuals to embrace the transformative potential of psychedelics and reject conventional societal norms in favor of personal and spiritual growth.

Leary's exploration of consciousness through psychedelics also led him to develop various techniques and practices aimed at optimizing the psychedelic experience. One such practice was the use of mantras, which are repetitive sounds or phrases that can induce a meditative state and enhance the effects of psychedelics. Leary believed that mantras could help individuals navigate the often chaotic and disorienting experiences induced by psychedelics, providing a focus for their attention and facilitating deeper introspection.

The use of mantras in Leary's psychedelic practice was influenced by his study of Hindu and Buddhist traditions, where mantras have long been used as tools for meditation and spiritual practice. Leary adapted these traditional practices to the context of psychedelic exploration, creating a fusion of Eastern spiritual techniques and Western psychological methods. This interdisciplinary approach reflected his broader philosophy of integrating diverse perspectives and knowledge systems to enhance human understanding and experience.

Leary's work was not without controversy, particularly his advocacy of psychedelics, which led to his dismissal from Harvard University and subsequent legal troubles. However, his ideas have continued to influence contemporary thought, particularly in the fields of psychology, technology, and spirituality. Leary's vision of a future where AI, cyberculture, and psychedelics converge to expand human consciousness remains a provocative and inspiring legacy.

In contemporary discussions about AI and consciousness, Leary's ideas provide a valuable framework for considering the ethical and philosophical implications of advanced technologies. His belief in the potential of AI to enhance human cognition challenges us to think about how we can harness these technologies in ways that promote human flourishing and well-being. Similarly, his insights into chaos theory and cyberculture encourage us to embrace the complexity and unpredictability of our digital age, seeing it as an opportunity for creativity and innovation.

Leary's work on psychedelics continues to resonate in today's growing interest in the therapeutic potential of these substances. Recent research has begun to validate many of Leary's claims about the benefits of psychedelics for mental health and personal growth, suggesting that these substances could play a significant role in addressing contemporary psychological and existential challenges. Leary's emphasis on the importance of set and setting, as well as his development of techniques like mantras, remains relevant for anyone interested in exploring the potential of psychedelics in a safe and intentional way.

In conclusion, Timothy Leary's contributions to the fields of AI computing, chaos theory, cyberculture, and psychedelics offer a rich and multifaceted perspective on the possibilities of human evolution and consciousness. His visionary ideas continue to inspire and challenge us to think beyond conventional boundaries, exploring new dimensions of technology, mind, and society. As we navigate the complexities of the 21st century, Leary's work reminds us of the potential for creativity, innovation, and spiritual growth that lies at the intersection of these dynamic and evolving fields.

43 ALIENS, MACHINE ELVES AND VISIBLE LANGUAGE

Terence McKenna, an influential figure in the realms of psychedelics and alternative thought, proposed a return to the values and experiences of ancient, pre-literate societies as a means to address the crises of modern civilization. Central to McKenna's philosophy was the belief that psychedelics, particularly tryptamines such as psilocybin and DMT, were instrumental in accessing realms of experience that modern humans had lost touch with.

McKenna's concept of the archaic revival is deeply intertwined with his experiences and theories regarding encounters with non-human intelligences, which he often described as "machine elves" or "aliens." These entities, according to McKenna, could be accessed through the use of psychedelics, offering insights and knowledge beyond ordinary human comprehension. In his view, these experiences were not merely hallucinations but interactions with a deeper reality, one that our ancestors might have regularly encountered in their altered states of consciousness.

The archaic revival, as McKenna saw it, was a necessary response to the alienation and ecological destruction wrought by modernity. He argued that by reconnecting with the archaic modes of consciousness, humans could find solutions to the problems facing the world. This revival involved embracing shamanic practices, a deep respect for nature, and the use of psychedelics to dissolve the boundaries of the ego and foster a sense of unity with the cosmos.

McKenna's ideas about machine elves and aliens emerged from his extensive experiences with psychedelics. He recounted numerous instances during his psychedelic journeys where he encountered entities that seemed to communicate with him. These beings, often described as machine elves or self-transforming elf machines, inhabited a realm that McKenna referred to as the "hyperspace" or "DMT space." In these experiences, the entities would engage with him, often through a form of communication that transcended language as we know it.

This form of communication, which McKenna termed "visible language," was a synesthetic experience where language took on a visual form. Words and ideas would manifest as three-dimensional, multi-colored objects that could be manipulated and understood in ways that verbal language could not convey. This concept of visible language was a key aspect of McKenna's vision of a transformed future, where human communication would evolve beyond the limitations of spoken and written language.

The notion of visible language ties back to McKenna's broader ideas about the evolution of consciousness. He believed that humanity was on the cusp of a major shift, a transformation that would be facilitated by psychedelics and the integration of archaic wisdom. In this new paradigm, visible language would enable a more direct and intuitive form of communication, reducing misunderstandings and fostering a deeper connection between individuals.

McKenna's encounters with these otherworldly entities and his experiences of visible language were not merely personal anecdotes but formed the foundation of his philosophical outlook. He saw these experiences as evidence of a vast, interconnected web of consciousness that transcended the material world. This perspective led him to challenge the dominant scientific and materialist worldview, advocating instead for a more holistic and mystical understanding of reality.

In advocating for the archaic revival, McKenna emphasized the importance of reclaiming our relationship with nature and the planet. He was deeply concerned about the ecological crisis and saw the revival of archaic values and practices as a means to heal the rift between humanity and the natural world. By embracing a more animistic worldview, one that sees all of nature as alive and imbued with spirit, McKenna believed that humans could foster a more sustainable and harmonious existence.

McKenna's vision was not without its critics. Some viewed his ideas as overly idealistic or lacking in scientific rigor. However, his work resonated with many who were disillusioned with the dominant cultural narrative and seeking alternative ways of understanding and experiencing reality. His emphasis on direct experience, personal transformation, and the exploration of consciousness struck a chord with those looking for deeper meaning and connection in their lives.

In the context of the archaic revival, McKenna also explored the implications of technological advancements. He saw technology as a double-edged sword, capable of both alienating us from nature and providing tools for reconnecting with it. He was particularly interested in the potential of virtual reality and other digital technologies to create new forms of experience and understanding. In McKenna's view, the integration of technology and archaic wisdom could lead to a new era of human development, where the boundaries between the natural and the artificial, the material and the spiritual, would dissolve.

Central to McKenna's philosophy was the idea that psychedelics were a key to unlocking these new possibilities. He often spoke about the "felt presence of direct experience," arguing that personal, firsthand encounters with the psychedelic realm were essential for genuine understanding and transformation. This emphasis on direct experience was a cornerstone of his advocacy for the archaic revival, as it encouraged individuals to explore their own consciousness and find their own truths, rather than relying solely on external authorities or established dogmas.

McKenna's fascination with machine elves and aliens also had a broader cultural significance. His descriptions of these entities and the realms they inhabited contributed to a growing interest in the idea of other dimensions and non-human intelligences. This interest intersected with various subcultures, including the New Age movement, the UFO community, and the burgeoning field of consciousness studies. McKenna's work helped to legitimize and popularize the exploration of these themes, inspiring others to investigate the boundaries of human perception and experience.

In conclusion, Terence McKenna's concept of the archaic revival, along with his experiences and theories regarding machine elves, aliens, and visible language, offers a provocative and visionary perspective on the potential for human transformation. His ideas challenge the conventional understanding of reality and invite us to explore the deeper dimensions of consciousness. By reconnecting with the wisdom of our ancestors and embracing the insights gained from psychedelic experiences, McKenna believed that humanity could find new ways to address the crises of modern civilization and move towards a more harmonious and enlightened future. His legacy continues to inspire and provoke thought, encouraging us to look beyond the familiar and explore the unknown realms of the mind and the universe.

44 DISCORDIANISM AND CONSPIRACY THEORY

Robert Anton Wilson, an influential American author and philosopher, played a pivotal role in popularizing Discordianism and conspiracy theories. His work, often blending satire and profound insight, explored the intersections of reality, perception, and belief systems. Discordianism, a modern, satirical religion, emerged in the late 1950s with the publication of the "Principia Discordia," co-authored by Greg Hill (Malaclypse the Younger) and Kerry Thornley (Lord Omar Khayyam Ravenhurst). Wilson, through his books and lectures, significantly contributed to the spread of Discordianism, infusing it with his unique perspective on reality and consciousness.

Discordianism posits that chaos and disorder are fundamental aspects of the universe, challenging the conventional dichotomy between order and chaos. It venerates Eris, the Greek goddess of chaos and discord, as its central deity. The religion employs humor, paradox, and absurdity to critique established beliefs and institutions, advocating for a more flexible and open-minded approach to life. Wilson's embrace of Discordianism is evident in his seminal work, "The Illuminatus! Trilogy," co-written with Robert Shea. This trilogy, blending science fiction, satire, and conspiracy theory, delves into the chaotic and interconnected nature of human existence, reflecting the core tenets of Discordianism.

Wilson's interest in conspiracy theories stemmed from his skepticism of authoritative narratives and his belief in the multiplicity of truths. He often asserted that our understanding of reality is shaped by the information we consume and the filters through which we interpret it. In "The Illuminatus! Trilogy," Wilson and Shea weave a complex tapestry of conspiracy theories involving secret societies, government cover-ups, and cosmic forces. This work exemplifies Wilson's view that belief in a singular, objective reality is an illusion, and that embracing uncertainty can lead to greater freedom and creativity.

Wilson's exploration of conspiracy theories extended beyond fiction. In his non-fiction works, such as "Cosmic Trigger: The Final Secret of the Illuminati," Wilson documented his personal experiences with altered states of consciousness, synchronicities, and paranormal phenomena. He often employed a method he called "model agnosticism," which entailed suspending judgment and remaining open to multiple interpretations of reality. This approach allowed him to explore various conspiracy theories without necessarily endorsing them, encouraging readers to question their assumptions and think critically.

Computers and the rise of the digital age played a significant role in the dissemination of Discordianism and conspiracy theories. The advent of personal computers and the internet provided new platforms for the exchange of ideas, allowing subcultures like Discordianism to flourish. Wilson, an early adopter of digital technology, recognized the potential of computers to transform human communication and consciousness. He saw the internet as a tool for decentralizing information and empowering individuals to seek out alternative perspectives.

In the context of Discordianism, computers facilitated the spread of the "Principia Discordia" and related texts, making them accessible to a global audience. Online forums and bulletin boards became spaces where Discordians could share their ideas, rituals, and humor, fostering a sense of community and collaboration. The internet also enabled the rapid proliferation of conspiracy theories, as individuals could easily publish and disseminate their views without the need for traditional gatekeepers like publishers or editors.

Wilson's engagement with computers and digital technology is evident in his writings. In "The Illuminatus! Trilogy," he and Shea imagined a world where computers and advanced communication networks played a crucial role in the machinations of secret societies and global conspiracies. This vision anticipated the internet's capacity to connect disparate individuals and ideas, creating a complex web of information and misinformation.

As computers became more integral to daily life, Wilson continued to explore their implications for society. In his later works, he examined the potential of computers to enhance human intelligence and creativity, advocating for the use of technology to expand consciousness and foster greater understanding. He also warned of the dangers of information overload and the erosion of privacy, presciently addressing issues that remain relevant in the digital age.

Wilson's influence on the discourse surrounding Discordianism and conspiracy theories cannot be overstated. His work challenged readers to question the nature of reality and embrace uncertainty, encouraging a playful and open-minded approach to life. By integrating humor, satire, and critical thinking, Wilson's contributions to Discordianism and conspiracy theory continue to resonate with those seeking alternative perspectives in an increasingly complex world.

In examining the broader cultural impact of Wilson's ideas, it's important to consider the role of computers in shaping contemporary society. The digital revolution has fundamentally altered how we access and process information, transforming the landscape of belief and knowledge. Computers, as tools for both creation and dissemination, have enabled the rapid spread of ideas, facilitating the growth of subcultures and the exchange of unconventional views.

The internet, in particular, has democratized access to information, allowing individuals to explore a vast array of perspectives. This has empowered movements like Discordianism, providing a platform for like-minded individuals to connect and collaborate. However, it has also led to the proliferation of conspiracy theories, as the decentralized nature of the internet makes it difficult to discern credible information from misinformation.

Wilson's legacy is intertwined with this digital evolution. His embrace of computers and the internet as tools for expanding consciousness reflects his broader philosophy of open-mindedness and exploration. By engaging with digital technology, Wilson anticipated many of the challenges and opportunities that define our current information age.

As we navigate the complexities of the digital world, Wilson's work offers valuable insights into the interplay between belief, information, and reality. His model agnosticism encourages a critical and flexible approach to the information we encounter, reminding us to question our assumptions and remain open to multiple interpretations. In a time when misinformation and polarization are rampant, Wilson's teachings are particularly relevant, advocating for a more nuanced and thoughtful engagement with the world.

Moreover, the humor and absurdity central to Discordianism provide a counterbalance to the often grim and divisive nature of conspiracy theories. By embracing the chaotic and unpredictable aspects of existence, Discordianism encourages a sense of playfulness and resilience. This perspective can be particularly valuable in an era where information overload and digital manipulation are pervasive.

In conclusion, Robert Anton Wilson's contributions to Discordianism and conspiracy theory are deeply intertwined with the rise of digital technology. His work highlights the potential of computers to transform our understanding of reality, challenging us to think critically and embrace uncertainty. As we continue to grapple with the implications of the digital age, Wilson's ideas offer a framework for navigating the complex and interconnected landscape of information, belief, and perception. By fostering a spirit of open-mindedness and humor, Wilson's legacy encourages us to approach the world with curiosity and creativity, embracing the chaos and complexity that define our existence.

45 CYBERPUNK AND SPECULATIVE FICTION

William Gibson is a name that resonates profoundly in the realm of speculative fiction and cyberpunk. His narratives are rich with intricate details, profound insights into technology and society, and a keen sense of the future's potential and perils. Gibson's work is not merely about futuristic gadgets or dystopian landscapes; it's a deep dive into the human condition in an age where technology is both a liberator and a tyrant.

Gibson's journey into the literary world began with his debut novel, "Neuromancer," published in 1984. This groundbreaking work did not just catapult him to fame but also crystallized the cyberpunk genre. "Neuromancer" is a complex tapestry of high-tech and low-life, painting a world where advanced technology coexists with societal decay. The protagonist, Case, is a washed-up console cowboy—a computer hacker—who is hired for one last job. This novel introduced readers to the concept of "cyberspace," a term Gibson coined to describe a virtual reality dataspace, which has since become a fundamental idea in understanding the internet and digital worlds.

Gibson's narratives often explore the symbiotic and sometimes parasitic relationship between humanity and technology. In his works, technology is not a distant, abstract concept; it is deeply interwoven with the characters' lives and identities. The human body and mind are often depicted as malleable, subject to enhancement or degradation by technological advancements. This theme is evident in "Neuromancer," where Case's neural damage is repaired to enable him to jack into cyberspace, blurring the lines between human capabilities and machine potential.

The world Gibson constructs in "Neuromancer" is one of stark contrasts and juxtapositions. The Sprawl, a massive urban environment stretching from Boston to Atlanta, is a place where corporate power reigns supreme, and individual freedom is scarce. Yet, amidst this dystopian backdrop, there is a vibrant subculture of hackers, street samurai, and cybernetic enhancements. Gibson's depiction of this world is a commentary on the trajectory of contemporary society, where technological advancements often come hand in hand with increasing social stratification and corporate dominance.

One of Gibson's strengths is his ability to anticipate future technological trends and their implications. His work often prefigures real-world developments, making his speculative fiction remarkably prescient. In "Neuromancer," for instance, the concept of cyberspace predates the widespread use of the internet, and his portrayal of artificial intelligence and virtual realities has proven to be remarkably accurate. This foresight is not merely a product of Gibson's imagination but also his deep understanding of the cultural and technological currents of his time.

Gibson's influence extends beyond literature into popular culture and technology. His ideas have permeated various media, including films, music, and video games. The "Matrix" trilogy, for example, owes a significant debt to Gibson's vision of virtual reality and the concept of jacking into a simulated world. Similarly, his influence can be seen in the aesthetics and themes of numerous cyberpunk films and novels that followed in the wake of "Neuromancer."

Gibson's subsequent works, such as "Count Zero" and "Mona Lisa Overdrive," continue to explore the themes introduced in "Neuromancer," expanding on the world and its characters. In these novels, Gibson delves deeper into the implications of artificial intelligence, corporate power, and the evolving nature of identity in a technologically saturated world. His characters are often caught in the crossfire of competing interests, struggling to navigate a world where reality is increasingly mediated by technology.

In "Count Zero," Gibson shifts the focus from a single protagonist to a broader cast of characters, each with their own motivations and trajectories. This multiplicity of perspectives allows him to explore the cyberpunk world from different angles, highlighting the interconnectedness of individuals within the vast technological landscape. The novel's plot revolves around a series of seemingly unrelated events that gradually converge, revealing a complex web of intrigue and manipulation.

"Mona Lisa Overdrive," the final installment of the Sprawl trilogy, continues this trend of interwoven narratives. The novel's title itself is a nod to the collision of art and technology, a recurring motif in Gibson's work. The story follows multiple characters, including a cybernetically enhanced assassin, a young girl with extraordinary abilities, and a reclusive artist. Through their intertwined fates, Gibson explores themes of transformation, control, and the search for meaning in a world where the boundaries between the virtual and the real are increasingly blurred.

Gibson's exploration of these themes is not limited to the Sprawl trilogy. His later works, such as the Bridge trilogy ("Virtual Light," "Idoru," and "All Tomorrow's Parties"), continue to examine the impact of technology on society and individuals. In these novels, Gibson shifts his focus to a near-future setting, where the remnants of a massive earthquake have created a lawless zone known as the Bridge. This setting serves as a microcosm of the broader societal upheavals caused by rapid technological change.

"Virtual Light" introduces readers to a world where augmented reality glasses, known as "virtual light" glasses, have become ubiquitous. These devices allow users to overlay digital information onto the physical world, creating a seamless blend of reality and virtuality. The novel's protagonist, Berry Rydell, is a former police officer turned security guard who becomes embroiled in a conspiracy involving these glasses. Through Rydell's journey, Gibson examines the implications of augmented reality and the ways in which technology can both empower and enslave.

In "Idoru," Gibson delves into the world of virtual celebrities and artificial intelligence. The novel follows Colin Laney, a data analyst with a unique ability to identify patterns in vast amounts of information. Laney is hired to investigate the enigmatic Idoru, a virtual pop star who has gained a massive following. Gibson's portrayal of the Idoru raises questions about the nature of identity and the potential for artificial entities to become genuine cultural phenomena. The novel's exploration of these themes is particularly relevant in today's world, where virtual influencers and AI-generated content are becoming increasingly prevalent.

"All Tomorrow's Parties," the final novel in the Bridge trilogy, brings together characters from the previous books in a climactic convergence. The novel's title alludes to the idea of multiple possible futures, a theme that runs throughout Gibson's work. In "All Tomorrow's Parties," the characters must navigate a world on the brink of transformation, where old structures are collapsing, and new ones are emerging. Gibson's depiction of this transitional period is both hopeful and cautionary, reflecting his nuanced understanding of technological progress and its potential consequences.

Gibson's exploration of technology and society is not limited to the near future. In his more recent works, such as the Blue Ant trilogy ("Pattern Recognition," "Spook Country," and "Zero History"), he examines the present and near-present, highlighting the ways in which technology shapes our contemporary world. These novels are set in a post-9/11 world, where global surveillance, corporate espionage, and digital culture have become pervasive. Through the eyes of his protagonists, Gibson delves into the complexities of modern life, revealing the often unseen forces that shape our reality.

In "Pattern Recognition," the first novel of the Blue Ant trilogy, Gibson introduces readers to Cayce Pollard, a marketing consultant with an unusual sensitivity to branding and logos. Cayce is hired to investigate a series of mysterious video clips that have been circulating on the internet, capturing the attention of a global audience. Through Cayce's journey, Gibson explores the power of media and the ways in which digital content can influence perception and reality. The novel's exploration of these themes is particularly relevant in today's world, where viral videos and social media have become central to our cultural landscape.

"Spook Country" continues the story of the Blue Ant trilogy, following a new cast of characters as they navigate the murky waters of espionage and digital art. The novel's protagonist, Hollis Henry, is a former rock star turned journalist who becomes embroiled in a conspiracy involving locative art—an art form that uses augmented reality to create site-specific experiences. Through Hollis's journey, Gibson examines the intersection of art, technology, and surveillance, revealing the ways in which these forces shape our understanding of space and place.

"Zero History," the final novel in the Blue Ant trilogy, brings together characters from the previous books in a complex web of intrigue and deception. The novel's title alludes to the idea of a world where history is being constantly rewritten, a theme that resonates with Gibson's exploration of digital culture and its impact on memory and identity. Through the eyes of his protagonists, Gibson delves into the complexities of modern life, revealing the often unseen forces that shape our reality.

In conclusion, William Gibson's work is a profound exploration of the interplay between technology and humanity. His novels are not merely speculative fiction; they are insightful commentaries on the present and future, revealing the ways in which technology shapes our lives and identities. Through his intricate narratives and richly imagined worlds, Gibson challenges readers to confront the potential and perils of technological progress, urging us to consider the implications of our ever-evolving relationship with the digital age. His contributions to the cyberpunk genre and speculative fiction continue to inspire and provoke, cementing his legacy as one of the most influential voices in contemporary literature.

46 POSTCYBERPUNK AND DIGITAL CULTURE

Neal Stephenson stands as a towering figure in the realm of postcyberpunk literature, a genre that evolved from the foundational works of cyberpunk but pushed the boundaries further, exploring the nuanced relationship between humanity and technology in the digital age. Stephenson's narratives are rich tapestries woven with intricate plots, deep dives into digital culture, and a prescient understanding of the evolving technological landscape. His works not only entertain but also provoke thought about the direction in which our society is headed.

One of Stephenson's most acclaimed novels, "Snow Crash," published in 1992, is a seminal work in postcyberpunk literature. It combines elements of action, satire, and deep technological speculation to create a narrative that is both thrilling and intellectually stimulating. The protagonist, Hiro Protagonist, is a hacker and pizza delivery driver in a dystopian future where the United States has fragmented into corporate city-states. The novel's title refers to a computer virus that infects both machines and humans, blurring the lines between the virtual and the physical. This concept of a virus that operates on multiple levels is a hallmark of Stephenson's ability to envision complex interactions between technology and society.

In "Snow Crash," Stephenson explores the Metaverse, a virtual reality successor to the internet. The Metaverse is a fully immersive digital space where people interact through avatars, conducting business, socializing, and even fighting in virtual duels. This concept has proven remarkably prescient, as it prefigures modern discussions about virtual reality, augmented reality, and the potential future of the internet. Stephenson's depiction of the Metaverse has inspired numerous technologies and platforms, including the development of virtual worlds and the concept of the "metaverse" that is now a buzzword in tech circles.

The themes in "Snow Crash" extend beyond technology into a critique of corporate power and cultural fragmentation. Stephenson portrays a world where governments have largely been supplanted by powerful corporations and private entities. This vision resonates with contemporary concerns about the influence of big tech companies and the erosion of public institutions. By extrapolating current trends into a hyperbolic future, Stephenson offers a cautionary tale about the potential consequences of unchecked corporate power.

Stephenson's ability to blend speculative fiction with sharp social commentary is also evident in "The Diamond Age: Or, A Young Lady's Illustrated Primer." Published in 1995, this novel explores nanotechnology and its implications for society. The story is set in a future where nanotechnology has transformed every aspect of life, from medicine to manufacturing. The protagonist, Nell, is a young girl who comes into possession of an interactive book designed to educate and empower her. This "primer" adapts to Nell's needs, teaching her survival skills and intellectual independence in a world divided by technological access and social class.

"The Diamond Age" delves into themes of education, empowerment, and the digital divide. Stephenson imagines a future where access to advanced technology determines one's social and economic mobility. The primer represents an ideal of personalized education, a tool that can bridge the gap between the privileged and the underprivileged. This concept is particularly relevant today, as debates about digital equity and the role of technology in education continue to evolve. Stephenson's vision of nanotechnology's potential, both utopian and dystopian, reflects his nuanced understanding of how technological advancements can both liberate and constrain.

Another significant work in Stephenson's oeuvre is "Cryptonomicon," published in 1999. This sprawling novel weaves together multiple timelines, exploring the connections between World War II codebreakers and modern-day cryptography enthusiasts. The novel's protagonists include Lawrence Waterhouse, a mathematical genius working on Allied cryptographic efforts during the war, and his grandson, Randy Waterhouse, who is involved in a contemporary project to create a data haven in Southeast Asia. The dual narratives highlight the enduring importance of cryptography and information security, themes that are increasingly relevant in today's digital age.

"Cryptonomicon" delves into the intricacies of cryptography, finance, and the power of information. Stephenson's meticulous research and detailed descriptions bring these complex subjects to life, making them accessible to readers without sacrificing their depth. The novel explores the idea that information is the ultimate currency, a concept that has only grown more pertinent as data has become a critical asset in the digital economy. Stephenson's exploration of these themes reflects his ability to anticipate the profound impact of digital culture on society and economics.

In "The Baroque Cycle," a trilogy comprising "Quicksilver," "The Confusion," and "The System of the World," Stephenson takes readers on a journey through the scientific and political revolutions of the 17th and 18th centuries. This historical fiction series is a departure from his more futuristic works but retains his signature blend of rich detail and complex plotting. The trilogy follows a diverse cast of characters, including historical figures like Isaac Newton and fictional adventurers like Jack Shaftoe. Through their stories, Stephenson explores the birth of modern science, the evolution of financial systems, and the interplay between technology and society.

"The Baroque Cycle" exemplifies Stephenson's ability to blend historical fiction with speculative elements, creating a narrative that is both educational and entertaining. His portrayal of the scientific revolution highlights the transformative power of knowledge and innovation. The trilogy's exploration of early financial markets and the development of the modern economy provides a historical context for understanding contemporary financial systems. Stephenson's meticulous attention to historical detail and his ability to weave complex narratives make "The Baroque Cycle" a landmark achievement in speculative fiction.

Stephenson's later works, such as "Anathem," "Reamde," and "Seveneves," continue to explore the intersections of technology, society, and culture. "Anathem," published in 2008, is a philosophical science fiction novel set on a parallel Earth where intellectuals live in monastic seclusion, dedicating themselves to the pursuit of knowledge. The novel's protagonist, Erasmus, embarks on a journey that challenges his understanding of reality and the nature of the universe. "Anathem" delves into themes of consciousness, cosmology, and the pursuit of truth, reflecting Stephenson's deep engagement with philosophical and scientific questions.

"Reamde," published in 2011, is a techno-thriller that explores the world of online gaming, cybercrime, and international intrigue. The novel's protagonist, Richard Forthrast, is the creator of a massively multiplayer online role-playing game (MMORPG) that becomes the target of a ransomware attack. The novel's fast-paced plot and complex characters reflect Stephenson's ability to craft compelling narratives that are deeply rooted in contemporary digital culture. "Reamde" examines the blurred lines between virtual and real-world conflicts, highlighting the ways in which digital environments can have tangible consequences.

In "Seveneves," published in 2015, Stephenson tackles the theme of human survival in the face of catastrophic events. The novel begins with the destruction of the moon, which triggers a chain of events that threatens to annihilate life on Earth. The story follows a diverse group of characters as they attempt to ensure the survival of the human race by creating a space-based refuge. "Seveneves" explores themes of resilience, innovation, and the enduring human spirit. Stephenson's meticulous attention to scientific detail and his ability to envision complex technological solutions make "Seveneves" a compelling exploration of humanity's potential to overcome existential threats.

Throughout his body of work, Stephenson has consistently demonstrated an ability to anticipate and engage with emerging technologies and cultural trends. His novels are not just speculative fiction; they are explorations of the human condition in a digital age. Stephenson's characters grapple with the implications of technological advancements, navigating worlds where the lines between reality and virtuality, human and machine, are increasingly blurred. His works challenge readers to think critically about the role of technology in shaping our future and to consider the ethical and societal implications of our digital age.

Neal Stephenson's influence extends beyond literature into the broader cultural and technological landscape. His ideas have inspired technologists, entrepreneurs, and futurists, contributing to ongoing discussions about the future of technology and society. Stephenson's ability to blend detailed technical knowledge with rich storytelling makes his work a valuable resource for understanding the complex interplay between technology and culture. As we continue to navigate the challenges and opportunities of the digital age, Stephenson's insights and narratives remain as relevant and thought-provoking as ever. His contributions to postcyberpunk literature and digital culture have cemented his legacy as one of the most influential and visionary writers of our time.

47 TRANSREALISM AND THE SINGULARITY

Rudy Rucker is a seminal figure in the field of speculative fiction, known for his unique approach to storytelling that blends elements of transrealism and singularity. His work often defies conventional genre boundaries, weaving together scientific concepts, philosophical inquiries, and deeply personal experiences. Rucker's narratives are characterized by their inventive use of technology and their exploration of the human condition through the lens of transrealism—a term he coined to describe fiction that incorporates autobiographical elements and fantastical elements in a seamless and transformative way.

Rucker's journey into the literary world began with his early works in the 1980s, where he established himself as a distinctive voice in speculative fiction. One of his most influential novels, "Software," published in 1982, is the first book in his "Ware" series. This novel introduces readers to Cobb Anderson, a retired computer scientist who created intelligent robots called boppers. The boppers, now living on the moon, have developed their own society and plan to offer immortality to humans by uploading their consciousness into robotic bodies. This concept of mind uploading and the exploration of artificial intelligence were groundbreaking at the time and continue to resonate in contemporary discussions about the future of human-machine integration.

"Software" is a vivid example of Rucker's ability to blend complex scientific ideas with compelling storytelling. The novel delves into themes of identity, consciousness, and the nature of life itself. By presenting a future where humans can transcend their biological limitations through technology, Rucker invites readers to ponder the ethical and philosophical implications of such advancements. The novel's exploration of the singularity—the hypothetical point in the future when technological growth becomes uncontrollable and irreversible, leading to unfathomable changes in human civilization—is both thought-provoking and prescient.

Rucker's exploration of the singularity continues in the subsequent books of the "Ware" series, including "Wetware," "Freeware," and "Realware." In "Wetware," published in 1988, Rucker delves deeper into the complexities of human-robot relationships and the potential for biological enhancement. The novel explores the concept of wetware—organic material that integrates with electronic systems—highlighting the blurred lines between organic and artificial life. Rucker's vivid descriptions and imaginative scenarios challenge readers to reconsider their understanding of what it means to be alive and conscious in a technologically advanced world.

"Freeware," published in 1997, expands on these themes by exploring the societal implications of widespread access to advanced technology. The novel depicts a future where people can modify their bodies and minds at will, creating a diverse and dynamic society. Rucker's depiction of this world is both utopian and dystopian, reflecting his nuanced understanding of the potential benefits and risks of technological progress. The characters in "Freeware" grapple with issues of identity, freedom, and the impact of technology on human relationships, providing a rich and multifaceted narrative that continues to resonate with readers.

In "Realware," the final book in the series, Rucker explores the concept of reality itself. Published in 2000, the novel delves into the nature of perception and the potential for technology to alter our understanding of the world. Rucker's imaginative scenarios and thought-provoking questions challenge readers to consider the implications of a reality that can be manipulated and transformed through technology. The "Ware" series as a whole is a testament to Rucker's ability to blend scientific speculation with deeply human themes, creating narratives that are both intellectually stimulating and emotionally engaging.

Rucker's contributions to transrealism are not limited to the "Ware" series. His novel "White Light," published in 1980, is a pioneering work in the genre, blending autobiographical elements with fantastical scenarios to explore the nature of reality and consciousness. The novel follows Felix Rayman, a mathematician who embarks on a journey through a multidimensional universe. Rucker's use of mathematical concepts and philosophical inquiries creates a rich and immersive narrative that challenges readers to reconsider their understanding of reality and the limits of human perception.

In "Spacetime Donuts," published in 1981, Rucker continues to explore the intersections of science and fiction. The novel presents a world where people can transform themselves into higher-dimensional beings, exploring the nature of existence and the potential for transcendence through technology. Rucker's imaginative scenarios and inventive use of scientific concepts create a narrative that is both entertaining and intellectually stimulating. His ability to blend personal experiences with speculative elements creates a unique and engaging storytelling style that has become a hallmark of his work.

Rucker's exploration of the singularity and transrealism extends beyond his novels into his short stories and essays. His collection "Gnarl!" published in 2000, features a diverse array of stories that explore the complexities of human existence in a technologically advanced world. Rucker's vivid imagination and deep understanding of scientific concepts create narratives that are both thought-provoking and entertaining. His essays, collected in "Seek!," published in 1999, offer insights into his creative process and the philosophical underpinnings of his work. Rucker's ability to blend scientific inquiry with personal reflection creates a rich and multifaceted body of work that continues to inspire readers and writers alike.

One of Rucker's most significant contributions to the field of speculative fiction is his ability to anticipate and explore emerging technological trends. His novel "Postsingular," published in 2007, presents a future where nanotechnology has transformed every aspect of life. The novel explores the concept of the singularity and its implications for humanity, delving into themes of identity, consciousness, and the nature of reality. Rucker's imaginative scenarios and vivid descriptions create a rich and immersive narrative that challenges readers to consider the potential impact of advanced technology on human civilization.

In "Hylozoic," the sequel to "Postsingular," published in 2009, Rucker continues to explore the implications of a world transformed by nanotechnology. The novel presents a future where all matter is sentient, creating a dynamic and interconnected universe. Rucker's exploration of this concept highlights his ability to blend scientific speculation with deeply human themes, creating narratives that are both intellectually stimulating and emotionally engaging. His vivid imagination and inventive use of scientific concepts create a unique and compelling vision of the future.

Rucker's contributions to speculative fiction extend beyond his writing into his work as a teacher and mentor. As a professor of computer science, Rucker has influenced a generation of students and writers, sharing his knowledge and passion for science and storytelling. His ability to blend scientific inquiry with creative expression has inspired countless readers and writers to explore the intersections of technology and humanity. Rucker's work as a teacher and mentor reflects his commitment to fostering creativity and innovation in the field of speculative fiction.

Rucker's influence can be seen in the work of contemporary writers and thinkers who continue to explore the themes of transrealism and the singularity. His imaginative scenarios and thought-provoking questions have inspired a new generation of writers to consider the implications of advanced technology for human civilization. Rucker's ability to blend scientific speculation with deeply human themes creates a rich and multifaceted body of work that continues to resonate with readers and writers alike.

In conclusion, Rudy Rucker's contributions to the field of speculative fiction are both profound and far-reaching. His unique approach to storytelling, blending elements of transrealism and the singularity, creates narratives that are both intellectually stimulating and emotionally engaging. Rucker's exploration of the intersections of technology and humanity challenges readers to consider the implications of advanced technology for human civilization. His vivid imagination, deep understanding of scientific concepts, and ability to blend personal experiences with speculative elements create a rich and multifaceted body of work that continues to inspire and provoke thought. As we continue to navigate the complexities of the digital age, Rucker's insights and narratives remain as relevant and thought-provoking as ever. His contributions to transrealism and the singularity have cemented his legacy as one of the most influential and visionary writers in the field of speculative fiction.

48 ECSTASY AND DEPRAVITY

In the gritty underbelly of modern society, where the neon lights of the city clash with the shadows of human depravity, Irvine Welsh's world unfolds. His narratives often delve into the darkest recesses of the human psyche, revealing a landscape marred by vice, addiction, and the relentless pursuit of euphoria. Welsh's novel "Ecstasy" is no exception, presenting a raw and unfiltered glimpse into the lives of individuals ensnared by the seductive allure of drugs and the chaos that ensues.

In "Ecstasy," Welsh explores the intricate dynamics of addiction, love, and the lengths to which people go to escape the banality of their everyday existence. The novel is a triptych of stories, each interconnected by the common threads of ecstasy and the consequences of its pursuit. Welsh's characters are not mere figments of imagination but rather reflections of the real people who populate the underbelly of society—flawed, broken, and yet, in their own way, deeply human.

The first story introduces us to Lloyd, a young man whose life revolves around the pulsating beats of rave culture and the euphoric highs of ecstasy. For Lloyd, the drug is more than just a means of escape; it's a gateway to a world where everything seems possible, where the mundane dissolves into a kaleidoscope of sensory overload. Yet, as the euphoria wanes, the harsh reality of his existence comes crashing down. Lloyd's journey is a poignant reminder of the transient nature of happiness and the price one pays for chasing the ultimate high.

Welsh's depiction of Lloyd's descent into addiction is unflinching, a stark portrayal of the human cost of drug abuse. Lloyd's relationships crumble, his sense of self erodes, and the once-bright future dims under the weight of his dependencies. The narrative is a brutal exploration of how ecstasy, both the drug and the emotion, can lead to a cycle of destruction that is difficult to break. Welsh's prose is visceral, each sentence a punch to the gut, leaving the reader both horrified and empathetic towards Lloyd's plight.

The second story shifts focus to Heather, a woman trapped in a loveless marriage with a controlling husband. Heather's life is a monotonous routine, devoid of passion and excitement. In her quest for liberation, she turns to ecstasy, seeking a reprieve from her oppressive reality. The drug offers her a taste of freedom, a brief moment of transcendence that allows her to rediscover her sense of self. However, this newfound freedom comes with its own set of challenges, as Heather grapples with the repercussions of her choices.

Welsh masterfully captures Heather's inner turmoil, her struggle to balance the fleeting joy of ecstasy with the long-term consequences of her actions. The narrative delves into the complexities of addiction, illustrating how the drug becomes both a source of solace and a catalyst for further despair. Heather's journey is a testament to the resilience of the human spirit, a stark reminder that even in the darkest of times, there is a glimmer of hope. Yet, Welsh does not offer easy solutions; instead, he presents a nuanced portrayal of addiction and recovery, one that is fraught with setbacks and moments of doubt.

The final story centers around a pharmaceutical executive, Samantha, whose life is a paradox of luxury and emptiness. On the surface, Samantha has it all—wealth, power, and prestige—but beneath the veneer of success lies a profound sense of dissatisfaction. Her life is a carefully constructed facade, masking the void within. In her quest for meaning, Samantha becomes involved in the development and distribution of a new designer drug, one that promises to revolutionize the world of recreational substances.

As Samantha delves deeper into the world of drug production, she is confronted with the ethical and moral dilemmas of her actions. Welsh paints a vivid picture of the corporate machinations and the human cost of the drug trade, highlighting the stark contrast between the pursuit of profit and the impact on individual lives. Samantha's journey is a sobering exploration of the consequences of unchecked ambition and the ways in which the pursuit of ecstasy can lead to both personal and societal downfall.

Through these interwoven narratives, Welsh constructs a tapestry of human experience, one that is rich in detail and unrelenting in its honesty. His characters are not heroes or villains but ordinary people caught in extraordinary circumstances. Welsh's writing is imbued with a sense of authenticity, each character's voice distinct and resonant, capturing the essence of their struggles and triumphs. The novel's structure allows for a multifaceted exploration of ecstasy, both as a drug and as a concept, revealing the myriad ways in which it shapes and distorts lives.

Welsh's portrayal of ecstasy is not merely confined to the realm of drug use; it extends to the broader human experience, encompassing the highs and lows of love, desire, and the quest for fulfillment. The novel is a meditation on the nature of happiness and the lengths to which people will go to attain it. Welsh's characters are united by their yearning for something more, something that transcends the ordinary and elevates them to a higher plane of existence. Yet, as the novel illustrates, this pursuit often comes at a great cost, one that is borne by the individual and society alike.

In "Ecstasy," Welsh does not shy away from depicting the darker aspects of human nature. His characters engage in acts of depravity, driven by their addictions and desires. The novel is rife with scenes of debauchery and excess, a reflection of the hedonistic impulses that drive human behavior. Welsh's writing is unapologetically graphic, his descriptions vivid and often unsettling, forcing the reader to confront the raw reality of addiction and its consequences.

Yet, amidst the darkness, there are moments of poignancy and beauty. Welsh's characters, despite their flaws and failings, are capable of love and redemption. The novel's exploration of the human condition is both brutal and compassionate, offering a glimpse into the depths of despair and the possibility of renewal. Welsh's ability to capture the complexity of human emotions is a testament to his skill as a writer, his prose both lyrical and hard-hitting.

"Ecstasy" is a novel that defies easy categorization. It is a work that challenges the reader to question their own perceptions of happiness and the means by which it is achieved. Welsh's unflinching portrayal of addiction and its impact on individuals and society is a powerful reminder of the fragility of the human spirit and the enduring quest for meaning. Through his characters, Welsh presents a stark yet empathetic view of the world, one that is both deeply unsettling and profoundly moving.

In the end, "Ecstasy" is a testament to the power of storytelling, a narrative that captures the essence of the human experience in all its messy, chaotic glory. Welsh's characters, flawed and broken, are a reflection of ourselves, their struggles and triumphs a mirror to our own. The novel is a journey into the heart of darkness, but it is also a celebration of the resilience of the human spirit and the enduring quest for something more. In Welsh's hands, the story of ecstasy becomes a powerful exploration of the human condition, a reminder that even in the depths of despair, there is always the possibility of redemption.

49 MYTHOLOGY AND STORYTELLING IN MODERN FICTION

Neil Gaiman, an iconic figure in contemporary literature, has an exceptional ability to weave mythology and storytelling into the fabric of modern fiction. His works are a testament to the enduring power of myth, demonstrating how ancient narratives can be revitalized and made relevant for today's readers. Gaiman's storytelling prowess lies in his deep understanding of mythological archetypes and his skillful adaptation of these elements into narratives that resonate with contemporary sensibilities.

Gaiman's fascination with mythology is evident in many of his works, most notably in "American Gods" and "The Sandman" series. In "American Gods," he creates a narrative where ancient deities coexist with modern gods, each representing different facets of contemporary life. This novel explores the shifting nature of belief and the way myths adapt to new contexts. The protagonist, Shadow Moon, finds himself entangled in a war between the old gods, who struggle to maintain their relevance, and the new gods, who symbolize modern obsessions such as media and technology. Through this conflict, Gaiman examines the resilience of myth and its ability to reflect and critique modern society.

"The Sandman" series, a cornerstone of graphic novel literature, further exemplifies Gaiman's mastery of mythological storytelling. The central character, Dream, is one of the Endless, a group of anthropomorphic beings who personify fundamental aspects of existence. Throughout the series, Gaiman intertwines various mythologies, folklore, and literary references, creating a rich tapestry that spans multiple dimensions and epochs. The character of Dream, also known as Morpheus, embodies the archetype of the ruler of the dream realm, drawing from diverse mythological traditions while remaining a distinctly modern creation. This blending of old and new allows Gaiman to explore themes of identity, destiny, and transformation in a deeply resonant manner.

Gaiman's approach to mythology is not merely about retelling ancient stories but about reinterpreting and recontextualizing them to speak to contemporary issues. His novel "Norse Mythology" is a retelling of the Norse myths, where he brings the tales of Odin, Thor, Loki, and other gods to life with his signature narrative voice. While remaining faithful to the original myths, Gaiman infuses them with a modern sensibility, making them accessible and engaging for a new generation of readers. This work highlights his belief that myths are not static relics of the past but living stories that can evolve and inspire.

In "Good Omens," co-authored with Terry Pratchett, Gaiman delves into the realm of religious mythology, blending it with humor and satire. The novel reimagines the biblical apocalypse, featuring an angel and a demon who team up to prevent the end of the world. Through this comedic and thought-provoking narrative, Gaiman and Pratchett explore themes of free will, morality, and the nature of good and evil. The playful use of religious mythology in "Good Omens" showcases Gaiman's ability to balance reverence for traditional stories with a willingness to subvert and reinterpret them.

Gaiman's storytelling is characterized by a deep empathy for his characters and a profound understanding of human nature. This empathy allows him to create complex, multidimensional characters who embody mythological archetypes while also being relatable to modern readers. In "Coraline," for instance, the titular character embarks on a journey that mirrors the hero's quest found in many myths. However, Coraline's story is uniquely her own, rooted in the fears and challenges of childhood. Gaiman uses the framework of myth to explore themes of bravery, identity, and the search for belonging, making Coraline's journey both timeless and deeply personal.

One of the hallmarks of Gaiman's work is his seamless blending of the mundane and the fantastical. He often sets his stories in familiar, contemporary settings, only to introduce elements of magic and myth that transform the ordinary into the extraordinary. This technique is evident in "Neverwhere," where the protagonist, Richard Mayhew, discovers a hidden, fantastical London beneath the streets of the city he thought he knew. Gaiman's ability to reveal the magical potential of everyday life underscores his belief in the power of stories to transform our perception of reality.

Gaiman's influence extends beyond his own writing; he is also an advocate for the importance of storytelling and myth in education and culture. In his speeches and essays, he frequently emphasizes the need for imagination and creativity in nurturing a literate and empathetic society. Gaiman believes that myths and stories are fundamental to our understanding of the world and ourselves, serving as tools for exploring complex ideas and emotions. His advocacy for the role of libraries and reading in personal and societal growth further underscores his commitment to the transformative power of stories.

In addition to his novels and graphic novels, Gaiman's work in other media, such as film, television, and theater, continues to expand the reach of his mythological storytelling. His adaptation of "American Gods" into a television series brought the novel's exploration of myth and modernity to a broader audience, while his work on films like "Stardust" and "Coraline" has introduced his unique blend of fantasy and mythology to viewers of all ages. These adaptations demonstrate Gaiman's versatility as a storyteller and his ability to translate the essence of myth into various forms of media.

Gaiman's storytelling is also marked by a profound respect for the source material of the myths he reinterprets. He approaches these ancient stories with a scholar's curiosity and a storyteller's imagination, seeking to preserve their core while making them resonate with contemporary audiences. This balance of fidelity and innovation is a key aspect of his success in bringing mythology to modern fiction. Gaiman's meticulous research and thoughtful adaptation process ensure that his retellings are both authentic and original, offering readers a fresh perspective on familiar tales.

Furthermore, Gaiman's engagement with mythology often involves a dialogue with his readers, encouraging them to explore and reinterpret these stories for themselves. He recognizes that myths are collective narratives, shaped by the contributions of many storytellers over time. By inviting readers into this ongoing conversation, Gaiman fosters a sense of shared ownership and participation in the storytelling process. This interactive approach to myth and storytelling reflects his belief in the communal nature of stories and their ability to connect people across time and space.

In conclusion, Neil Gaiman's integration of mythology and storytelling in modern fiction exemplifies the enduring relevance of ancient narratives in contemporary culture. Through his novels, graphic novels, and adaptations, Gaiman revitalizes myths, making them accessible and meaningful for today's readers. His empathetic characterizations, seamless blending of the mundane and the fantastical, and commitment to the transformative power of stories underscore his unique contribution to literature. Gaiman's work not only entertains but also invites readers to explore the depths of myth and imagination, enriching their understanding of the world and themselves.

50 AI BOOM AND ARCHITECTURE

Sam Altman, a name synonymous with innovation and foresight in the realm of artificial intelligence, has played a pivotal role in the AI boom that is reshaping various industries, including architecture. As the CEO of OpenAI, Altman has been instrumental in driving the development of advanced AI models that are not only transforming how we interact with technology but also revolutionizing fields that have traditionally been dominated by human creativity and expertise.

The AI boom, characterized by rapid advancements in machine learning and neural networks, has permeated the architecture industry in profound ways. Traditionally, architecture has been a discipline that combines art and science to create functional and aesthetically pleasing structures. However, the integration of AI is pushing the boundaries of what is possible, enabling architects to explore new forms, optimize designs, and enhance the overall efficiency of their projects.

One of the most significant impacts of AI in architecture is in the area of design optimization. Neural networks can analyze vast amounts of data, including historical building designs, environmental conditions, and user preferences, to generate innovative solutions that meet specific criteria. For instance, AI can suggest the most efficient spatial layouts, materials, and construction methods to minimize costs and environmental impact while maximizing functionality and aesthetic appeal. This capability allows architects to make data-driven decisions that enhance the quality and sustainability of their designs.

Moreover, AI-powered tools can assist architects in the early stages of design by generating multiple design iterations based on predefined parameters. This process, known as generative design, involves creating numerous design options and refining them through iterative cycles until the optimal solution is found. By automating this labor-intensive process, AI frees up architects to focus on more creative and strategic aspects of their projects. Generative design not only accelerates the design process but also opens up new possibilities for innovation, as AI can explore design solutions that may not have been considered by human designers.

The integration of AI in architecture also extends to the construction phase. AI algorithms can predict potential challenges and inefficiencies in construction projects, allowing for proactive measures to be taken to mitigate risks. For example, AI can analyze construction schedules, resource allocation, and site conditions to optimize project timelines and reduce delays. This predictive capability is particularly valuable in large-scale projects where even minor delays can lead to significant cost overruns.

Another area where AI is making a substantial impact is in the realm of sustainability. As the world grapples with the effects of climate change, the need for sustainable building practices has never been more urgent. AI can analyze environmental data to design buildings that are energy-efficient and environmentally friendly. For instance, AI can optimize building orientation, window placement, and insulation materials to reduce energy consumption and improve indoor air quality. Additionally, AI can monitor and manage building systems in real-time, ensuring that they operate at peak efficiency and reducing the building's overall carbon footprint.

The use of AI in architecture is not limited to new construction projects. It is also being applied to the renovation and retrofitting of existing structures. AI can assess the structural integrity of older buildings, identify areas that require reinforcement, and suggest the most effective renovation strategies. This capability is particularly valuable in preserving historical buildings, where maintaining the original architectural features while ensuring modern safety standards is a delicate balance. By leveraging AI, architects can develop renovation plans that honor the building's heritage while enhancing its functionality and safety.

One of the most exciting aspects of the AI boom in architecture is its potential to democratize the field. AI-powered design tools can make sophisticated architectural capabilities accessible to a broader audience, including non-experts. For instance, individuals and small businesses can use AI tools to design their own spaces without needing extensive architectural knowledge. This democratization of design empowers more people to engage in the creative process and realize their vision for their environments.

Despite the numerous benefits of AI in architecture, there are also challenges and ethical considerations that need to be addressed. One of the primary concerns is the potential displacement of human labor. As AI takes on more tasks traditionally performed by architects and construction workers, there is a risk of job loss and economic disruption. It is essential to ensure that the integration of AI in architecture is managed in a way that complements human skills rather than replaces them. This may involve retraining and upskilling workers to adapt to new roles in an AI-enhanced industry.

Another ethical consideration is the issue of data privacy and security. AI systems rely on vast amounts of data to function effectively, and the architecture industry is no exception. Ensuring that this data is collected, stored, and used responsibly is crucial to maintaining public trust. Additionally, there is a need for transparency in how AI algorithms make decisions, particularly in areas that affect public safety and well-being. Architects and AI developers must work together to establish guidelines and standards that promote ethical AI use in the industry.

Sam Altman's vision for AI and its potential to transform industries is being realized in the architectural field. His leadership at OpenAI has been instrumental in developing advanced AI models that are now being applied to architectural design, construction, and sustainability. The AI boom is enabling architects to push the boundaries of creativity, efficiency, and sustainability, resulting in buildings that are not only aesthetically pleasing but also environmentally friendly and cost-effective.

As we look to the future, the continued integration of AI in architecture promises to bring even more innovations and advancements. Emerging technologies such as augmented reality (AR) and virtual reality (VR) are likely to further enhance the design process, allowing architects and clients to visualize and interact with their projects in immersive ways. AI-driven smart buildings, equipped with sensors and automated systems, will become more prevalent, offering enhanced comfort, security, and energy efficiency.

The evolution of AI in architecture is a testament to the transformative power of technology and the vision of leaders like Sam Altman. By harnessing the capabilities of AI, the architecture industry is entering a new era of innovation and possibility. As we navigate this exciting frontier, it is essential to balance technological advancements with ethical considerations, ensuring that the benefits of AI are realized in a way that enhances human creativity and well-being.

In conclusion, the AI boom, driven by pioneers like Sam Altman, is reshaping the architecture industry in profound ways. From design optimization and generative design to sustainability and construction management, AI is enabling architects to achieve new levels of efficiency, creativity, and environmental responsibility. As we embrace these advancements, it is crucial to address the ethical challenges and ensure that AI serves as a tool to enhance human potential rather than replace it. The future of architecture, powered by AI, promises to be an exciting and transformative journey, redefining the way we design and interact with our built environment.

51 THE SINGULARITY AND ARTIFICIAL INTELLIGENCE

Ray Kurzweil, a renowned futurist and inventor, has long been an advocate for the potential of artificial intelligence (AI) to revolutionize human existence. His vision is centered around the concept of the singularity, a hypothetical future point at which technological growth becomes uncontrollable and irreversible, resulting in unforeseeable changes to human civilization. Kurzweil's ideas about the singularity are rooted in his belief in the Law of Accelerating Returns, which posits that the rate of technological progress is exponential, not linear. According to Kurzweil, this exponential growth means that advancements in AI and other technologies will occur at an increasingly rapid pace, leading to a future where machines surpass human intelligence.

Kurzweil's predictions about the singularity are both ambitious and controversial. He envisions a world where AI becomes deeply integrated into every aspect of human life, fundamentally altering our bodies, minds, and societies. One of the key milestones in this journey, according to Kurzweil, is the development of strong AI, also known as artificial general intelligence (AGI). Unlike current AI systems, which are designed for specific tasks, AGI would possess the ability to understand, learn, and apply knowledge across a wide range of domains, much like a human being. Kurzweil believes that we are on the cusp of achieving AGI and that its arrival will catalyze the singularity.

One of the most significant implications of the singularity is the potential for AI to enhance human intelligence. Kurzweil foresees a future where humans and machines merge, creating a hybrid intelligence that far surpasses the capabilities of our current biological brains. This concept, often referred to as the "cyborg" or "transhumanist" vision, involves the use of technologies such as brain-computer interfaces and neural implants to augment human cognition. Kurzweil predicts that by the 2030s, we will begin to see the widespread adoption of these technologies, enabling us to connect our brains directly to the cloud, access vast amounts of information instantaneously, and communicate telepathically.

The implications of such enhancements are profound. Kurzweil suggests that augmented intelligence could lead to dramatic improvements in memory, learning, and problem-solving abilities. This, in turn, could accelerate scientific and technological innovation, leading to breakthroughs in fields such as medicine, energy, and space exploration. Furthermore, Kurzweil believes that the merging of human and machine intelligence will enable us to transcend our biological limitations, potentially extending human lifespans indefinitely. He is a proponent of the idea that death is a solvable problem and that advances in biotechnology and AI could ultimately lead to the elimination of aging and disease.

However, Kurzweil's vision of the singularity is not without its critics. Some experts argue that his timeline for achieving AGI and the singularity is overly optimistic, pointing to the significant technical and ethical challenges that remain. Developing AGI requires not only significant advancements in computational power and algorithms but also a deeper understanding of human cognition and consciousness. Critics also raise concerns about the potential risks associated with creating machines that surpass human intelligence. There is the possibility that such machines could act in ways that are unpredictable or harmful, leading to scenarios where humans lose control over AI systems.

In response to these concerns, Kurzweil emphasizes the importance of ethical considerations and the need for rigorous oversight in the development of AI technologies. He advocates for the establishment of guidelines and frameworks to ensure that AI is developed and deployed in ways that are safe, transparent, and aligned with human values. Kurzweil is optimistic that with careful planning and collaboration, we can harness the power of AI to create a future that is beneficial for all of humanity.

Another critical aspect of Kurzweil's vision is the impact of AI on the economy and the nature of work. As AI and automation technologies continue to advance, there is growing concern about the displacement of human jobs and the potential for widespread unemployment. Kurzweil acknowledges these challenges but argues that the singularity will also create new opportunities and industries that we cannot yet imagine. He envisions a future where AI takes over routine and mundane tasks, freeing humans to focus on more creative, strategic, and fulfilling work.

This transition, according to Kurzweil, will require significant adjustments in education and workforce training, as well as social and economic policies to support those affected by automation.

Kurzweil also explores the philosophical and existential implications of the singularity. The idea of merging with machines and achieving digital immortality raises profound questions about the nature of identity, consciousness, and what it means to be human. Kurzweil believes that as we integrate more closely with technology, we will need to rethink our definitions of self and society. He suggests that the singularity will lead to a new era of human evolution, where our biological and digital selves become intertwined, creating a collective intelligence that transcends individual limitations.

The concept of the singularity has inspired significant debate and speculation, both within the scientific community and in popular culture. While some view Kurzweil's predictions as overly speculative or even utopian, others see them as a plausible extension of current technological trends. Regardless of one's perspective, Kurzweil's ideas have undoubtedly sparked important conversations about the future of AI and its potential to transform human society.

Kurzweil's contributions to the field of AI extend beyond his predictions about the singularity. As an inventor and entrepreneur, he has played a key role in advancing technologies that have practical applications today. His work on speech recognition, optical character recognition, and text-to-speech synthesis has had a significant impact on industries ranging from healthcare to education to entertainment. Kurzweil's inventions have made it possible for people with disabilities to access information and communicate more effectively, demonstrating the positive potential of AI to improve human lives.

In addition to his technological innovations, Kurzweil is also a prolific author and speaker, sharing his vision of the future with audiences around the world. His books, including "The Singularity Is Near" and "How to Create a Mind," have become influential works in the field of futurism and have inspired many to explore the possibilities of AI and the singularity. Through his writing and public speaking, Kurzweil seeks to demystify complex technological concepts and make them accessible to a broader audience, encouraging more people to engage with and shape the future of AI.

Kurzweil's optimism about the potential of AI is grounded in his belief in the inherent creativity and resilience of humanity. He argues that throughout history, humans have continually adapted to new technologies and used them to overcome challenges and improve their quality of life. Kurzweil sees the singularity as the next chapter in this ongoing story, a transformative moment that will unlock unprecedented opportunities for human progress. He envisions a future where AI enhances our abilities, extends our lifespans, and enables us to explore and understand the universe in ways that are currently beyond our reach.

As we move closer to the singularity, the questions and challenges raised by Kurzweil's vision will become increasingly relevant. The rapid pace of technological advancement demands thoughtful and proactive engagement from scientists, policymakers, and society as a whole. By exploring the potential benefits and risks of AI, we can work towards a future that harnesses the power of these technologies to create a more just, equitable, and prosperous world.

In conclusion, Ray Kurzweil's vision of the singularity and the future of artificial intelligence presents both exciting possibilities and significant challenges. His predictions about the exponential growth of technology and the potential for merging human and machine intelligence have sparked important discussions about the future of humanity. While there are valid concerns about the feasibility and risks of achieving the singularity, Kurzweil's optimistic outlook serves as a reminder of the transformative power of human ingenuity and the potential for AI to enhance our lives in profound ways. As we navigate the complexities of this technological frontier, Kurzweil's ideas provide a valuable framework for thinking about the future and the role of AI in shaping our destiny.

SECTION SIX

SPECIAL TOPICS AND INTERDISCIPLINARY STUDIES

Special topics and interdisciplinary studies have always intrigued scholars and enthusiasts alike, especially when these fields converge to explore the intricate and often mysterious aspects of human experience. One such convergence occurs at the intersection of virtual reality (VR), dreams, psychology, enjoyment, and the pursuit of perfecting mental states. These domains, each rich with their own complexities, offer fascinating insights when studied together, revealing new dimensions of understanding human consciousness and mental well-being.

Virtual reality, a technology that creates immersive digital environments, has revolutionized how we perceive and interact with simulated worlds. Its applications extend far beyond entertainment, reaching into therapeutic and psychological realms. VR has the unique capability to induce states of ecstasy and profound enjoyment, akin to the experiences one might have in dreams or during heightened moments of mental clarity. This ability to transport users to entirely different realities provides a fertile ground for psychological studies focused on how these experiences affect the mind and emotions.

Dreams, those elusive and often enigmatic narratives that unfold during sleep, have fascinated humanity for millennia. They represent a state of consciousness where the mind explores scenarios and emotions in a manner that is unbound by the physical limitations of the waking world. Dreams can evoke powerful feelings of joy, fear, love, and sorrow, making them a compelling subject for psychologists seeking to understand the workings of the human mind. The parallels between the immersive experiences provided by VR and the vivid landscapes of dreams offer a unique opportunity for interdisciplinary research. Both can create a sense of presence and involvement that blurs the line between reality and imagination.

Psychology, the scientific study of the mind and behavior, plays a crucial role in deciphering the impacts of VR and dreams on mental states. Psychologists explore how these experiences influence our emotions, cognitive processes, and overall mental health. VR, for instance, has been utilized in exposure therapy to treat phobias by gradually immersing patients in controlled virtual environments that simulate their fears. This method allows individuals to confront and overcome their anxieties in a safe and manageable way, highlighting the therapeutic potential of VR.

Enjoyment and the pursuit of happiness are central themes in both dreams and VR experiences. The sense of pleasure derived from these states can be deeply enriching, contributing to a person's overall sense of well-being. In dreams, people often find themselves in scenarios that fulfill their desires and aspirations, leading to feelings of joy and contentment upon awakening. Similarly, VR can provide immersive experiences that allow users to engage in activities they find pleasurable, from exploring fantastical worlds to achieving goals they might not be able to pursue in real life.

The quest for perfecting mental states involves understanding and enhancing these moments of enjoyment and clarity. Techniques such as mindfulness, meditation, and positive psychology aim to cultivate a state of mental well-being that can be sustained over time. VR has the potential to be a powerful tool in this pursuit. By creating environments that promote relaxation and focus, VR can help individuals practice mindfulness and meditation in a controlled and engaging setting. This technological approach to mental health can complement traditional methods, offering new pathways to achieving a balanced and fulfilling life.

Mental health, a crucial aspect of overall well-being, can significantly benefit from the interdisciplinary study of VR, dreams, and psychology. The ability to simulate therapeutic scenarios in VR provides a valuable resource for mental health professionals. For example, VR can be used to create simulations for cognitive-behavioral therapy (CBT), allowing patients to practice coping strategies and problem-solving skills in a virtual space before applying them in real-life situations. This kind of intervention can be particularly effective for treating conditions such as PTSD, anxiety disorders, and depression.

Moreover, the study of dreams offers insights into the subconscious mind, revealing underlying thoughts, fears, and desires that might not be apparent in waking life. Analyzing dreams can help psychologists understand their patients better, providing clues about their mental state and emotional well-being. When combined with VR, the therapeutic potential is amplified. VR can be used to recreate dream scenarios, allowing individuals to explore and confront their subconscious in a controlled environment. This fusion of dream analysis and VR therapy can lead to breakthroughs in understanding and treating complex psychological issues.

Enjoyment, as a psychological construct, is intricately linked to motivation and overall life satisfaction. Positive experiences in VR can reinforce the pursuit of meaningful activities and goals. By providing a safe space to explore and achieve, VR can boost self-efficacy and confidence, encouraging individuals to translate these virtual successes into real-world accomplishments. This reinforcement can play a critical role in recovery and rehabilitation, especially for individuals dealing with trauma or chronic mental health conditions.

The interdisciplinary approach to studying these topics also highlights the importance of a holistic understanding of human experience. By examining the intersections of VR, dreams, psychology, and enjoyment, researchers can develop more comprehensive models of mental health and well-being. This integrated perspective can lead to innovative treatments and interventions that address multiple facets of mental health simultaneously, providing more effective and personalized care.

In the realm of perfecting mental states, the focus often shifts to optimizing the conditions that lead to peak experiences and flow states. Flow, a concept introduced by psychologist Mihaly Csikszentmihalyi, describes a state of complete immersion and engagement in an activity, often leading to a sense of fulfillment and productivity. VR can facilitate flow by creating environments that challenge and engage users at the right level, promoting concentration and enjoyment. This capability makes VR a valuable tool for enhancing performance in various fields, from education to professional development and beyond.

As we continue to explore the potential of VR and its impact on mental states, it is essential to consider the ethical implications of this technology. Ensuring that VR experiences are designed with user well-being in mind is crucial. Developers and researchers must prioritize creating content that is not only engaging but also supportive of mental health. Additionally, understanding the long-term effects of prolonged VR use on the brain and behavior is vital for developing guidelines and best practices for safe and beneficial usage.

The future of interdisciplinary studies in VR, dreams, and psychology promises to be a rich and exciting field of research. As technology advances, the possibilities for creating more immersive and realistic virtual experiences will expand, offering new avenues for exploration and treatment. The ongoing collaboration between technologists, psychologists, and other experts will be key to unlocking the full potential of these innovations.

In conclusion, the convergence of VR, dreams, psychology, enjoyment, and the quest for perfecting mental states represents a fascinating and rapidly evolving area of study. By leveraging the unique strengths of each field, researchers can gain deeper insights into human consciousness and develop new methods for enhancing mental health and well-being. The interdisciplinary approach not only enriches our understanding of these complex topics but also opens up new possibilities for innovation and improvement in how we care for our minds. As we move forward, the continued integration of these disciplines will undoubtedly lead to exciting discoveries and transformative changes in how we experience and understand the human mind.

52 METAPHYSICS AND SPECULATIVE FICTION

"Maze of Death" by Philip K. Dick, a work that delves into the depths of metaphysics and speculative fiction, offers a unique lens through which to examine the concepts of reality, artificial intelligence, and virtual reality. Dick, renowned for his exploration of the human psyche and the nature of reality, crafts a narrative that is as much about the internal struggles of its characters as it is about the external, often fantastical, environments they inhabit.

In "Maze of Death," the characters are confined to a remote planetary colony, where they await a spaceship to transport them to their final destination. This seemingly straightforward plot is complicated by the introduction of a religious belief system called "The Tenets," which the colonists adhere to. These tenets, provided by an enigmatic entity known as the Mentufacturer, shape their understanding of their existence and the world around them. This belief system functions as a metaphor for the various ways humans seek to make sense of their lives and the universe, touching upon the metaphysical questions of purpose, meaning, and the nature of reality.

Dick's portrayal of reality in "Maze of Death" is characteristically fluid and uncertain. The characters' experiences on the planet are punctuated by inexplicable phenomena and shifting perceptions, blurring the line between what is real and what is illusory. This ambiguity is a hallmark of Dick's work, challenging readers to question the reliability of their own perceptions and the stability of the reality they inhabit. The novel's setting and events suggest that reality is not a fixed, objective construct but rather a subjective experience shaped by individual consciousness and belief.

Artificial intelligence plays a crucial role in "Maze of Death," particularly in the form of the tenets and the Mentufacturer. The tenets can be seen as an artificial construct, a system designed to provide order and meaning in an otherwise chaotic and unpredictable universe. The Mentufacturer, as the source of these tenets, represents an external intelligence that shapes and controls the characters' beliefs and actions. This relationship echoes contemporary discussions about the influence of AI on human thought and behavior, raising questions about autonomy, free will, and the potential for AI to manipulate or enhance human cognition.

The concept of virtual reality is also intrinsic to the novel's exploration of metaphysics and speculative fiction. The characters' experiences on the planet can be likened to a virtual reality simulation, where their perceptions and interactions are mediated by an underlying system (the tenets) that dictates the parameters of their existence. This parallels modern VR technology, which creates immersive environments that can alter and shape users' experiences. In "Maze of Death," the boundaries between reality and simulation are porous, underscoring the idea that our understanding of reality is mediated by the tools and systems we use to interpret it.

Dick's exploration of these themes is not merely speculative but also deeply philosophical. The novel invites readers to contemplate the nature of existence and the ways in which our beliefs, technologies, and perceptions construct the reality we experience. The characters' journey through the maze of their own minds and the external environment serves as a metaphor for the human quest for understanding in an often inscrutable universe.

One of the central themes of "Maze of Death" is the notion of entropy and decay. The planetary colony is a microcosm of a universe in decline, where the characters' efforts to impose order and meaning are constantly thwarted by the inherent chaos of their environment. This reflects Dick's broader preoccupation with the fragility of human constructs and the inevitability of decay, both physical and metaphysical. The characters' struggles to maintain their faith in the tenets amidst the disintegration of their surroundings mirror the human condition, where the search for meaning and stability is often at odds with the unpredictable and entropic nature of reality.

The novel's ending, where the true nature of the characters' existence is revealed, further complicates the distinction between reality and illusion. The revelation that the characters are part of a larger experiment or simulation orchestrated by an external intelligence forces readers to reconsider the nature of their experiences and the reality they inhabit. This twist is a quintessential Philip K. Dick maneuver, designed to unsettle and provoke thought about the fundamental nature of existence and the limits of human understanding.

In the context of AI and VR, "Maze of Death" anticipates many contemporary debates about the ethical and philosophical implications of these technologies. The novel's depiction of the tenets as a form of AI that shapes human belief and behavior resonates with current discussions about the role of algorithms and artificial intelligence in influencing decision-making and perception. Similarly, the characters' experiences in the planetary colony can be seen as an early exploration of the potential and pitfalls of virtual reality, highlighting the ways in which immersive environments can blur the line between the real and the simulated.

Dick's work often reflects his own struggles with mental illness and his fascination with altered states of consciousness. In "Maze of Death," the characters' shifting perceptions and the ambiguity of their reality can be interpreted as a metaphor for the experience of psychosis, where the boundaries between reality and illusion become indistinct. This personal dimension adds a layer of poignancy to the novel's exploration of metaphysics, as it reflects the author's own quest for meaning and stability in a world that often seemed chaotic and incomprehensible.

The philosophical questions raised by "Maze of Death" are as relevant today as they were when the novel was first published. As we grapple with the implications of AI and VR technologies, Dick's exploration of reality, belief, and perception offers a valuable framework for considering the ethical and existential challenges these technologies pose. The novel's depiction of a reality mediated by artificial constructs and external intelligences serves as a cautionary tale about the potential for technology to shape and control human experience, while also highlighting the enduring human quest for understanding and meaning.

"Maze of Death" is a testament to Philip K. Dick's genius as a speculative fiction writer and his ability to weave complex metaphysical themes into compelling narratives. The novel's exploration of reality, AI, and VR continues to resonate with readers and scholars, offering a rich tapestry of ideas and questions that challenge our understanding of the nature of existence and the role of technology in shaping our perceptions. Through the lens of speculative fiction, Dick invites us to ponder the mysteries of the universe and our place within it, reminding us that the quest for meaning is a journey that is as much about the questions we ask as the answers we find.

53 PERFORMANCE ART AND ELECTROCLASH

Fisher Spooner, an enigmatic and genre-defying duo, emerged at the turn of the 21st century, captivating audiences with their unique blend of performance art and electroclash music. Formed in 1998 by Warren Fischer and Casey Spooner, the group quickly became a sensation in the underground art and music scenes. Their work is an amalgamation of theatrical performance, electronic beats, and provocative visuals, which collectively challenge and redefine the boundaries of conventional music and art.

The origins of Fisher Spooner can be traced back to New York City's vibrant and eclectic arts scene. Warren Fischer, a classically trained musician, and Casey Spooner, a performance artist, met while both were involved in various art projects. Their shared interest in pushing the envelope and exploring the intersection of different artistic mediums led to the formation of Fisher Spooner. From the outset, the duo aimed to create a multimedia experience that was as visually compelling as it was sonically innovative.

Fisher Spooner's debut album, "#1," released in 2001, was a landmark in the electroclash movement. Electroclash, characterized by its fusion of 1980s synthpop, new wave, and punk rock elements with contemporary electronic dance music, provided the perfect backdrop for Fisher Spooner's avant-garde sensibilities. The album featured tracks like "Emerge," which became an anthem of the genre. "Emerge" is a pulsating, high-energy track with minimalist lyrics and a hypnotic beat, encapsulating the essence of electroclash while also showcasing Fisher Spooner's unique artistic vision.

What set Fisher Spooner apart from other acts was their commitment to performance art. Their live shows were extravagant spectacles, incorporating elaborate costumes, choreographed dance routines, and theatrical staging. Casey Spooner, the frontman, often appeared in outlandish outfits, combining elements of glam rock, drag, and avant-garde fashion. This visual flamboyance was not just for show; it was a deliberate artistic choice that added layers of meaning to their performances. Each show was a meticulously crafted piece of performance art, blurring the lines between concert and theatrical production.

The visual aspect of Fisher Spooner's work was just as important as the music itself. They collaborated with a range of visual artists, designers, and choreographers to create a cohesive and immersive experience. For instance, their music videos, such as the one for "Emerge," were highly stylized and visually striking, often featuring surreal and provocative imagery. These videos were not merely promotional tools but integral components of their artistic expression.

Fisher Spooner's commitment to integrating various art forms extended to their approach to marketing and distribution. In the early 2000s, they were pioneers in utilizing the internet and social media to connect with their audience and distribute their work. This was at a time when the music industry was grappling with the rise of digital platforms and the decline of traditional record sales. Fisher Spooner's innovative use of technology allowed them to reach a global audience and build a dedicated fan base, despite operating outside the mainstream music industry.

Their follow-up albums, "Odyssey" (2005) and "Entertainment" (2009), continued to explore and expand the boundaries of electroclash and performance art. "Odyssey" marked a shift towards a more polished and accessible sound, while still retaining the experimental edge that defined their earlier work. The album featured collaborations with high-profile producers like Mirwais Ahmadzaï and Linda Perry, which helped to broaden their appeal and introduce their work to new audiences. "Entertainment," on the other hand, returned to a more raw and experimental approach, with tracks that were both sonically challenging and visually provocative.

Throughout their career, Fisher Spooner remained committed to challenging societal norms and pushing the boundaries of artistic expression. Their work often addressed themes of identity, gender, and sexuality, using their platform to question and subvert traditional notions of conformity and acceptance. This was particularly evident in their live performances, where the blending of masculine and feminine elements, along with the use of drag and androgyny, created a space for exploring and celebrating diverse identities.

In addition to their work as Fisher Spooner, both Warren Fischer and Casey Spooner have pursued individual artistic projects. Warren Fischer has continued to compose and produce music, while Casey Spooner has expanded his work in performance art and theater. Their individual pursuits have further enriched their collaborative work, bringing new perspectives and ideas to the Fisher Spooner project.

Fisher Spooner's influence on the electroclash movement and contemporary performance art cannot be overstated. They played a crucial role in bringing the underground electroclash scene into the mainstream consciousness, and their innovative approach to integrating music, visual art, and performance has inspired countless artists across various disciplines. Their legacy is evident in the work of contemporary musicians, performance artists, and visual artists who continue to push the boundaries of their respective fields.

One of the most remarkable aspects of Fisher Spooner's career is their ability to evolve and adapt while remaining true to their artistic vision. Over the years, they have navigated the ever-changing landscape of the music and art worlds, consistently producing work that is both relevant and groundbreaking. This adaptability is a testament to their creativity and dedication to their craft.

In recent years, Fisher Spooner has continued to explore new avenues for their artistic expression. Their 2018 album, "Sir," produced by R.E.M.'s Michael Stipe, marked a significant departure from their earlier work, with a more introspective and intimate approach. The album delves into themes of love, heartbreak, and self-discovery, reflecting the personal experiences and growth of the artists. "Sir" received critical acclaim for its emotional depth and maturity, further cementing Fisher Spooner's reputation as innovative and influential artists.

Fisher Spooner's journey is a testament to the power of collaboration and the endless possibilities that arise when different artistic disciplines intersect. Their work challenges audiences to think beyond conventional categories and appreciate the rich tapestry of human creativity. As pioneers of electroclash and performance art, Fisher Spooner has left an indelible mark on the cultural landscape, inspiring future generations of artists to explore, experiment, and redefine the boundaries of art and music.

In conclusion, Fisher Spooner's impact on the worlds of performance art and electroclash is profound and enduring. Their innovative fusion of music, visual art, and theatrical performance has set a new standard for what is possible in contemporary art. As they continue to evolve and explore new artistic horizons, Fisher Spooner's legacy will undoubtedly inspire and influence the next generation of artists and creators, ensuring that their groundbreaking work remains a vital part of the cultural dialogue for years to come.

54 THE INTERSECTION OF TECHNOLOGY AND MORAL RESPONSIBILITY

In the rapidly evolving landscape of technology, cybersecurity and ethics have become inextricably intertwined, shaping not only how we protect information but also how we define moral responsibility in the digital age. Cybersecurity involves the practices and technologies used to safeguard data, networks, and systems from cyberattacks, unauthorized access, and data breaches. Ethical considerations in this realm address the moral implications of these practices, the responsibilities of those who safeguard data, and the impact of cybersecurity measures on individuals' rights and privacy.

At the heart of cybersecurity is the protection of sensitive information from malicious actors. This involves deploying a range of tools and strategies, such as firewalls, encryption, intrusion detection systems, and regular security audits. The primary goal is to ensure the confidentiality, integrity, and availability of data. However, as cybersecurity measures become more sophisticated, so too do the ethical dilemmas they present. For instance, the use of advanced surveillance technologies can effectively detect and prevent cyber threats but also raises significant privacy concerns. Balancing the need for security with the right to privacy is a fundamental ethical challenge in cybersecurity.

One of the key ethical principles in cybersecurity is the concept of informed consent. Individuals have a right to know how their data is being collected, used, and protected. Organizations must be transparent about their data practices and obtain consent from users before collecting or processing their information. This principle is not only a legal requirement under various data protection regulations, such as the General Data Protection Regulation (GDPR) in Europe but also a moral imperative. Respecting users' autonomy and rights fosters trust and promotes ethical behavior in the digital ecosystem.

Another important ethical consideration is the duty to protect data. Organizations that collect and store personal data have a moral obligation to implement robust cybersecurity measures to prevent data breaches and cyberattacks. Failure to do so can result in significant harm to individuals, including financial loss, identity theft, and emotional distress. The ethical duty to protect data extends beyond legal compliance; it encompasses a broader responsibility to safeguard individuals' well-being and trust in digital services.

The rise of artificial intelligence (AI) and machine learning in cybersecurity adds another layer of ethical complexity. AI-driven cybersecurity tools can analyze vast amounts of data, detect anomalies, and respond to threats in real-time. While these technologies offer significant benefits, they also pose ethical risks. For example, AI algorithms can inadvertently perpetuate biases present in the data they are trained on, leading to unfair or discriminatory outcomes. Ensuring that AI systems are designed and deployed ethically requires careful consideration of the potential biases and impacts on different user groups.

Ethical hacking, also known as penetration testing, is another area where cybersecurity and ethics intersect. Ethical hackers use their skills to identify vulnerabilities in systems and networks, helping organizations strengthen their security posture. While their intentions are noble, ethical hackers must adhere to strict guidelines and obtain permission before conducting tests. Unauthorized access, even with good intentions, can result in legal repercussions and ethical breaches. The practice of ethical hacking highlights the importance of operating within legal and ethical boundaries while striving to improve cybersecurity.

The ethical responsibility of cybersecurity professionals extends to their conduct and decision-making processes. Professionals in this field often have access to sensitive information and powerful tools that can be misused. Ethical codes of conduct, such as those established by professional organizations like the International Information System Security Certification Consortium (ISC)^2, provide guidelines for ethical behavior. These codes emphasize principles such as integrity, confidentiality, and respect for privacy, guiding professionals in making ethical decisions and maintaining public trust.

Cybersecurity incidents, such as data breaches and cyberattacks, often have far-reaching ethical implications. When a breach occurs, organizations face ethical decisions about how to respond. Promptly notifying affected individuals, cooperating with regulatory authorities, and taking steps to mitigate harm are all ethical responsibilities. Transparency and accountability are crucial in handling cybersecurity incidents, as they demonstrate a commitment to ethical principles and help rebuild trust.

The ethical considerations in cybersecurity also extend to the broader societal impact of cyber threats and security measures. For example, the implementation of widespread surveillance technologies to enhance security can lead to a surveillance state, eroding civil liberties and privacy. Policymakers and cybersecurity experts must navigate these ethical dilemmas, ensuring that security measures do not come at the expense of fundamental rights and freedoms. Balancing security and privacy requires a nuanced approach that considers the ethical implications of surveillance and data collection practices.

Cybersecurity ethics also involves addressing the digital divide and ensuring equitable access to cybersecurity resources and education. Marginalized communities and developing countries often lack the resources and infrastructure to implement robust cybersecurity measures. This disparity creates ethical challenges, as these communities become more vulnerable to cyber threats. Promoting digital inclusion and providing access to cybersecurity education and resources are essential steps in addressing these ethical concerns and fostering a more secure and equitable digital world.

The role of ethics in cybersecurity is further highlighted by the increasing prevalence of cyber warfare and state-sponsored cyberattacks. Nations engaging in cyber warfare must consider the ethical implications of their actions, including the potential harm to civilians and critical infrastructure. International norms and agreements, such as the Tallinn Manual on the International Law Applicable to Cyber Warfare, seek to establish ethical guidelines and legal frameworks for cyber operations. Adhering to these guidelines is crucial for maintaining ethical standards and preventing the escalation of cyber conflicts.

In the realm of corporate cybersecurity, ethical considerations are closely linked to corporate social responsibility (CSR). Companies have a responsibility to protect not only their own data but also the data of their customers, employees, and partners. Ethical corporate practices in cybersecurity include investing in robust security measures, conducting regular security assessments, and fostering a culture of security awareness. Companies that prioritize cybersecurity ethics demonstrate their commitment to social responsibility and build stronger relationships with stakeholders.

The intersection of cybersecurity and ethics also influences the development of cybersecurity policies and regulations. Policymakers must consider the ethical implications of regulations, ensuring that they protect individuals' rights and promote fairness. For example, regulations that mandate data breach notifications empower individuals to take protective measures and hold organizations accountable. Ethical policymaking in cybersecurity involves a careful balance between protecting public safety and respecting individual rights.

Education and training play a vital role in promoting cybersecurity ethics. Integrating ethical principles into cybersecurity curricula helps prepare future professionals to navigate the complex ethical landscape of the field. Ethical training programs emphasize the importance of integrity, transparency, and respect for privacy, equipping professionals with the skills to make ethical decisions in their careers. Continuous education and professional development in cybersecurity ethics are essential for keeping pace with evolving technologies and ethical challenges.

As technology continues to advance, the ethical considerations in cybersecurity will become increasingly complex. Emerging technologies, such as quantum computing and the Internet of Things (IoT), present new ethical challenges and opportunities. For example, quantum computing has the potential to break current encryption methods, raising ethical questions about the security of sensitive data. Ensuring that these technologies are developed and deployed ethically requires ongoing dialogue and collaboration among cybersecurity experts, ethicists, policymakers, and other stakeholders.

In conclusion, the intersection of cybersecurity and ethics is a critical area that shapes how we protect information and define moral responsibility in the digital age. Cybersecurity measures must balance the need for security with the rights to privacy and autonomy, addressing ethical dilemmas such as informed consent, the duty to protect data, and the potential biases of AI technologies. Ethical hacking, the conduct of cybersecurity professionals, and the societal impact of cyber threats all highlight the importance of ethical considerations in this field. Promoting digital inclusion, addressing the ethical implications of cyber warfare, and integrating ethical principles into education and policymaking are essential steps in fostering a secure and ethical digital world. As technology evolves, the ethical challenges in cybersecurity will continue to grow, requiring ongoing commitment to ethical principles and collaboration among diverse stakeholders.

55 THE FUTURE OF IMMERSIVE EXPERIENCES

Virtual Reality (VR) and Augmented Reality (AR) have transformed the landscape of immersive experiences, blurring the lines between the digital and physical worlds in unprecedented ways. The journey of these technologies from their conceptual origins to their current sophisticated implementations illustrates a rapid evolution, poised to redefine various sectors such as entertainment, education, healthcare, and beyond.

VR, characterized by its ability to create entirely digital environments, immerses users in a computer-generated realm that feels convincingly real. When donning a VR headset, users can find themselves transported to any location or scenario, from exploring distant planets to participating in historical events. This level of immersion is made possible through a combination of high-resolution displays, spatial audio, and haptic feedback systems, which together simulate a multi-sensory experience. The psychological impact of such immersion can be profound, providing users with a sense of presence that traditional media cannot achieve.

Meanwhile, AR enhances the physical world by overlaying digital information onto real-world environments. Unlike VR, which requires complete isolation from the physical surroundings, AR integrates seamlessly with the user's immediate environment. Through devices like smartphones, tablets, or specialized AR glasses, digital objects appear to coexist with real ones, enabling interactive experiences that augment everyday life. For instance, AR can transform a simple walk in the park into an educational journey, with historical facts and virtual wildlife appearing along the path.

The entertainment industry has been a primary driver of VR and AR adoption. Video games, for instance, have leveraged VR to create more immersive gameplay experiences. Games like "Beat Saber" and "Half-Life: Alyx" showcase how VR can elevate engagement, making players feel as though they are part of the game world. These experiences are not only more engaging but also physically interactive, often requiring players to move and act within the virtual space, thus bridging the gap between digital play and physical activity.

Beyond gaming, VR has found applications in virtual tourism and storytelling. With VR, users can visit iconic landmarks, ancient ruins, or even underwater environments without leaving their homes. This capability has been particularly beneficial during the global pandemic, providing a safe alternative to physical travel. Filmmakers and content creators are also exploring VR as a medium for narrative experiences, offering audiences new ways to engage with stories by placing them at the center of the action.

AR, on the other hand, has seen widespread use in mobile applications. Games like "Pokémon Go" have demonstrated the mass appeal of AR by encouraging players to explore their real-world surroundings in search of virtual creatures. This blending of the virtual and physical worlds not only enhances gameplay but also promotes physical activity and social interaction. Additionally, AR has become a valuable tool in retail, where apps allow customers to visualize products in their homes before making a purchase. Furniture retailers like IKEA have pioneered AR applications that enable users to see how a piece of furniture would look in their space, thus aiding in decision-making and reducing the need for returns.

In education, VR and AR offer revolutionary potential for immersive learning experiences. Traditional teaching methods often struggle to convey the complexity of certain subjects, such as anatomy or historical events. VR can overcome these limitations by providing 3D visualizations and interactive simulations. For example, medical students can use VR to practice surgical procedures in a risk-free environment, gaining hands-on experience without the consequences of real-world mistakes. History students can virtually step into reconstructed ancient cities, gaining a deeper understanding of historical contexts through exploration.

AR also enhances education by bringing textbooks and classroom materials to life. With AR apps, students can scan textbook pages to see 3D models, animations, and additional information. This interactive approach not only makes learning more engaging but also caters to different learning styles, as students can interact with content in ways that suit them best.

The healthcare industry stands to benefit significantly from VR and AR technologies. In VR, exposure therapy for conditions like PTSD and phobias can be conducted in a controlled, virtual environment, allowing patients to confront their fears safely. Pain management is another area where VR shows promise; immersive experiences can distract patients from pain during procedures or chronic pain episodes. For rehabilitation, VR can provide engaging exercises tailored to a patient's needs, making the recovery process more enjoyable and effective.

AR is also making strides in healthcare, particularly in surgical procedures and diagnostics. AR can overlay vital information, such as patient vitals and 3D anatomical structures, directly onto a surgeon's field of view, enhancing precision and reducing the risk of errors. For medical training, AR can provide interactive, real-time guidance during procedures, helping trainees learn complex techniques more effectively.

The business and industrial sectors are increasingly adopting VR and AR for various applications. In manufacturing, AR can assist workers by overlaying assembly instructions and safety information onto physical equipment, improving efficiency and reducing errors. VR simulations can be used for training employees in hazardous environments, providing a safe way to practice without exposure to real-world risks.

Remote collaboration has also been transformed by these technologies. VR meeting platforms allow team members from around the world to gather in a shared virtual space, enhancing the sense of presence and interaction compared to traditional video conferencing. AR can facilitate remote assistance, where experts can guide on-site workers through complex tasks by overlaying instructions and annotations onto their field of view.

Despite their transformative potential, VR and AR face several challenges that need to be addressed for wider adoption. The cost of high-quality VR and AR hardware remains a barrier for many consumers and businesses. Additionally, issues such as motion sickness in VR and the limited field of view in AR devices need further refinement. Content creation for these platforms is also more complex and resource-intensive compared to traditional media, requiring specialized skills and tools.

Privacy and security concerns are significant, particularly with AR, which often requires access to cameras and location data. Ensuring that user data is protected and that applications do not become invasive will be crucial for maintaining public trust.

Looking ahead, the future of VR and AR is promising, with ongoing advancements in technology and expanding applications. The development of lighter, more comfortable, and affordable hardware will make these technologies more accessible. Improvements in display resolution, field of view, and tracking accuracy will enhance the realism and usability of VR and AR experiences.

The integration of artificial intelligence (AI) will further expand the capabilities of VR and AR. AI can enable more realistic interactions with virtual characters, personalize learning experiences, and enhance the accuracy of

AR overlays. For instance, AI-driven AR applications could provide real-time language translation or context-aware information, enriching everyday activities.

As 5G networks become more widespread, the enhanced connectivity will support more robust and seamless VR and AR experiences, particularly for mobile and cloud-based applications. This will enable more complex and data-intensive applications, such as large-scale multiplayer VR games or real-time AR collaboration tools.

In conclusion, VR and AR represent the future of immersive experiences, offering transformative potential across various sectors. While challenges remain, ongoing technological advancements and innovative applications are driving these technologies toward mainstream adoption. As VR and AR continue to evolve, they will increasingly shape how we interact with digital and physical worlds, creating new opportunities for engagement, learning, and productivity.

CONCLUSION

The convergence of visionaries, futurists, and neural networks heralds a new era in cultural theory and aesthetics, where the boundaries between human creativity and machine intelligence blur. This transformative period, characterized by postmodern and contemporary sensibilities, is reshaping our understanding of art, design, and expression in the 21st century.

Artificial intelligence, particularly advanced models like GPT, has become a cornerstone of this evolution. These models, trained on vast datasets, can generate human-like text, create art, compose music, and even participate in complex problem-solving. As AI continues to trend across various media platforms, its influence on culture and aesthetics becomes increasingly profound. This evolving relationship between AI and creativity is akin to navigating a digital aether, where algorithms serve as both guides and co-creators.

Critics and scholars have long debated the implications of AI in the arts. Some view it as a revolutionary tool that democratizes creativity, while others caution against the potential loss of human touch and authenticity. Drama ensues as these discussions often highlight the tension between traditional artistic values and the emerging role of virtual intellect.

Reality and virtuality are now in constant interplay. AI can simulate lifelike interactions, generate realistic visuals, and even create immersive experiences that rival reality itself. This virtual intellect is not just enhancing existing media but also creating entirely new forms of artistic expression. As these technologies evolve, so does the cultural landscape, continuously updating our collective memory and understanding of art and aesthetics.

In this dynamic environment, the role of visionaries and futurists is more critical than ever. They are the ones who can navigate the complexities of AI, understand its potential, and harness it to enhance human creativity. By pushing the boundaries of what is possible, they help to define the future of aesthetics and cultural theory.

The fusion of AI and human creativity offers a glimpse into a future where technology and art are inseparable. As we continue to explore this uncharted territory, it is essential to remain vigilant about the ethical implications and strive to maintain a balance between innovation and tradition. This balanced approach will ensure that the evolving landscape of aesthetics remains vibrant, inclusive, and reflective of the diverse tapestry of human experience.

In conclusion, the integration of AI into the arts represents a significant milestone in our cultural evolution. By enhancing our creative capabilities and expanding our aesthetic horizons, neural networks and AI technologies are transforming how we perceive and interact with art. As visionaries and futurists continue to explore these possibilities, they will shape a future where technology enhances the beauty and complexity of human creativity, ensuring that the cultural landscape of the 21st century is as rich and diverse as it is innovative.

56 LANGUAGE, POLITICS, AND MEDIA

Noam Chomsky, a towering figure in the fields of linguistics, cognitive science, and political commentary, has made profound contributions that resonate across diverse disciplines. His pioneering work in the realm of language has fundamentally reshaped our understanding of human cognition. Chomsky's theory of generative grammar, introduced in the 1950s, posits that the ability to generate language is innate to humans, governed by a universal grammar inherent in the human mind. This idea challenged the prevailing behaviorist theories of the time, which viewed language acquisition as a product of environmental stimuli and conditioning.

Chomsky's contributions to linguistics extend beyond his theories of syntax. He delved deeply into the philosophical underpinnings of language, arguing that understanding language involves understanding the structures of the human mind. His work has influenced not only linguistics but also psychology, cognitive science, and artificial intelligence. At the Massachusetts Institute of Technology (MIT), where Chomsky has spent much of his career, he has influenced countless students and scholars, fostering an environment of rigorous intellectual inquiry and innovation.

In addition to his academic pursuits, Chomsky is renowned for his incisive political commentary. He has been a vocal critic of U.S. foreign policy, corporate power, and the media. Chomsky's political writings, characterized by their clarity and depth, scrutinize the intersections of power, economics, and public discourse. His book "Manufacturing Consent," co-authored with Edward S. Herman, is a seminal work that explores how media serves the interests of dominant, elite groups, shaping public perception and discourse in ways that maintain existing power structures. This critique of media complicity in the propagation of state and corporate interests continues to be relevant in an era dominated by 24-hour news cycles and social media.

Chomsky's analysis of media extends into the digital age, where the proliferation of information technologies has transformed how news and information are disseminated. He has expressed concerns about the concentration of media ownership and the potential for new technologies, such as machine learning and artificial intelligence, to be used for surveillance and control. These concerns highlight the need for critical engagement with the ways in which technology intersects with power and society.

At MIT, Chomsky's influence is felt not only in the field of linguistics but also in the burgeoning fields of computer science and artificial intelligence. His ideas about the structure and function of language have informed research in natural language processing (NLP), a subfield of AI focused on the interactions between computers and human language. NLP technologies, which include applications like language translation, sentiment analysis, and conversational agents like GPT (Generative Pre-trained Transformer), are grounded in the principles of linguistics and cognitive science that Chomsky helped to establish.

Machine learning, a core component of AI, leverages vast amounts of data to train models capable of performing complex tasks. In the context of natural language, machine learning algorithms can analyze and generate human-like text, enabling advancements in various applications from chatbots to automated content generation. However, Chomsky has critiqued some aspects of machine learning, arguing that while these systems can mimic certain aspects of human cognition, they lack the deeper understanding of language and meaning that humans possess. This critique points to the ongoing debate about the capabilities and limitations of AI in replicating human intelligence.

The development of GPT and similar models represents a significant milestone in AI research. These models, trained on extensive datasets, can produce coherent and contextually relevant text, demonstrating a form of linguistic proficiency. However, Chomsky's insights remind us that such systems are ultimately statistical models, lacking the intrinsic understanding and intentionality that characterize human language use. This distinction underscores the complexity of human cognition and the challenges inherent in creating truly intelligent machines.

Chomsky's contributions to the field of aesthetics, though less widely recognized, are also noteworthy. His exploration of the nature of creativity, particularly in the context of language, intersects with broader questions about the nature of artistic expression and human creativity. He argues that the creative use of language is a fundamental aspect of human nature, reflecting the innate capacities of the human mind. This perspective aligns with his broader view that humans are not merely passive recipients of external stimuli but active agents capable of generating novel and meaningful expressions.

In the realm of aesthetics, Chomsky's ideas resonate with contemporary debates about the role of technology in art and creativity. The advent of AI-generated art and music challenges traditional notions of creativity, raising questions about authorship, originality, and the nature of artistic expression. While AI can produce works that mimic human creativity, the question remains whether these creations possess the same depth of meaning and intentionality as those produced by human artists. Chomsky's emphasis on the innate capacities of the human mind provides a critical lens through which to view these developments, suggesting that true creativity involves more than the mere replication of patterns.

Chomsky's interdisciplinary influence extends beyond academia, touching on issues of profound societal importance. His critiques of political and economic power structures resonate in contemporary discussions about inequality, social justice, and the role of intellectuals in society. He has consistently advocated for the responsibility of intellectuals to speak truth to power, challenging unjust systems and advocating for a more equitable and democratic society. This commitment to social justice is reflected in his extensive body of work, which spans topics from the Vietnam War to neoliberal globalization.

In his political writings, Chomsky often emphasizes the importance of grassroots activism and collective action. He argues that meaningful social change comes from the efforts of ordinary people working together to challenge oppressive systems. This perspective aligns with his broader view of human nature as inherently creative and capable of transformative action. By highlighting the power of collective agency, Chomsky provides a hopeful vision of the potential for positive change, even in the face of formidable challenges.

Chomsky's critique of media and political power is particularly relevant in the digital age, where the boundaries between information and misinformation are increasingly blurred. The rise of social media platforms has democratized access to information but has also facilitated the spread of false and misleading content. Chomsky's insights into the mechanisms of propaganda and media manipulation offer valuable tools for critically assessing the information we consume and for fostering a more informed and engaged citizenry.

In conclusion, Noam Chomsky's contributions to the fields of linguistics, politics, and media have left an indelible mark on contemporary thought. His groundbreaking theories of language have revolutionized our understanding of human cognition, while his incisive political commentary has challenged dominant power structures and advocated for social justice. At MIT, his influence continues to inspire new generations of scholars and researchers, fostering a culture of intellectual rigor and critical inquiry. As we navigate the complexities of the digital age, Chomsky's insights into the intersections of language, technology, and power remain as relevant as ever, offering a critical lens through which to understand and engage with the world. His work underscores the importance of intellectual and creative agency, reminding us of the profound capacities of the human mind and the enduring power of collective action.

57 FINAL REFLECTIONS: SYNTHESIS OF THE THEMES AND FUTURE DIRECTIONS IN CULTURAL THEORY

As we stand on the precipice of a new era defined by rapid technological advancements and the AI boom, it is essential to synthesize the themes that have emerged and consider the future directions in cultural theory. The integration of neural networks, artificial intelligence, and machine learning into creative and aesthetic practices has not only transformed these fields but also raised profound questions about the nature of creativity, authenticity, and the human experience.

One of the most significant themes is the augmentation of human creativity through AI. Tools like OpenAI's GPT, under the leadership of visionaries like Sam Altman, have demonstrated the potential of AI to generate human-like text, art, music, and more. This collaboration between humans and machines challenges traditional notions of authorship and creativity, suggesting a future where AI serves as a partner rather than a mere tool.

The role of visionaries and futurists in this landscape cannot be overstated. These individuals are at the forefront of exploring how AI can enhance human potential. They push the boundaries of what is possible, using neural networks to create novel forms of expression and design. Their work highlights the importance of maintaining a balance between leveraging AI's capabilities and preserving the unique qualities of human creativity.

In cultural theory, the postmodern and contemporary sensibilities of the 21st century are characterized by a skepticism of grand narratives and an embrace of plurality and diversity. AI's ability to analyze vast datasets and generate new insights aligns with these sensibilities, offering a tool for exploring the complexities of human experience and cultural production. As AI becomes more integrated into creative processes, it will undoubtedly influence the direction of cultural theory, prompting new questions and frameworks for understanding art and aesthetics.

The AI boom has also sparked a broader conversation about the ethics and implications of machine intelligence in the arts. Critics and scholars debate the potential loss of human touch in AI-generated works and the ethical considerations of using AI in creative fields. These discussions are crucial for ensuring that the development and deployment of AI technologies are aligned with ethical principles and societal values.

Looking to the future, the evolving relationship between AI and human creativity will likely lead to new forms of artistic expression and cultural production. Virtual intellects, capable of simulating lifelike interactions and creating immersive experiences, will continue to push the boundaries of what is possible in art and design. As these technologies evolve, they will update our collective memory and understanding of aesthetics, continuously reshaping the cultural landscape.

One of the key directions in cultural theory will be the exploration of how AI can democratize access to creative tools and opportunities. By making sophisticated design and artistic tools available to a broader audience, AI can help to level the playing field and foster greater inclusivity in the arts. This democratization has the potential to uncover new talents and perspectives, enriching the cultural tapestry.

In conclusion, the synthesis of these themes reveals a dynamic and rapidly evolving landscape in cultural theory and aesthetics. The integration of AI, championed by visionaries like Sam Altman and exemplified by tools like ChatGPT, is transforming how we create and engage with art. As we navigate this new frontier, it is essential to balance innovation with ethical considerations, ensuring that the future of aesthetics and cultural theory remains vibrant, inclusive, and reflective of the diverse experiences and values of humanity. The AI boom represents not just a technological revolution but a cultural one, with the potential to enhance and expand the boundaries of human creativity in profound and exciting ways.

www.ingramcontent.com/pod-product-compliance
Lightning Source LLC
Chambersburg PA
CBHW081145130726
47996CB00009B/2997